Tainted Souls and
Painted Faces

Reading
WOMEN
Writing

a series edited by
Shari Benstock and Celeste Schenck

Reading Women Writing is dedicated to furthering international feminist debate. The series publishes books on all aspects of feminist theory and textual practice. *Reading Women Writing* especially welcomes books that address cultures, histories, and experience beyond first-world academic boundaries. A complete list of titles in the series appears at the end of the book.

Tainted Souls and Painted Faces

THE RHETORIC OF FALLENNESS IN VICTORIAN CULTURE

Amanda Anderson

Cornell University Press

ITHACA AND LONDON

First published 1993 by Cornell University Press.

International Standard Book Number 0-8014-2781-9 (cloth)
International Standard Book Number 0-8014-8148-1 (paper)
Library of Congress Catalog Card Number 93-17254
Printed in the United States of America
Librarians: Library of Congress cataloging information appears
on the last page of the book.

⊗ The paper in this book meets the minimum requirements of
the American National Standard for Information Sciences—
Permanence of Paper for Printed Library Materials, ANSI Z39.48–1984.

For my parents,
Sara A. Anderson and
Philip E. Anderson

Contents

Acknowledgments

I am grateful to the Program for the Study of Cultural Values and Ethics at the University of Illinois, which provided fellowship support for the writing of this book during 1990–91. I also thank the Department of English at the University of Illinois for providing released time during 1991–92.

This book has benefited from the support and thoughtful criticism of many teachers, colleagues, and friends. I thank Harry Shaw, Jonathan Culler, Mark Seltzer, and Mary Jacobus for their careful and challenging readings of an earlier version of this manuscript. For their incisive responses to portions of the manuscript, and for helpful conversations about my work, I also thank Phil Barrish, Sabrina Barton, Nina Baym, Liz Bohls, Judy Frank, Peter Garrett, Carol Neely, Jeff Nunokawa, Bob Parker, Adela Pinch, Jack Stillinger, Sasha Torres, and Paula Treichler. I am especially grateful to Michael Bérubé and Janet Lyon, who both gave rigorous, detailed responses to the entire manuscript at a time when I had lost all distance on it. My greatest debt of all is to Allen Hance, for his untiring readings of multiple drafts, his rigorous intellectual challenges, and, not least, his sustaining companionship.

I owe a special thanks to Cary Nelson for his help at a crucial stage in this project, and to Richard Wheeler for the many ways in which he has supported this book. I am also grateful to Bernhard Kendler and Liz Holmes of Cornell University Press, and to Shari Benstock and Celeste Schenck, the series editors. Chapter 4 previously appeared as "D. G. Rossetti's 'Jenny': Intersubjectivity, Agency, and the Prostitute," *Genders* 4 (1989): 103–21, and a shorter version of the Afterword was published as "Cryptonormativism and Double Gestures: The Politics of Post-structuralism," *Cultural Critique* 21 (1992): 63–95. Sections of the Introduction previously appeared as "Prostitution's Artful Guise," *Diacritics* 21: 2–3 (1991): 102–22. I am grateful to these journals and to their respective publishers, the University of Texas Press, Oxford University Press, and Johns Hopkins University Press, for permission to use the material here.

AMANDA ANDERSON

Urbana, Illinois

Tainted Souls and

Painted Faces

Introduction

In an 1850 review article for the *Westminster Review* entitled "Prostitution," W. R. Greg writes, "Of all the social problems which philosophy has to deal with, this is, we believe, the darkest, the knottiest, and the saddest."[1] Greg's essay draws on several contemporary accounts of prostitution, both investigative and fictional, and in many ways actively seeks to discredit commonly held views on the condition and fate of prostitutes. But his description of prostitution as a vexing problem for philosophy reflects something distinctive about the scope and nature of mid-Victorian approaches to sexual "fallenness." Indeed, I argue in this book that depictions of prostitutes and fallen women in Victorian culture typically dramatize predicaments of agency and uncertainties about the nature of selfhood, character, and society. My purpose is to isolate and describe a pervasive rhetoric of fallenness in mid-Victorian culture, one that constitutes sexually compromised women as lacking the autonomy and coherence of the normative masculine subject. This rhetoric is shaped through interactions between Victorian ideologies of gender and several other historical factors: tensions between materialist and idealist understandings of the self and of moral action, debates on social reform and character transformation, and, not least, preoccupations with the relation between social identities and aesthetic forms. Through close analyses of social and literary texts from the mid-Victorian period, I demonstrate that the Victorian conception of fallenness, represented predominantly by the figures of the fallen

1. [W. R. Greg], "Prostitution" 448.

woman and the prostitute, must be reinterpreted as culturally more central and analytically more complex than has previously been recognized. As my readings show, the fallen woman is less a predictable character than a figure who displaces multiple anxieties about the predictability of character itself.

Most studies of Victorian prostitution acknowledge the fluidity of the term "fallen woman," its application to a range of feminine identities: prostitutes, unmarried women who engage in sexual relations with men, victims of seduction, adulteresses, as well as variously delinquent lower-class women. A wide umbrella term, the designation cuts across class lines and signifies a complex of tabooed behaviors and degraded conditions.[2] What tends to remain constant in depictions of fallenness, however, is the attenuated autonomy and fractured identity of the fallen figure. In fact, some of the most familiar epithets for sexually immoral Victorian women—the "painted" woman, the "public woman," the woman who "loses her character"—succinctly express the larger informing assumptions about the nature of the fallen state, its failure to present or maintain an authentic, private, or self-regulating identity. By my account, the shadowy and marginal appearances of the fallen, in both literary and nonliterary texts, frequently serve less as moral exempla of vice than as uneasy reminders of more general cultural anxieties about the very possibility of deliberative moral action: to "fall" is, after all, to lose control. Mechanization, degrading urban environments, social determination, laws of causation, commodification, the disruptions of desire, the constraints of cultural forms and narratives—these are the forces that, singly or jointly, lurk behind portrayals of the sexually stigmatized.

The contexts for Victorian debates on the nature of agency and selfhood are multiple—philosophical, scientific, religious, medical, political, and literary. The concept of fallenness is of course religious in origin, and it was used as a religious category by many evangelical

2. In her study of constructions of femininity in Victorian culture, Lynda Nead makes a sharp class distinction between the prostitute and the fallen woman, arguing that the prostitute was a part of the dangerous classes, while the fallen woman was "fallen" precisely because she had once been a member of respectable society. This distinction does apply in some instances but is more distorting than clarifying. The system of prostitution was often presented as a microcosm of society, with differentiated classes; more significant, the condition of "fallenness" was often ascribed to women of the lower classes, including prostitutes. See Nead, *Myths of Sexuality* 94–96.

commentators on prostitution and by many believing Victorian writers. But my readings emphasize the ways fallenness was rearticulated to secular and scientific paradigms during the Victorian era and ultimately served to loosen religious and ethical moorings. As elaborated in Augustinian theology, the condition of fallenness derives from the act of original sin. But although fallenness traces to an act of will, no amount of remorse or repentance enables us to transcend our fallen state through our own resolution. One can hope for a divine, uplifting act of grace, but such a dispensation will come only if one is among the predetermined number of the elect. This concept of fallenness, which was taken up in its essentials by Calvinism, lays stress on the predetermined nature of our moral condition, and itself seriously challenges vocabularies of moral agency and responsibility, as evidenced in the heated theological debates that attended the rise of protestantism. I explore how the concept of fallenness, traditionally exercised by questions of moral agency, came to figure an emergent set of threateningly secular determinisms, despite the continued use of religious imagery and concepts.[3]

Perhaps the broadest context for an understanding of agency and selfhood in Victorian Britain was the philosophical debate between idealism and materialism, a debate that, to greater and lesser degrees of explicitness, conditioned discussions of moral reform, character, and gender. The radical political traditions of the utilitarians and the Owenites subscribed to versions of the materialist doctrine of necessity, according to which human action conformed to discoverable laws of causation and could be formed and guided by educators. A materialist understanding of the self likewise informed the influential sciences of phrenology and physiognomy, as well as leading doctrines in medicine and psychology. And in the second half of the century, evolutionism and social evolutionism identified forms of natural law that, it was surmised, would lend certainty and pre-

---

3. Although I am here drawing attention to the significance of religious fallenness, the intricate and complex relation between religious and social determinism in Victorian culture is not the particular focus of this book, which concentrates more exclusively on establishing a relation between fallenness and secular determinisms. However, my interpretation of Gaskell's *Ruth* in Chapter 3 does address some important facets of this topic. For useful analyses of the relation between religious and social thought in Victorian culture, particularly as it relates to languages of determinism and the new social sciences, see Catherine Gallagher, *The Industrial Reformation of English Fiction* 36–61; Frank Mort, *Dangerous Sexualities* 30–32; and John R. Reed, *Victorian Will* 29–79.

dictability to a culture whose traditional moral and religious frames had been significantly dislodged. The deep commitment to moral and social transformation that lay behind many scientific and materialist approaches, however, was alternately consoled and troubled by the idea of uniform laws of causation. Consoled, because it seemed that if one could only discover the laws that determined character, one could make the world over into a harmonious and morally elevated community (or, in the case of more quietist evolutionary models such as Herbert Spencer's, rest assured that society would evolve to perfection). Troubled, because if character were both determined and infinitely malleable, then a coherent conception of moral action was undermined, and cherished notions of rationality, individuality, and autonomy were threatened with obsolescence. In response to precisely these concerns, idealists such as Coleridge and Carlyle insisted on the notion of a morally autonomous subject and explicitly endorsed a spiritual philosophy. Their purpose was to protect the individual and the moral sphere from an encroaching and degrading materialism that was seen to imperil the human soul and the spiritual community.

In Chapter 1, I first offer an extended discussion of Victorian debates over selfhood and agency, using the works of John Stuart Mill to highlight the emergence of social science and to introduce Victorian arguments about the nature of character. I then consider how these wider philosophical and political debates shaped mid-century accounts of prostitution and fallenness, which were themselves a subset of early sociological and statistical approaches to poverty, public health, and social morality. In general terms, I argue that approaches to fallenness manifest the most extreme and unsettling ramifications of the materialist approaches to character and individual identity. This chapter is intended to provide a social and intellectual introduction to the category of fallenness, and to set the context for ensuing chapters on Charles Dickens, Elizabeth Gaskell, Dante Gabriel Rossetti, and Elizabeth Barrett Browning.

The time frame covered by the study is roughly 1840 to 1860, the middle decades of the century, although I treat some earlier traditions and texts that influenced cultural debates during these decades.[4] I chose this time period because it saw, simultaneously, the

4. In my discussion of Mill, I refer to some texts written after 1860, but within

elaboration of scientific approaches to morality, society, and character, the proliferation of discourses on prostitution, and a burgeoning literary interest in narratives of the fall. My analysis does not extend into the era of the Contagious Diseases Acts, a period that has been treated in depth by Judith R. Walkowitz.[5] While the debates over the Acts engage and contest many facets of the earlier discourses on fallenness, they are more directly about the state politics of prostitution; my book focuses instead on the manifold cultural meanings of fallenness during a time when prostitution did not yet occupy the political center stage.

The Question of Agency

Through its elaboration of fallenness as a historical category with a distinctive rhetoric, this project significantly revises previous approaches to Victorian prostitution and ideologies of gender. Accounts that have followed in the wake of the Foucauldian project of reconstructing the history of sexuality interpret discourses on prostitution as part of a multipronged production and administration of specific sexualities and subjectivities. Studies by Walkowitz, Lynda Nead, and Linda Mahood analyze sexual discourses and policies as complex technologies of power directed at women and the lower classes, revising the Foucauldian model so as to take gender and political resistances more fully into account.[6] I do not dispute the idea that administrative apparatuses in the nineteenth century managed social subjects through the production of a range of sexual identities and subject-positions, among them the prostitute and the hysteric. My discussion in Chapter 1 in fact describes the construction of "the prostitute" as a new social identity or status within the context of early sociology and "moral statistics." Likewise, this study

the context of his mid-century concerns with character and agency. And D. G. Rossetti's "Jenny" is somewhat anomalous, with drafts spanning from 1848 to 1870.

5. Judith R. Walkowitz, *Prostitution and Victorian Society*.

6. Walkowitz, *Prostitution and Victorian Society*; Nead, *Myths of Sexuality*; and Linda Mahood, *The Magdalenes*. In her new and richly textured study of "dangerous sexualities" in 1880s London, Walkowitz amplifies the model of her earlier work to consider the ways diverse late Victorian social actors participated in discourses on sexuality and political issues. See Judith R. Walkowitz, *City of Dreadful Delight*; also see Mort, *Dangerous Sexualities*.

builds on Foucauldian and other cultural analyses of the prostitute's symbolic relation to the urban environment and to the disease, degraded material conditions, and political threats often associated with it.[7]   ∧

What I believe has been insufficiently explored in the Foucauldian-inspired approaches to prostitution, which are often highly attentive to the histories of institutions, social policies, and class relations, is the rhetorically supple and historically overdetermined conception of fallenness as attenuated autonomy. Walkowitz, Nead, and Mahood, it is true, have importantly amplified the Foucauldian approach so as to stress not only the processes of social control directed at the prostitute but also the forms of social protest and critique focused on this figure.[8] But while their approach reconfigures the fallen woman's position within the social field, it does not directly investigate fallenness as a charged site for Victorian concerns with the question of agency itself, ones that include but are not exhausted by apprehensions of the power of environment over character. As I demonstrate, the discourses on fallenness, which clearly serve to codify behaviors, negotiate political threats, and wage political protests, also constitute an intricate and overdetermined engagement with some of the most vital and consequential Victorian ideas about agency, representation, and social transformation.[9]

7. Walkowitz, Nead, and Mahood all read representations of the prostitute as displacing political tensions between the classes and expressing concerns with the communication of disease and the moral contaminations associated with the urban environment and the "social residium." Partly building on Walkowitz's study, but also incorporating a Bakhtinian analysis, Peter Stallybrass and Allon White similarly argue that the prostitute was the "privileged category in a metonymic chain of contagion which led back to the culture of the working classes." Stallybrass and White, *The Politics and Poetics of Transgression* 138. Also see Nancy Armstrong, *Desire and Domestic Fiction* 161–202.

8. Walkowitz does this through her careful reconstruction of the political battles over the Contagious Diseases Acts, Nead and Mahood by recovering the critiques of prostitution in the Owenite tradition. For a briefer but excellent description of the role of the prostitute in Victorian understandings of their urban and social conditions, see Deborah Epstein Nord, "The Urban Peripatetic." Françoise Basch, in an earlier study that treats both literary and nonliterary genres, also emphasizes the elements of social critique in depictions of fallen women and prostitutes; see Basch, *Relative Creatures*.

9. For an approach that interprets the prostitute as more directly posing questions of agency, although within the context of American naturalism and turn-of-the-century American culture, see Mark Seltzer's discussions of the prostitute as a "statistical person" and a figure focusing questions of mechanism, culturalism, and social constitution. Seltzer, *Bodies and Machines* 65, 99, 106. And in her new book, which

Of course, historians and cultural critics have not failed to remark that Victorian discourses characteristically construct the prostitute as one who lacks agency. Indeed, Walkowitz identifies and then contests this dominant depiction, discrediting the widely held Victorian notion that prostitutes and fallen women were destined for a "downward path" of disease, decay, despair, and death. By demonstrating that Victorian prostitutes exercised control over their trade and formed powerful communities and alliances, Walkowitz not only refutes Victorian views but also engages a prominent debate within the feminist historical tradition, which has itself been pulled between victimological models stressing the suppression of women under patriarchal culture, and cultural feminist models that celebrate women's marginalized practices and subcultures. Ironically, however, the form taken by questions of agency within our current disciplines can sometimes mask the historically specific concerns with agency that the debates on fallenness were themselves enacting. While Walkowitz, Nead, and Mahood all point to tensions between moralism and environmentalism in early British sociology, their accounts do not sufficiently reconstruct the context for Victorian discussions of character and selfhood, relying instead upon a generalized and ultimately unexamined notion of agency.

A related problem has occurred within feminist literary criticism, not only in images-of-women criticism, which identifies denials of agency as simply unrealistic, but also in later feminist analyses. For example, in *Woman and the Demon: The Life of a Victorian Myth*, Nina Auerbach interprets representations of the fallen woman as both conveying and dispelling a myth of powerful womanhood that centrally inhabited the Victorian cultural imagination.[10] Yet despite her invocation of cultural myths and her historically sensitive treatment of "character," Auerbach often conceives of the relation between women and representation as curiously unmediated, casting femininity as directly empowered or suppressed through representation. The latter notion, that feminine subjectivity or sexuality can be sup-

explores sexual narratives in the context of late Victorian constructions of gender, power, and urban public spaces, Walkowitz incorporates and analyzes understandings of gender and class identity deriving from several discursive genres: fictional, journalistic, psychological, scientific. Walkowitz's study has multiple foci and is concerned to draw out the discourses that were being generated in the late Victorian period, which saw a more complex challenge to earlier approaches to feminine sexual transgression. See Walkowitz, *City of Dreadful Delight*.

10. Nina Auerbach, *Woman and the Demon* 150–84.

pressed or trapped by representation, appears in several feminist literary critics, among them Helena Michie and Naomi Schor; Michie argues that in Victorian cultural representations "the prostitute's body is dressed, defaced, and erased."[11] These approaches assume a suppression of femininity loosely analogous to the denials of agency that are examined in the images-of-women tradition, even as they approximate Luce Irigaray's more complex philosophical claim that women are caught within oppressive phallocentric representations, "hemmed in, cathected by tropes."[12] Both the Anglo and French paradigms of feminist critique are highly sensitive to portrayals of attenuated autonomy or fractured identity, yet often do not situate them sufficiently within specific social and intellectual contexts.[13] This is also the case in Lacanian approaches, where representations of fallen subjectivity are easily assimilable to the concept of feminine "lack."[14]

I am not suggesting that we could somehow denude ourselves of our own contemporary theoretical concerns and apprehend Victorian fallenness in its pristine state, uninflected by subsequent historical, aesthetic, and intellectual developments. On the contrary, our contemporary investments in questions of agency, subjectivity, and social transformation light up hitherto obscured aspects of the Victorian approach to fallenness, enabling us to interpret it anew. My point in discussing recent approaches is simply to indicate their failure to mediate sufficiently between their own theoretical horizon

11. Helena Michie, *The Flesh Made Word* 62; Naomi Schor, *Breaking the Chain.*

12. Luce Irigaray, *Speculum of the Other Woman* 142–43.

13. For other literary criticism specifically treating the prostitute and fallen woman in nineteenth-century Britain, much of it within the images-of-women tradition, see George Watt, *The Fallen Woman in the 19th-Century English Novel*; Pierre L. Horn and Mary Beth Pringle, eds., *The Image of the Prostitute in Modern Literature*; Laura Hapke, "He Stoops to Conquer"; Beth Kalikoff, "The Falling Woman in Three Victorian Novels" and "Victorian Sexual Confessions"; Angela Leighton, " 'Because Men Made the Laws.' " For literary accounts that more fully treat the social and intellectual context, see Basch, *Relative Creatures*; Sally Mitchell, *The Fallen Angel*; Elizabeth K. Helsinger, Robin Lauterbach Sheets, and William Veeder, *The Woman Question* 3:111–70; Mariana Valverde, "The Love of Finery"; Nord, "The Urban Peripatetic."

14. For an extended psychoanalytic account of representations of prostitution, one that employs the model of repressed femininity yet opens it out onto a richer consideration of social and historical factors, see Charles Bernheimer, *Figures of Ill Repute.* For a further discussion of Bernheimer and psychoanalysis, see my review of Bernheimer's book, "Prostitution's Artful Guise." Joseph Allen Boone also produces a psychoanalytic account of denied agency in his analysis of narratives of seduction in the English novel; see Boone, *Tradition Counter Tradition* 99–113.

and the intellectual and social horizons of Victorian discourse. In my interpretations, I cultivate a hermeneutic approach that fosters self-consciousness about the historical development of approaches to agency. And ultimately, I question the cogency of those models of agency informing the Foucauldian and psychoanalytic approaches, insofar as they reproduce the very problems—at once philosophical and ethical—that afflict the understanding of social and individual identity within the Victorian rhetoric of fallenness. As I elaborate further toward the end of the Introduction, my own perspective integrates elements of feminist critique, hermeneutic method, and Jürgen Habermas's approach to intersubjectivity.

Tainted Souls, Painted Faces

Of especial importance for literary history is the way in which fallenness, as a category of determined identity, was taken up within the aesthetic register. This is a topic frequently neglected or subordinated within social accounts of prostitution and Victorian ideologies of gender. But I show that aesthetic manifestations of threats to autonomy often appear alongside or further symbolize more strictly social manifestations of determined subjectivity. As a fated, false, or "painted" character, the fallen woman reveals concerns about the formal rendering of character and occasions crises about the readability of subjects. Most prominently, fallenness is assimilated to narrative itself, identified or equated with a "downward path." In the realist novel, for example, fallen women often highlight the coercive logic of the conventional narratives or genres through which literary character is rendered.[15] The fallen woman's extreme predicament allows other forms of characterization to appear less determined; if she's so trapped, the narrative logic implies, the protagonist and the other privileged characters must be free. The notion that a woman has "lost her character" is uncannily precise in this formal sense. "Lost characters" underwrite seemingly "free" characters, not only in social terms, by making their social ascension seem uncontrived or a result of their own agency, but also in an epistemological sense, by making them seem more "real," less

15. For discussions of the way narrative requirements determine identity, see Cynthia Chase, *Decomposing Figures* 157–95; Jonathan Culler, *The Pursuit of Signs* 169–88.

"painted." In *David Copperfield*, for example, fallen women displace the fear that character may be determined by either social forces or narrative exigency. As I argue in Chapter 2, they serve to suggest that Copperfield's "personal" history issues out of his own will and steady application. The fallen women are fatally written, but Copperfield writes himself.

The economy between masculine and feminine character in *David Copperfield* and other novels reveals that "fallen" characters highlight a tension between plot and character that is constitutive of realist fiction. It is not that fallen women are somehow textually determined while other characters are not— after all, at a certain level all literary characters are "false" and "fictional" and constituted by narrative. Yet within the constructed fictions of many nineteenth-century realist texts, the fallen woman appears as both hyperdetermined and disturbingly "false" (painted, melodramatic, histrionic); this portrayal in turn creates an effect of greater verisimilitude around the nonfallen. Realist fiction was one primary mode through which subjectivity was given form in the nineteenth century; it helped to shape cultural models of self-understanding. By exploring aesthetic manifestations of "fallen subjectivity," I hope to show both how Victorian conceptions of the self were gendered and how literary genres and popular cultural forms were themselves experienced as dangers or constraints. These constraints frequently become most visible in depicted encounters between fallen women and other characters, who often perceive the fallen woman as a text that is already written rather than an agent capable of dialogical interaction. In such instances, the fallen woman can evoke not only crises of readability but also larger concerns about the relation between people and books, between living encounters and reading, and between social and aesthetic experience.

In some cases, such as Thackeray's *Vanity Fair*, "impure" feminine characters are aligned not with constraining narratives but with active storytelling and theatricality, even becoming doubles for the author in various ways. One might be tempted to argue, in light of this fact, that the more prevalent punishing narratives are defensive reactions against the transgressor's perceived capacity to create fictions and recreate the self. But what tends to obtrude more in representations of fallenness, as opposed to portrayals of more potent feminine transgressors such as Becky Sharp, is not the perception that the woman is an artist but rather the uneasy apprehension that the author is himself fallen.[16] In other words, the fallen woman is construed as subject to a number of threatening determinations—social, economic, cultural—that the author himself wishes to ward off. Yes, authors jealously guard their autonomy and capacity to write themselves in a way that the prostitute or fallen character cannot, but not usually because the fallen character threatens to appropriate that capacity. More commonly, the fallen character reminds the author that he can never fully own himself, and that his own history, as well as the story he tells about that history, is determined by a number of forces beyond his control.[17] Hence my definition of fallenness as determinism rather than open-ended aesthetic capacity or other transformative power or energy.[18]

The transformative prostitutional capacity receives fuller representation in nineteenth-century French novels than it does in English ones, mainly because in France there were not such taboos against representing actual prostitutes (as opposed to the more muted fallen woman) or women associated with the theater (a profession often linked with prostitution). Accordingly, it is no accident that Thackeray gives Becky Sharp French heritage or that she ends up living in France, nor is it insignificant that in the first chapter of *Vanity Fair*, Becky flaunts her French and hurls Johnson's dictionary out of her carriage: these details signal her distance from the realm of fallenness, however immoral she may be. Likewise, when working actresses appear in mid-Victorian fiction, they are often exotic, powerful, and threatening, as for example Madame Laure in *Middlemarch*, Vashti in *Villette*, or Alcharisi in *Daniel Deronda*.[19] In the case of the fallen, however, theatricality or storytelling is less a process that the woman controls than something that controls her.

16. For a related discussion of the author-as-whore metaphor in Victorian culture, see Catherine Gallagher, "George Eliot and *Daniel Deronda*."

17. My pronoun use here reflects the fact that such scenarios are usually (though not necessarily) gendered in the manner indicated.

18. Nina Auerbach's chapter on fallen women in *Woman and the Demon* compensates for the ubiquity of downward-path narratives, and retains the notion of transformative feminine power, by privileging visual art and iconographic moments within fictional texts, claiming that "an explicit narrative . . . abases the woman" while "an iconographic pattern . . . exalts her" (168).

19. For reconstructive historical and social analyses of actual working actresses, see Tracy C. Davis, *Actresses as Working Women*, and Mary Jean Corbett, *Representing Femininity* 107–29. For a discussion of representations of prostitution in nineteenth-century France that elaborates the concept of transformative prostitutional capacity, see Bernheimer, *Figures of Ill Repute*.

Among the works under consideration in this book, only Elizabeth Barrett Browning's *Aurora Leigh* depicts a fallen woman who effectively appropriates the power of self-expression and self-definition commanded by the text's protagonist (and she only does so, interestingly, once the scene shifts from London to Paris).[20]

The powerful cultural dominance of the idea of fallenness as a predelineated narrative appears not only in literary works of the period but also in the contemporary social debates I discuss in Chapter 1. A minority of reformers faulted other social commentators for allowing an unrealistic, specifically literary depiction of the "harlot's progress" to set back reform efforts and distort cultural knowledge, but others confidently cited literary texts and narratives to support their faith in the downward path. Indeed, some argued against punitive legislation for prostitution by invoking the absolute dependability of the punishing consequences that the "fall" set in motion.[21] Those who challenged the notion that the fall produced a predictable and accelerated decline cited the findings of Alexandre Parent-Duchâtelet's *De la prostitution dans la ville de Paris* (1836). A massive statistical and analytic account of what, due to police regulation, was the best-documented working-class profession in France, Parent-Duchâtelet's study refutes the prevalent belief in the downward-path trajectory, demonstrating that prostitution was for most practitioners a transient occupation, adopted for two or three years and frequently leading to marriage. Parent-Duchâtelet's argument was endorsed in England by William Acton and others, though many who otherwise borrowed his findings significantly dropped the idea of transience. The transience claim is supported by the research of Walkowitz, whose own extensive historical study, as I have discussed, establishes that prostitutes exerted considerable control over their fate. I myself do not intend in this book to intervene into the historical debate over the lived experience of actual prostitutes; rather, I examine, across a wide spectrum of cultural texts and practices, the multiple determinisms represented by the category of fallenness.

20. For a discussion of differences between French and English literary depictions of prostitution, see Peter Brooks, *Reading for the Plot* 143–70.

21. See E. M. Sigsworth and T. J. Wyke, "A Study of Victorian Prostitution and Venereal Disease" 88, 94.

Purity and Fallenness

In Chapter 1, I argue that fallenness should be understood principally in relation to a normative masculine identity seen to possess the capacity for autonomous action, enlightened rationality, and self-control. This argument raises the question of how fallenness fits into the broader opposition between masculine and feminine identity in Victorian culture, an opposition most powerfully expressed in the doctrine of the separate spheres. In its classic formulation, this doctrine assigns man to the public sphere of individual exertion, business, and politics, and relegates woman to the private, domestic sphere of the affections. As an oxymoronic "public woman," the Victorian prostitute immediately troubles this structuring gender opposition and casts into question the idea of natural feminine "purity" that supports the dominant doctrine. In her influential work on the Victorian ideology of gender, in fact, Mary Poovey has argued that variously public and impure women serve as unsettling reminders of an aggressive female sexuality that the dominant culture sought to disavow and suppress, since it upset the structuring binary opposition between masculinity and a sexless, maternal femininity.

For Poovey, the feminine domestic ideal emerges as the single cultural image most requisite to the coherence and efficacy of Victorian ideological reproduction. Her textual analyses repeatedly demonstrate what she at one point calls the "epistemological centrality of woman's self-consistency to the oppositional structure of Victorian ideas."[22] And, on the level of domestic practices, the faithful middle-class wife serves as a crucial psychological anchor, providing a ground for personal identity and warding off the destabilizing effects of transgressive desire. In Poovey's reading of *David Copperfield*, for example, the feminine domestic ideal consolidates masculine identity and guides the narrative of individual fulfillment that underwrites bourgeois ideology:

> Because her domestic authority—indeed, her self-realization—depended on her ability to regulate her own desire, the faithful woman as wife anchored her husband's desire along with her own, giving it an object as she gave him a home. In this model, self-regulation

22. Mary Poovey, *Uneven Developments* 9.

was a particularly valuable and valued form of labor, for it domesticated man's (sexual) desire in the private sphere without curtailing his ambition in the economy.[23]

In exploring the self-regulating subjectivity assigned to virtue in the nineteenth century, Poovey extends Nancy Armstrong's work on the centrality of the female subject, and of feminine forms of power and surveillance, to the development and consolidation of bourgeois identity.[24] For both Poovey and Armstrong the ascendance of the middle class was supported ideologically through the rearticulation of the concept of virtue from a public, aristocratic locus to a private and feminized sphere. The emergent middle-class ideology, which privileged the efforts, capacities, and worth of "autonomous individuals," challenged the status-based aristocratic ideology precisely by valorizing a model of identity or interiority based on a private, carefully guarded feminine virtue.[25]

While these approaches contribute significantly to feminist studies through their recasting of cultural constructions of femininity, the stress on virtue and purity diminishes the cultural work performed by the Victorian category of fallenness. Armstrong does analyze depictions of the "monstrous" woman in mid-Victorian England, arguing that this figure displaces class threats in Dickens, Gaskell, and Thackeray, but the analysis is subordinated to her master narrative, which, in her own words, "links the history of British fiction to the empowering of the middle classes in England through the dissemination of a new female ideal."[26] And Poovey may assert that a "contradiction between a sexless, moralized angel and an aggressive, carnal magdalen was . . . written into the domestic ideal as one of its constitutive characteristics," but this approach effectively reduces impurity to transgressive sexuality, and fallenness becomes merely the sexualized underside of the domestic ideal.[27] My readings suggest that fallenness took on a life of its own in the period that

23. Poovey, *Uneven Developments* 115.
24. Armstrong, *Desire and Domestic Fiction.*
25. Lynda Nead's *Myths of Sexuality* also claims that the production of a "norm of respectable femininity" was central to the self-definition of the middle class. And Michael McKeon, in *The Origins of the English Novel 1600–1740*, emphasizes the ideological centrality of the concept of virtue, more broadly tracing its inextricable connections to social, ethical, and epistemological issues.
26. Armstrong, *Desire and Domestic Fiction* 9.
27. Poovey, *Uneven Developments* 11.

Poovey singles out for study and, ironically, that the category of fallenness can be understood only if one is careful not to reduce it to female sexuality. If feminine virtue could symbolize or help promote normative models of inherent, autonomous, or self-regulating identity, fallenness represented manifold challenges to those models and did not bespeak simply a form of aggressivity or sexuality that threatened to disrupt a symbolic purity.[28] Moreover, the relation between the categories of purity and fallenness took highly complex forms, with purity sometimes figuring and shoring up coherent, normative forms of identity, sometimes figuring alternate or ideal conceptions of identity, and sometimes displaying—as selflessness or sympathy—the attribute of attenuated agency that typically defines fallenness.

In criticizing a too-exclusive concentration on fallenness as transgressive sexuality, I don't mean to suggest that fallenness had no sexual referent or that no traces of suppressed sexual desire surround representations of fallen women; and of course one dominant fear behind the perceived contaminating power of the prostitute was the fear of sexually transmitted disease.[29] This book, however, self-consciously moves beyond a restrictively sexual meaning of fallenness, establishing the significance of displaced versions of fallenness to the cultural self-understandings of Victorians. In this sense my project too is Victorian, following the displacements that a prevailing attitude of censorship seemed to invite. But this approach derives not from any affinity with Victorian prudishness, or from a fetishistic disavowal of female sexuality, but rather from a commitment to reconstructing fallenness in terms of its own cultural horizons. A repressive approach to feminine sexuality undeniably informs the construction of gender in Victorian Britain, but repression was accompanied by a proliferation of metaphoric meanings of fallenness,

28. In a separate article on Victorian prostitution, Poovey uses W. R. Greg's article to elaborate more fully the symbolic function of the prostitute within bourgeois ideology, claiming that, as an available sexual resource, she served as "both the symbol and site of 'natural' class inequity and exploitation" but also inevitably raised the specter of social unrest. To counter this representation, according to Poovey, Greg defines the prostitute as innately moral, thereby aligning the lower-class prostitute with the virtuous middle-class woman and shoring up the gender ideology that is seen to stabilize class difference. While this view does begin to play out distinctly social threats that the Victorian prostitute can figure, it does not isolate or explore the category of fallenness. See Mary Poovey, "Speaking of the Body." For a very different approach to Greg, see my discussion in Chapter 1.

29. See Walkowitz, *Prostitution and Victorian Society* 48–65.

a virtual epidemic that formally resembled but by no means referred exclusively to fears of sexual or physical contamination. To distance such metaphoric meanings from a posited ultimate reference such as sexuality or the body allows us better to reconstruct the range of their cultural purposes.

Rhetoric and Theory

I have selected authors and texts that illustrate some of the most dramatic instances of the Victorian rhetoric of fallenness as well as some of the most significant challenges to it. In my desire to elaborate the more distinctly formal predicaments enacted through the rhetoric of fallenness, I have chosen several genres for close study, including the industrial novel, the autobiographical novel, the dramatic monologue, the novel-in-verse, social commentary, and journalism. After analyzing philosophical and social contexts in the first chapter, I turn to Dickens, who not only wrote novels in which fallenness figures prominently but also managed a fallen women's refuge for ten years. Because of Dickens's acute interest in the reformation of character and in the forces of modernization that threatened autonomy and private selfhood, he serves as a crucial introductory figure for the discussion of fallenness as a broad social and aesthetic category. Moreover, his writings feature a trope that commonly structures the rhetoric of fallenness, one that itself enacts a question of agency. This is the trope of metalepsis, in which the fallen figure is transformed from an effect into a cause, or vice versa. If on the one hand the fallen woman is seen as victimized or even constituted by forces that exceed her control—the force of a degrading urban milieu, the inescapability of pre-scripted downward paths—on the other hand she can serve as a threatening manifestation of those very forces that constituted her. The pervasive trope of metalepsis reflects just how contaminating fallenness was perceived to be: any distanced view of the fallen woman as victim could easily transmute into an anxious apprehension that she would communicate her condition to others. It also shows in a heightened way how fully assimilated the fallen figure's identity was to larger determining forces, how profoundly allegorized and reified this figure was in the cultural imaginary. Oscillating between victim and threat, effect and cause, the fallen woman both represented and precipitated multifaceted problems of agency.[30]

Throughout, I have chosen to analyze literary texts in which the fate of fallen characters is thematically central, such as Dickens's *David Copperfield*, Gaskell's *Ruth*, and Barrett Browning's *Aurora Leigh*. *Ruth* provides added interest because it explicitly thematizes the relation between religious and social versions of fallenness. I have also favored texts in which the convergence of political and aesthetic interests is particularly marked, such as Gaskell's *Mary Barton* and, again, *Aurora Leigh*. As I demonstrate, the prostitute Esther in *Mary Barton* occasions some of Gaskell's most extreme anxieties about the efficacy of reformist fiction, her fear that transforming the lives of the poor into pathos-inducing stories will promote a readerly quietism, while *Aurora Leigh*'s Marian Erle is pivotal to Barrett Browning's attempt to forge a rapprochement between philanthropy and art, and between intersubjective and aesthetic experience. In my chapters on Gaskell and Barrett Browning, moreover, I try to indicate social and cultural reasons why texts by middle-class women might articulate dilemmas and solutions differently from those by middle-class men.

I devote one chapter to an extended reading of D. G. Rossetti's poem "Jenny," a monologue describing a scholar's ruminations during a visit to a prostitute, who herself remains half asleep and semi-reclined throughout the poem. This text serves in many ways as a touchstone for this book, displaying in myriad ways the multiple forms of uncertain agency—economic, sexual, epistemological—ascribed to the Victorian prostitute. It also serves as

30. The metaleptical reversals I describe are implicitly acknowledged by Nead's dual approach to representations of the prostitute: her argument that on the one hand the prostitute represents threatening social forces, and on the other she is cast as a victim. Similarly, Mort refers to the "expansive logic" of early social medicine in Britain: "Immoral conduct was the direct result of the filth, squalor and disease of the urban working-class environment. But immorality—conceived as a general lack of self-reliance and improper habits—was also cited as one of the principal *causes* of disease." Mort, *Dangerous Sexualities* 29. In their discussion of the prostitute and other lower-class figures who haunt the bourgeois imaginary, Stallybrass and White discuss this same strategy in more strictly rhetorical terms: across literary and non-literary texts, they demonstrate, metonymic associations between subjects and their social environments are supplanted by metaphoric ones. For example, if at first reform-minded Victorians acknowledge or even insist that social conditions produce the filth surrounding the poor, this view typically devolves into a metaphorical identification of the poor with the degrading environment itself. Stallybrass and White, *The Politics and Poetics of Transgression* 131.

a touchstone because it powerfully dramatizes the speaker's inability to achieve any kind of mutuality or reciprocity with the (in this case, literally) fallen figure. The speaker's repeated objectifications of Jenny exemplify a more general cultural tendency to reify the fallen, to cast them as irredeemably other. Indeed, I read the poem as a virtual negation of dramatic monologue, insofar as the speaker recurringly suppresses impulses to actually speak to the prostitute. As we shall see at other crucial moments in the chapters, depicted encounters with fallen women typically insist on their own "failure": seen as a fantasmatic threat, the woman remains unheeded; seen as a victim, she becomes an object of condescending pity.

As I have indicated, such reifying representations helped to stabilize dominant models of selfhood, to contain and moralize what were really pervasive concerns about individual and social identity. Somehow, the idea that circumstances determine character, or that acts bring inexorable consequences, was made less threatening if one could point to a form of character that seemed incapable of influencing its fate in any way. Many writers thus chose to reserve more idealist conceptions of the self for their masculine or pure characters, while invoking forms of materialism and determinism when conceiving of fallen women. In fact, in some representations of fallen women, distinctly modern forms of paralyzing self-consciousness are visited upon the fallen as part of their punishment. But this tendency to marginalize what were felt to be threatening determinisms raises a larger question: are we to interpret Victorian fallenness as a distorted and false understanding of human agency, or, alternately, as a disavowed or even inadvertent truth? It's clear that many Victorians wanted to cordon off the condition of fallenness, reserving for their respectable selves the prerogatives of deliberative action and coherent identity. Yet from another perspective the fallen woman can appear simply as an exaggeration of those more modern forms of identity that were being circulated through the discourses of radicalism, the emergence of sociological understanding, and myriad literary genres investigating the status of subjectivity and character.

Ultimately, the question whether or not to endorse the model of fallen subjectivity dovetails with another question of theoretical import for this project. I earlier emphasized the importance of reconstructing specifically Victorian notions of agency while remaining self-conscious about the unavoidable and indeed productive ways in which contemporary concerns frame one's interpretations of the past. I think it equally important to be as explicit as possible about the normative principles that animate one's critical approach, especially when that critical approach makes recurrent appeal to political and ethical values. To the extent that I locate a negative process of othering integral to the rhetoric of fallenness—one that reifies, objectifies, and otherwise thwarts depictions of reciprocal interaction—I am myself appealing to intersubjective ideals of recognition and respect that need to be duly acknowledged. It is possible of course to insist that fallen characters are constituted through lamentable processes but nonetheless reveal a truth about subjectivity: its fundamental constructedness, dividedness, or absence (to itself and others). But my readings assume instead that although conceptions of fallenness derive from the mutually constitutive forms of power and knowledge that attend modernity, we nonetheless do not need to reproduce these extreme and potentially objectivist conceptions as an absolute fact about subjectivity, as Foucauldian approaches risk doing. The new philosophies and social theories of the early and mid-Victorian period forwarded the possibility of social critique when they rendered visible the many ways that social forces and cultural narratives condition and mediate human action. Unfortunately, however, they also often promoted atomistic and mechanistic models of agency. The Victorian rhetoric of fallenness took up these models, often entrenching them further by opposing an illusory ideal of autonomy to an extreme determinism characteristically gendered as feminine.

The rhetoric of fallenness thus counts for me not as disavowed or inadvertent truth but rather as a historically situated and ultimately distorted projection of our nonetheless irreducibly social subjectivities. In my view, our understanding of subjectivity must acknowledge the constitutive force of intersubjective practices; identity must be understood as constituted in and through ongoing relations with others, even as we acknowledge and analyze our places within larger systems. The rhetoric of fallenness, by extending the implications of atomistic social theory, distortedly allows a systems perspective to dominate its understanding of social life, thereby not only pro-

ducing a mechanistic determinism but also preventing the elaboration of identity as relational and intersubjective. I emphasize the
historical determinants of this disabling mode of understanding and
locate those moments where Victorian writers reconceive social and
aesthetic determinisms.

As we shall see, only when writers give the intersubjective character of subjective identity its due can they begin to indicate the
social ideals that will redress the negative effects of the rhetoric of
fallenness. Here my approach is informed by Habermas, who argues
that only by acknowledging the primacy of intersubjective practices,
and by becoming self-reflexive about the regulative ideals that guide
communicative action, can we properly understand, or begin to
transform, the social world. And like that of Habermas, my approach
to depictions of intersubjective relations is both reconstructive and
critical; accordingly, I use the word "intersubjective" both descriptively (to refer simply to the interpersonal and social relations that
I analyze) and normatively (to evoke various socially constituted
ethical and political ideals). However, I do not feel that Habermas
gives due recognition to nonrational aspects of social interaction. I
try to indicate, both through my critical stance and by drawing out
revisionist moments in Victorian texts, forms of intersubjectivity that
privilege not only rational dialogue but also sympathetic reciprocity
and social indeterminacy. And I conclude my discussions of Victorian literary texts with Elizabeth Barrett Browning because she goes
furthest toward a radical revision of the dominant discourse, using
a developed notion of reciprocal recognition to challenge reifying
approaches to fallenness.

Drawing out key revisionist moments among Victorian writers,
moments that articulate or at least gesture toward ideals of intersubjective reciprocity and social participation, is one of the principal
ways this book seeks to clarify the ethical and political implications
of the rhetoric of fallenness. In the Afterword, I more directly extend
such considerations to our own theoretical horizons. In broadest
terms, I aim to identify to what extent the dominance of a systems
perpective, which in some sense conditions the elaboration of fallen
subjectivity in Victorian culture, shapes poststructuralist paradigms
in cultural criticism. My analysis of contemporary approaches to
subjectivity and critiques of othering is here more directly informed
by Habermas's theory of communicative action and his general attempt to establish the dialectical relation between the critique of

systemic domination and the invocation of intersubjective ideals. By adopting Habermas and Habermasian-inspired approaches, I claim to show that the conceptions of selfhood and agency employed in poststructuralist cultural criticism are not consistent with the ethical ideals that animate its political critiques.

1

Mid-Victorian Conceptions of Character, Agency, and Reform: Social Science and the "Great Social Evil"

In the sixth and final book of his *System of Logic*, John Stuart Mill shifts his attention from the science of logic to "the logic of the moral sciences," setting forth a series of propositions for the development of a new science, ethology, which will establish the laws that determine the formation of human character. For Mill, the science of ethology will in turn provide the necessary foundation for a more broadly conceived science of society, insofar as the character of society ultimately derives from "the laws of individual human nature."[1] Mill's remarks in Book VI of the *Logic* remain somewhat sketchy and tentative, more in the manner of a prospectus than a complete demonstration, and he had hoped to extend the ideas in a later work, which he never in fact wrote. But precisely because of the methodical way in which Mill circles round and never quite secures his new science, the beginning of Book VI serves as a particularly apt introduction to mid-Victorian conceptions of agency and selfhood, and of individual and social identity. Mill's distinctive style of internal debate, his addiction to arguing both sides of the question, dramatizes the philosophical and social predicaments that inform Victorian debates on individual character and social reform.[2]

1. "The laws of the phenomena of society are, and can be, nothing but the laws of the actions and passions of human beings united together in the social state. Men, however, in a state of society, are still men; their actions and passions are obedient to the laws of individual human nature. . . . Human beings in society have no properties but those which are derived from, and may be resolved into, the laws of the nature of individual man." John Stuart Mill, *A System of Logic Ratiocinative and Inductive* 879 (originally published in 1843).
2. Mill is often used to dramatize debates and contested issues in Victorian cul-

This chapter is intended to set the context for an understanding of the Victorian category of fallenness, which I identified in the Introduction as a historically determined, and typically gendered, conception of attenuated autonomy or fractured identity. In order to introduce the cultural context for the analysis of fallenness, I begin with Mill's discussion of character, setting it in relation not only to the broader Victorian intellectual milieu but also to Mill's approaches to selfhood and agency in *On Liberty, The Subjection of Women,* and the *Autobiography*. I show how Mill negotiates the tension between materialist and idealist conceptions of the self, and I identify the assumptions about gender that underlie and trouble Victorian debates on the determinants of character and human action. In this context I then analyze nonliterary accounts of prostitution in the Victorian period.

A Science of Human Nature

Mill's project in the final book of the *Logic* is to set the "sciences of man" on a firm foundation by applying "the methods of Physical Science" to the study of human nature and society. In order for this positivistic project to be possible, Mill tells us in his "Introductory Remarks," a first and potentially fatal objection must be dispelled. "Are the actions of human beings, like all other natural events, subject to invariable laws? Does that constancy of causation, which is the foundation of every scientific theory of successive phenomena, really obtain among them?" Mill devotes the following chapter, "Of Liberty and Necessity," to an extended demonstration that these questions can in fact be answered in the affirmative. In thus defending the doctrine of philosophical necessity, however, Mill takes pains to distinguish it from a mechanical determinism, with which it is often, in his view, erroneously equated. For Mill, the claim

---

ture, for precisely this reason. Raymond Williams, for example, devotes a chapter of *Culture and Society* to Mill's essays on Bentham and Coleridge, noting that "Mill's attempt to absorb, and by discrimination and discarding to unify, the truths alike of the utilitarian and the idealist positions is, after all, a prologue to a very large part of the subsequent history of English thinking: in particular, to the greater part of English thinking about society and culture." Williams, *Culture and Society, 1780–1950* 49. Maurice Mandelbaum identifies a similar coming together in Mill of two defining traditions of nineteenth-century thought, the materialist and the idealist. See Mandelbaum, *History, Man, and Reason* 9.

embodied in the doctrine of philosophical necessity is simply that any human conduct is ultimately intelligible as the effect of a complex interplay among disposition, character, and circumstances:

> Correctly conceived, the doctrine called Philosophical Necessity is simply this: that, given the motives which are present to an individual's mind, and given likewise the character and disposition of the individual, the manner in which he will act might be unerringly inferred: that if we knew the person thoroughly, and knew all the inducements which are acting upon him, we could foretell his conduct with as much certainty as we can predict any physical event.

This doctrine, according to Mill, need not conflict with our "feeling of freedom," our sense that we perform our acts voluntarily. Indeed, to know fully the circumstances and character of another person is precisely to know how he or she shall "will to act in a particular case": "We may be free, and yet another may have reason to be perfectly certain what use we shall make of our freedom."[3]

Although the doctrine of necessity *need* not conflict with our "feeling of freedom," it turns out that it frequently does. For Mill, reason and analysis can demonstrate with clarity that the doctrine of necessity is not a fatalism, yet the imagination conceives the case differently and ascribes a "mysterious compulsion" to the relation between cause and effect, where all that really obtains is "uniformity of order" or "mere constancy of succession." "Even if the reason repudiates, the imagination retains, the feeling of some more intimate connexion, of some peculiar tie, or mysterious constraint exercised by the antecedent over the consequent." Ultimately, Mill insists that this melodramatic conception of causation, which is evoked most frequently by the critics of necessitarianism, does not obtain even in the physical world of inanimate objects, as "the best philosophical authorities" recognize (a reference to Hume and his followers).[4] But of more interest is his remark that this misconception

---

3. Mill, *Logic* 833, 835, 836–37.
4. Mill, *Logic* 837–38. In the 1872 edition of the *Logic*, Mill substituted "necessitarian(s)" for "necessarian(s)" throughout. I use his later preference throughout this chapter, though it should be noted that the other variant appears frequently in Victorian texts.

nonetheless "exist[s] more or less obscurely in the minds of most necessitarians, however they may in words disavow it."[5]

That Mill himself was susceptible to an anxious fatalism is well documented in the *Autobiography*. While the famous mental crisis Mill describes undergoing in 1826–27 is not exclusively about questions of determinism, in looking back Mill senses that prior to his discovery of poetry and the "internal culture of the individual," he had been a "mere reasoning machine," his feelings worn away by "the habit of analysis." Likewise, he is deeply impressed when he later discovers that his companions at that time had viewed him as a " 'made' or manufactured man." More important for present purposes, we also learn in the *Autobiography* that Mill was subject to subsequent periods of dejection in which "the doctrine of what is called Philosophical Necessity weighed on my existence like an incubus. I felt as if I was scientifically proved to be the helpless slave of antecedent circumstances; as if my character and that of all others had been formed for us by agencies beyond our control, and was wholly out of our own power."[6] Mill goes on to report that, after devoting much time to the subject, he was finally able to see his way clear to the arguments that he would present most fully in the *Logic*, arguments that extend beyond the defense of moral freedom I have already sketched. Briefly, Mill cuts through the Gordian knot of necessity by asserting that although our characters are determined by circumstances, we ourselves are able to influence those very circumstances that determine us. As E. P. Thompson might put it, though we are all made characters, we participate in our own making.

Mill's accounts of his own bouts of dejection in the *Autobiography*, as well as his sympathetic discussion of how liable even the most rational necessitarians are to feelings of fatalism, genuinely acknowledge the force of deterministic thinking even as they claim to have transcended it. Although he believes strongly that he has reasoned through the problem, Mill does not disavow his own grapplings with a dispiriting fatalism to which, in his view, everyone is vul-

5. Mill, *Logic* 838. Mill believed that a significant cause of the misconceptions surrounding the doctrine of necessity was the word "necessity" itself, and he advocated abandonment of the "inappropriate" and "pernicious" term. See *Logic* 839–42.

6. John Stuart Mill, *Autobiography* 147, 111, 141, 163, 175–77. The *Autobiography* was originally published posthumously, in 1873.

nerable. Yet a strange gendered image appears in the passage from the *Autobiography*: the doctrine of philosophical necessity, we are told, "weighed on [his] existence like an incubus." Originally a personified representation of the nightmare, an incubus is an evil demon supposed to descend upon people during sleep and especially to have sexual intercourse with women. The image thus casts Mill's own apprehension of being a fully determined subject in explicitly sexual and feminine terms: for Mill, to feel that he lacks autonomy as a deliberative, rational subject is tantamount to being sexually ravaged while he remains unconscious and helpless. Significantly, Mill does not use the term *succubus*, which would have allowed him to retain a masculine subject-position.

Mill here produces an intellectualist version of the rhetoric of fallenness, which more generally constitutes fallen women as subjects whose characters have "been formed . . . by agencies beyond [their] control." The supple logic that informs this rhetoric is most tellingly revealed in such reversals as this, where the experience of being determined is portrayed in sexualized, feminine terms. In fact, a muted version of this same rhetoric appears in the passage from the *Logic* in which Mill describes the erroneous apprehension of necessity. In the act of imaginative feeling that overshadows rational conviction, one conceives of the relation between antecedent and consequent as a "more intimate connexion," a "peculiar tie," a "mysterious constraint."[7] My suggestion here is not that Mill seeks to relegate fatalism to a discredited feminine realm of the imagination or feelings—after all, it is the insistent "feeling of freedom" that will require Mill's own repudiation of a too-stark determinism. Rather, I wish to emphasize that Mill imagines determinism as a kind of excessive intimacy, which then transmutes, through the mediating word "tie," into a form of constraint. One might be tempted to read this description of the power of antecedents over consequents as Mill's displaced anxiety about deriving a little too directly from his own paternal antecedent, his experience of the filial "tie" as a little too constraining.[8] But the evocation of a relation at once unfamiliar

7. Mill, *Logic* 837–38.
8. Janice Carlisle makes precisely this argument. In general, she reads Mill's intellectualist traumas of determinism as displacements of more specific problems in his relationships and career. Thus she interprets Mill's agonized grapplings with the doctrine of necessity as a generalized and abstract representation of a dilemma that

("peculiar," "mysterious") and intimate conforms more generally to the rhetorical pattern I am identifying. In an oblique way, Mill here once again figures the alienating apprehension of oneself as the mere effect of prior causes in terms of an inappropriate intimacy.

Mill's reelaboration of the doctrine of necessity, and in particular the form his theory of character begins to assume, further develops the ways in which gendered categories govern Victorian approaches to the question of agency. In the *Logic* Mill explicitly criticizes the Owenite doctrine of the formation of character; and, as I shall take up later, he also seeks to revise or recast principles that inform the associationism of his father and the Benthamites.

The Owenites were a group of early socialist reformers who subscribed to the writings of Robert Owen, a Welsh factory owner who first became known for his experiments in labor management at the Scottish cotton factory of New Lanark. Owen documents his transformation of the New Lanark factory in his *Essays on the Formation of Human Character*. As he tells it, when he first assumed the stewardship of the factory, the population "possessed almost all the vices and very few of the virtues of a social community. Theft and the receipt of stolen goods was their trade, idleness and drunkenness their habit, falsehood and deception their garb, dissensions civil and religious their daily practice; they united only in a zealous systematic opposition to their employers." By Owen's account, his managerial intervention is simple, bloodless, and instantly successful. He merely reveals to the workers that they will derive "immediate benefits" if they alter their conduct, demonstrating that their present behavior produces a host of evils. Appealing to their reason, Owen explains that a cultivated habit of industry, along with sympathy, friendship, and understanding, "would soon render that place a paradise, which, from the most mistaken principles of action, they now made the abode of misery." These simple truths are adopted, and the community is transformed: the workers "became industrious, temperate, healthy; faithful to their employers, and kind to

"found its more immediate and palpable embodiment in the question of vocation." In submitting to a career at the East India Company, a career chosen as well as shared by his father, Mill sensed not only that he had forfeited control over his own vocation but that he was not participating in the active life of politics, the sphere that most engaged his intellectual interest. Carlisle, *John Stuart Mill and the Writing of Character* 70–71.

each other." Or, more epigrammatically, "They were taught to be rational, and they acted rationally."[9]

Owen primarily intends his utopian narrative to illustrate a radical conception of character formation, one that can justify the most ambitious and far-reaching projects of social transformation. As he puts it in the famous passage from the *Essays,*

> Every day will make it more and more evident that the character of man, is, without a single exception, always formed for him; that it may be, and is, chiefly created by his predecessors; that they give him, or may give him, his ideas and habits, which are the powers that govern and direct his conduct. Man, therefore, never did, nor is it possible he ever can, form his own character.[10]

This passage seems to imply a hopeless determinism, but Owen actually derives from it a principle that functions as a lever of social change. All those who participate in the act of governing—whether as national leaders, factory owners, or educators—should serve as omnipotent predecessors who mold and shape the characters of those they govern. Owen's use of a genealogical model thus does not so much insist that we are the hapless victims of whatever characters our predecessors chose to give us as justify the unlimited aspirations of a paternalistic project of reform.

Furthermore, even though Owen explicitly states that "the true and sole origin of evil" is the belief that men form their own characters, his program for rational enlightenment does not forsake entirely the principle of *self*-transformation.[11] This tension between free will and determinism, which ultimately assumes the form of an outright contradiction in Owen, appears frequently across Victorian radical and reformist literature. As Catherine Gallagher has shown, it stems from a series of not easily reconciled tendencies in the social discourse of the period.[12] In order to counter moralizing discourses that blamed workers or the poor for their miserable conditions, social critics stressed the environmental determination of character. But

---

9. Robert Owen, *Essays on the Formation of Human Character* 20, 21, 23. The essays were originally published in 1812.

10. Owen, *Essays* 39.

11. Owen, *Essays* 39.

12. For a discussion of this contradiction in Victorian discourses on abolition and industrial reform, see Catherine Gallagher, *The Industrial Reformation of English Fiction* 3–35. I am indebted in the discussion that follows to Gallagher's analysis.

this emphasis, which was often motivated by a desire to promote sympathy and understanding, risked shading into a social determinism that could only lament the tragic plight of the poor. Partly to dispel this effect, and partly to convince others that transformation was possible, critics simultaneously stressed the workers' capacity for enlightened self-control and self-transformation. While many, like Owen himself, adopted a paternalistic rhetoric in which the rulers showed the childlike workers how best to conduct themselves, such a stance could not sustain itself without some appeal to the workers' own rational participation in the project of character transformation. This participative aspect comes out most strongly in Owen when he describes reformation of character through rational education. Although educators are bound to encounter strong resistance from previously inculcated misconceptions, ultimately the truth will prevail, transforming the objects of reform into agents of reform.

> Let them [the students under the present system of education] begin to think calmly on these subjects, to examine their own minds, and the minds of all around them, and they will become conscious of the absurdities and inconsistencies in which their forefathers have trained them; they will then abhor the errors by which they have been so long abused; and with an earnestness not to be resisted, they will exert their utmost faculties to remove the cause of so much misery to man.[13]

Thus, even though the Owenites primarily portray character as a product of external forces, their program of character reform nonetheless requires them to preserve intact some notion of rational autonomy.

Immediately evident from this discussion is the centrality of the category of "character" itself. Despite the larger social agendas and ideals driving radical and reformist discourses, the dominant concern remains the transformation of individual character. Although Mill seeks to recast the concept of character formation that informs Owenism, he still privileges the individual as the fundamental unit of social analysis and the primary locus of social change. As we shall see, the category of character is a contested term in Victorian debates

13. Owen, *Essays* 71.

over selfhood, inflected in very different ways by different writers. Indeed, the term itself becomes an object of struggle, as differing camps seek to claim it for their own. In his own discussions of character, Mill is drawn in two directions at once, toward the scientific approach to human action that is represented by Benthamism, and toward more idealist emphases on "internal culture," as represented by Coleridge and Carlyle. By exploring his attempt to balance these two ways of thinking about selfhood and character, we can more clearly see the terms of the debate he was attempting to resolve.

Mill's interpretation of Owenism in the *Logic* takes as fundamental and overriding Owen's principle that one never forms one's own character; as a consequence, the Owenites are "the sect which in our own day has most perseveringly inculcated and most perversely misunderstood" the doctrine of necessity. As we know, Mill contests the Owenite principle of character formation by calmly pointing out that while circumstances influence character, characters can themselves influence circumstances. One cannot directly will to be different from what one is, but then, neither did those who helped shape us directly will our characters into existence: "They made us what they did make us, by willing, not the end, but the requisite means; and we, when our habits are not too inveterate, can, by similarly willing the requisite means, make ourselves different." Mill then addresses a potential further objection to his position. For the Owenite, to say that we can "will" to change our characters need not alter the fact that we are externally determined, for in such an event our own desire to change has presumably itself been imposed on us by circumstances. Mill's response to this idea is signally difficult to follow, but the distinction he appears to draw is that between "education" and "experience." The desire to change our characters *is* formed for us, Mill concedes, but "not, in general, by our organization, nor wholly by our education, but by our experience; experience of the painful consequences of the character we previously had: or by some strong feeling of admiration or aspiration, accidentally aroused."[14]

In order to understand Mill's drift here, we must detour through the traditions of utilitarianism and associationism. The doctrine of necessity that Mill seeks to vindicate in face of the distortions of

14. Mill, *Logic* 840–41.

Owenite theory derives from a philosophical tradition extending from James Mill and Bentham back through Priestley, Hartley, Hume, and Locke. One of the defining features of this tradition is the rejection of any belief in innate ideas and, correspondingly, the privileging of education and experience as the decisive determinants of human action and development. Ideas, rather than springing up spontaneously in the mind, are the result of sensations and complex processes of association that accrue through experience.[15] But if associationist philosophy emphasized the malleability of human nature, it also subscribed to a hedonistic psychology that held that people tend to pursue pleasure and avoid pain. In the hands of some of its practitioners (Bentham, particularly) this principle became rigidified into a more substantive theory of human nature as essentially egoistic. It is excesses of this kind of "sole motive" theorizing that Mill criticizes in the *Logic* as examples of the "geometrical, or abstract method," a method that he traces back to Hobbes.[16] Mill's recasting of the doctrine of utilitarianism insists on a more expansive notion of pleasure and interests, incorporating the idea that one can derive pleasure from disinterested activity and the cultivation of character and virtue.[17]

Even though Mill seeks to demonstrate that on correct interpretation, the doctrine of necessity is simple, clear, and unproblematic, the tradition that he invokes itself manifests the same tensions that characterize Owenism and reformist literature more generally. Indeed, Mill seems to use Owenism as a philosopher's whipping boy in order partly to protect the tradition represented by his father. For the doctrine of associationism, with its essentially passive conception of subjectivity, itself risked understanding character as the mere product of conditioning. Mill himself testifies in the *Autobiography* that the associationist education to which his father subjected him turned him into a "mere reasoning machine." Much like Owenism, then, the tradition of philosophical necessity experienced difficulties

15. There were considerable differences among individual associationists. For example, as Mandelbaum explains, Locke held onto some form of nativism in his claim that the mind's own operations could not be interpreted in terms of the effects of experience, whereas Berkeley, Hume, and Hartley took a more radical stance. For a detailed discussion of the associationist tradition, see Mandelbaum, *History, Man, and Reason* 147–62.

16. Mill, *Logic* 887–94.

17. See John Stuart Mill, *Utilitarianism* 210–13. *Utilitarianism* was originally published in 1861.

in reconciling its foundational principles (of the reasons for action and the power of external conditions) with its desire to promote moral betterment. In order to resolve this tension between fact and value, Bentham and James Mill argued for a species of moral education that would teach self-interested individuals to identify (associate) their own interests with the interests of the greatest number. Others claimed that such identifications would come about more naturally through experience, that the painful results of conflicts of interest would teach individuals that nakedly egoistic acts were productive not of pleasure but of pain.[18] Hence, egoistic impulses would gradually be transmuted into the virtuous desire to secure the greater good of the community. But in these cases, virtue is either contingent upon external conditioning or derivative of a more basic self-interest. Such resolutions did not satisfy Mill, who sought to establish a more inward and beneficent conception of virtue.

We are now in a better position to analyze Mill's awkward solution to the Owenite dilemma. His focus on the painful teaching of experience follows from the associationist tradition, and this derivation is confirmed by the swerve into the notion of accidental arousals of strong feelings of admiration or aspiration—by the sudden admission, in other words, of the force of contingent associations. Yet Mill is also struggling here to move beyond the discourse of associationism, and his emphasis on character is indicative of the direction he wishes to take. For note that Mill refers not to the painful consequences of our previous actions, but to the painful consequences of our previous character. That is, Mill begins to elaborate a model whereby the individual regulates and cultivates his or her own character. This accent on self-cultivation, or "the internal culture of the individual," profoundly affects the "science" of human nature that Mill elaborates. By allowing for a seat of judgment and autonomous rationality that exceeds, monitors, and seeks to alter character, Mill is able to retain both the notion of a "made" or "formed" character (which is central to his new science) and the possibility for moral agency. But, perhaps inevitably, he begins to replicate the very dilemmas he intends to sublate.

18. As the necessitarian Charles Bray writes, "We are made to suffer for that which is already done, that the further evil may be prevented which would ensue from the repetition of the offence." Bray, *The Philosophy of Necessity* 179. For further discussion of the place of this argument in the associationist tradition, see Mandelbaum, *History, Man, and Reason* 158.

For Mill, moral agency is demonstrated in our capacity to "modify our character *if we wish*." Mastering habits and temptations confirms this capacity, and our conviction that we have realized our own previous attempts at altering our character "[renders] our consciousness of freedom complete." And if we cannot achieve such absolute moral progress, then we must at least feel that "our wish, if not strong enough to alter our character, is strong enough to conquer our character when the two are brought into conflict in any particular case of conduct." Here the impasse reveals itself most sharply, though Mill's prose and style of argumentation remain distinctly unruffled. For suddenly, the question of the formation of character is mooted by an appeal to a form of consciousness that can stand apart from, and hence transcend, character: the "power of the mind" or "the feeling of moral freedom."[19] Mill generates a split self, one part free, one part made.[20]

By the end of the chapter, the category of character has been recast so as to itself comprise the separate governing faculty that earlier took character as its preformed yet still malleable object. In an elaboration of the critique of utilitarianism, Mill argues that not only likings and aversions but also "purposes," constituted by "habits of willing," serve as motives for human action. He then proclaims, "It is only when our purposes have become independent of the feelings of pain or pleasure from which they originally took their rise, that we are said to have a confirmed character. 'A character,' says Novalis, 'is a completely fashioned will.' "[21] This remark is similar to the famous passage in *On Liberty*: "A person whose desires and impulses are his own—are the expression of his own nature, as it has been developed and modified by his own culture—is said to have a character. One whose desires and impulses are not his own, has no character, no more than a steam-engine has a character."[22]

The transformations undergone by the concept of character reveal its privileged, protected status: before pursuing the science of human nature and showing how human action follows universal laws of

19. Mill, *Logic* 841.
20. Alan Ryan argues that Mill's position generates a kind of spectator-self: "the agent disappears, to be replaced by a spectator of events occurring at a location which we somehow continue to call 'him.' " Ryan, *John Stuart Mill* 130. Also see Carlisle, *John Stuart Mill and the Writing of Character* 23.
21. Mill, *Logic* 842–43.
22. John Stuart Mill, *On Liberty* 264. *On Liberty* was originally published in 1859.

causation, Mill presents a reconstructed doctrine of necessity, one in which character is less the object of universal laws than the index of human purposiveness and rational control. And while Mill ostensibly focuses on the laws of individual human nature so that he may build up toward a science of society, his remarks on character indicate a program of moral betterment that is distinctly atomistic, the individual's relation to him- or herself seeming to take precedence over any larger program of reform. We have seen why this is so: if the individual is not accorded primacy as the locus and agent of change, then character risks becoming something that is manufactured externally. In laying the ground for a science of human nature, therefore, Mill does not in the least mean to deny the dignity of the individual; on the contrary, he wishes to incorporate into his scientific approach to society an aesthetic conception of self-crafted character. But this also means that Mill's science of character doesn't really solidify. As Janice Carlisle has shown, Mill's initial and tentative ethological analyses in the *Logic* generate only a series of clichés, and he really does not get much beyond the rudimentary claim that human action is subject to a complex of causes, which include among them circumstances, previous character, physical organization, and, of course, one's desire to alter the circumstances that determine one's character.[23]

Mill's writings on character and the science of society attempt to reconcile what were frequently seen by Victorian contemporaries as two incompatible approaches to selfhood and agency: the materialist and the idealist. The materialists included the utilitarians, the followers of the doctrine of necessity, the Owenites, the positivists: all those who conceived of character as externally determined and all those who denied the possibility of a self-sufficient moral consciousness. They were generally eager to apply scientific methods to the study of human nature and society, and were optimistic about the possibility for reform based on the principle of the malleability of character. The idealists included Coleridge, Carlyle, James Martineau, and all those, generally under the influence of German romanticism and idealism, who subscribed to a notion of character as self-created.[24] These writers found the general tenets of the mate-

---

23. Carlisle, *John Stuart Mill and the Writing of Character* 123–67; also see Ryan, *John Stuart Mill* 133–47.
24. See Mandelbaum, *History, Man, and Reason*, for an extended discussion of how

rialists pernicious and morally repugnant. To approach the human soul scientifically and instrumentally was merely to extend the negative effects of an increasingly materialistic, industrialized, and mechanized society.

That Owen could cheerfully employ metaphors in which workers were "vital machines" and character transformation could be calculated with "mathematical precision" horrified people like James Martineau, who himself fled from an early embrace of the doctrine of necessity.[25] In the preface to his *Types of Ethical Theory*, Martineau affirms "the secret misgivings which [he] had always felt at either discarding or perverting the terms which constitute the vocabulary of character,—'responsibility,' 'guilt,' 'merit,' 'duty.' " Disputing both the doctrine of necessity and evolutionist approaches, Martineau argues that "moral existence" is constituted by "the presence of a self-conscious, free, and reflecting subject."[26]

As the famous essays on Bentham and Coleridge reveal more explicitly, Mill thought that both sides of the debate over "moral existence" had something valuable to contribute. Mill praises Bentham for his powerful practical understanding of society, yet faults him severely for neglecting the nobility of character and the importance of "self-culture": "Man is never recognized by him as a being capable of pursuing spiritual perfection as an end; of desiring, for its own sake, the conformity of his own character to his standard of excellence, without hope of good or fear of evil from other source than his own inward consciousness." For Mill, "the regulation of [the human being's] outward actions," founded on an understanding of the laws of the formation of character, is a crucial part of morality, but it must be combined with "self-education" in order to work properly.[27]

James Martineau's "secret misgivings" and Mill's carefully elaborated middle ground attest to the profound defamiliarization brought on by the debates over the formation of character and the transformation of society, particularly through the "perversion" of an older moral vocabulary. The utilitarian view considers actions

these traditions inform nineteenth-century British and continental thought more generally.

25. Owen, *Essays* 30, 10.

26. James Martineau, *Types of Ethical Theory* xii–xiii, xv.

27. John Stuart Mill, "Bentham" 95, 98. "Bentham" was originally published in 1838.

vicious or virtuous insofar as they are productive of misery or happiness, pain or pleasure; the idea of an internal moral nature is abandoned. Responsibility becomes the duty to recognize and remember what causes are productive of which effects, and henceforth to remove causes that issue in pain and to apply causes that promote pleasure.[28] In countering such arguments, Mill protects the notions of inward consciousness and virtuous character, defining virtue in terms of freedom. For Mill, the cultivation of virtue is made possible by our moral freedom; and correlatively, we can be assured of our freedom only if we successfully cultivate our virtue. Thus, directly after his statement in the *Logic* that moral freedom consists in being able to conquer our character when it comes into conflict with our wishes, Mill adds, "And hence it is said with truth, that none but a person of confirmed virtue is completely free."[29]

If virtue is correlated with self-control, freedom, and self-consistency, it should come as no surprise that the person who lacks these qualities is not vicious but rather determined. Thus, in *On Liberty*, the failure to make one's desires and impulses one's own means not that one is evil but that one is a machine ("a steam engine"). And here we can begin to see the significance of the category of fallenness in the discourse of the Victorian period, even though Mill does not himself invoke the term. If one does not oversee the development of one's own character, then one is destined to be driven by forces that exceed rational consciousness, whether these be external circumstances or internal promptings. The absence of virtue becomes the absence of "character," which is another name for coherent and self-regulated identity. It is the argument of this book that Victorian discursive practices frequently gendered this opposition, such that women were far more liable to the lapses of control that defined a character as "lost" or "ruined." And although a specific form of selfless virtue was allotted to women, it is crucial to understand that fallenness was predominantly defined in opposition to a masculine ideal of rational control and purposive action.

---

28. "But if philosophical necessity be true, what becomes of all the distinctions between virtue and vice? If all actions are necessary, are not all equally virtuous and vicious? They would undoubtedly be so if there were no difference between pleasure and pain, happiness and misery; but so long as there is this difference, the inherent distinction between actions must continue, as they tend either to one state or another." Bray, *The Philosophy of Necessity* 190.

29. Mill, *Logic* 841. This sentence was not added until the 1868 edition, but it merely renders explicit a series of connections that Mill has been tacitly assuming.

In fact, the ideal of feminine virtue, insofar as it neglects "the internal culture of the individual," can actually promote rather than prevent fallenness. Mill implies as much in *The Subjection of Women*: "All women are brought up from the very earliest years in the belief that their ideal of character is the very opposite to that of men; not self-will, and government by self-control, but submission, and yielding to the control of others."[30] Women are likely to fall, and when they do, it won't be out of any power of choice, since choice is dependent on self-control.

Mill must be credited for his trenchant critiques of the unequal position of women in his society; moreover, his use of the incubus image in the *Autobiography* reveals a sympathetic identification with a feminized subject-position, rather than the kinds of misogynistic disavowal that frequently attend representations of fallenness. Nonetheless, *The Subjection of Women* risks casting women as somehow more subject to external conditioning than men, and hence more "artificial":

> I consider it presumption in any one to pretend to decide what women are or are not, can or cannot be, by natural constitution. They have always hitherto been kept, as far as regards spontaneous development, in so unnatural a state, that their nature cannot but have been greatly distorted and disguised; and no one can safely pronounce that if women's nature were left to choose its direction as freely as men's, and if no artificial bent were attempted to be given to it except that required by the conditions of human society, and given to both sexes alike, there would be any material difference, or perhaps any difference at all, in the character and capacities which would unfold themselves.[31]

Women's nature is "greatly distorted and disguised" because they have been subjected and thereby rendered artificial; to free them would allow an as-yet-unimaginable character to "unfold" itself. It is not the organic metaphor of blighted growth that is significant here. Mill elsewhere employs an organic concept of individual development that is gender neutral, and that is deployed specifically

---

30. John Stuart Mill, *The Subjection of Women* 271. This essay was originally published in 1869.
31. Mill, *The Subjection of Women* 304–5.

against mechanistic conceptions of character and human nature.[32] The more telling point of Mill's remarks about Victorian feminine character is a not fully examined assumption of women's greater susceptibility, malleability, and artificiality: less that they need to recover their true nature than that they are too easily manufactured.

Mill's reconstruction of virtue and character reveals that what was being threatened by the contemporary philosophies of necessity and utilitarianism was not so much cherished notions of goodness but rather vital investments in autonomy and integral selfhood. Hence, what jeopardizes virtue in Mill's schema is not active or deliberate viciousness but rather a conception of subjectivity and human behavior that challenges the very possibility of moral agency. Mill does not himself use the term *fallenness* or extensively elaborate a gendered category of attenuated autonomy. Still, his general discussions of virtue and the formation of character illuminate how concepts of freedom and determinism inflect the representation of fallenness in Victorian culture.

Also relevant to a broader understanding of Victorian fallenness is Mill's critique of the distinct social and interpersonal consequences that follow from an overly deterministic conception of human nature. As I discussed above, Mill criticized Bentham for failing to acknowledge the nobility and cultivation of character as essential to any program of moral education. Equally memorable, however, is Mill's critique of Bentham's lack of sympathy, and his concomitant emphasis, in the essay on Coleridge, on "a strong and active principle of cohesion among the members of the same community or state."[33] Because strict empirical observation dominates his approach to human nature, Bentham lacks "the power by which one human being enters into the mind and circumstances of another," a power Mill associates with poetry, drama, and history. Bentham's personal failure also translates into a failure of his general philosophy, which does not acknowledge the sympathetic aspect of human actions, their degree of "lovableness."[34] Using the example of Brutus' sent-

32. In *On Liberty*, for example, Mill writes, "Human nature is not a machine to be built after a model, and set to do exactly the work prescribed for it, but a tree, which requires to grow and develope [sic] itself on all sides, acccording to the tendency of the inward forces which make it a living thing" (263).

33. John Stuart Mill, "Coleridge" 134–35. "Coleridge" was originally published in 1840.

34. Mill, "Bentham" 92, 112.

encing of his sons, Mill argues that although the action was morally right, there was nothing lovable about it, because it involved the suppression of human ties of affection.

Mill's discussion of Bentham does not itself integrate sympathy into morality, retaining lovableness as a separate quality; still, it draws attention to the privileging of egoistic motives in the philosophies of necessity and utilitarianism. And in later works, Mill gives sympathy a central role, arguing for its importance in the moral cultivation of character. As he writes in the *Autobiography*, the discovery of Wordsworth during his crisis not only taught him to find happiness in "tranquil contemplation" but inspired interest in "the common feelings and common destiny of human beings." Mill correspondingly criticizes the denigration of the sympathies in most English thinkers, who "almost seem to regard them as necessary evils, required for keeping men's actions benevolent and compassionate."[35] Likewise, in *The Subjection of Women* he proclaims, "We are entering into an order of things in which justice will again be the primary virtue; grounded as before on equal, but now also on sympathetic association; having its root no longer in the instinct of equals for self-protection, but in a cultivated sympathy between them."[36]

I discussed earlier the kinds of problems that ensue when philosophers of necessity attempt to reconcile the self-interested character of human action with ideals of moral betterment, the latter of which require that one attend to the greater good of the community or state. To accord equal primacy to "sympathetic" or "disinterested" feelings is one way to solve those problems, and this alternative is enacted not only by Mill but also by others such as Charles Bray.[37] It is also central to the theories of social evolution, in which

35. Mill, *Autobiography* 153, 157.
36. Mill, *The Subjection of Women* 294.
37. Although an atomistic egoism predominates, the emphasis on the sympathetic feelings is not entirely missing from the philosophies of James Mill and Bentham, as Elie Halevy demonstrates in his exhaustive study of the Benthamite tradition. First, Bentham does admit extrapersonal motives for actions and includes among his list of pleasures the pleasures of association. More important, James Mill and Bentham generate a theory about the progress of sympathy in the individual, its development from simple to complex forms (love of parents to love of humanity), an approach that anticipates the social evolutionists. Briefly, James Mill and Bentham suggest that the more one gets enmeshed in larger social communities, the more difficult it becomes to separate sympathetic feelings from egoistic ones, and eventually one can't help but act morally. However, this line of argument remains nascent because neither

"consensus" between parts of an organically conceived social whole blurs into moral values such as "sympathy" and "solidarity."[38]

Sympathy also occupies a tenuous and sometimes highly vexed place in many Victorian depictions of fallenness. The outcast status of the fallen woman is often felt, by her and by others, to be absolute: one can feel compassion, one can lament her downfall, but reciprocal sympathy of the sort extolled and heralded by Mill in *The Subjection of Women* remains almost entirely unimaginable. And, of course, many commentators deny the possibility of *any* kind of sympathetic encounter, even of the most patronizing or nonreciprocal sort, arguing that fallenness entails exile, isolation, and radical attenuation of social ties. As the second half of this chapter shows, even those who argue most strenuously for compassionate rescue do so precisely because they see how powerfully the prevalent discourse militates against it.

There are several reasons why the fallen woman was constructed as either inaccessible to, or profoundly in need of, sympathy. On the most basic level, her sexual lapse, which upset revered conceptions of feminine "purity," provoked moral repugnance on the one hand and pleas for mercy on the other. But I want to suggest a less obvious reason for the profound tensions and problems generated whenever sympathy and fallenness were spoken of together. The extreme model of determined selfhood represented by fallenness itself derives from an atomistic and sometimes even mechanistic worldview, one unable to theorize intersubjective bases of selfhood and agency. These paradigms enforce the fallen woman's radical exile from the possibilities for sympathetic encounters, and they are a primary reason why the image of the unredeemable fallen woman is so marked and profound in mid-Victorian culture.

It is important, however, to distinguish fallenness from the understanding of vice that likewise derives from hedonistic atomism. In a number of associationist and, later, evolutionist models, virtue consists of the development of the disinterested feelings from out of a primary egotism. Accordingly, vice becomes correlated with

---

Mill nor Bentham wants to argue that one acts morally by nature. See Elie Halevy, *The Growth of Philosophic Radicalism* 465, 471–73.

38. For a discussion of the link between "consensus" and sympathy in Comte, Spencer, Mill, Eliot, and Lewes, see Suzanne Graver, *George Eliot and Community* 153–55. Also see Herbert Spencer, *Social Statics* 448.

recalcitrant self-interest, and it can be attributed to both men and women.

Victorian domestic ideologues named particular feminine vices that women should guard against: vanity, caprice, self-indulgence, artifice.[39] These vices evoke a prevalent cultural conception of the self-centered or egoistic woman, and we have numberless literary representations of such types: Rosamond in *Middlemarch*, Blanche Ingram in *Jane Eyre*, Becky Sharp in *Vanity Fair*, to name but a few. These women are distinguished from the *fallen*, however morally castigated they may be, largely because they retain a resilient agency; they are, in fact, notable for their power. As a victim, the fallen woman may come metaleptically to symbolize those forces that determined her, but she does not typically function as a villainous or vicious agent. As I have stressed, fallenness displaces threats to autonomy and discrete identity, to cherished forms of masculine selfhood. Fallenness, with its insistent emphasis on a self driven or fractured by external forces, challenges the very possibility of a self-regulated moral existence.

Fallenness is thus fundamentally opposed to the ideal of a masculine subject capable of controlling itself and influencing its surrounding circumstances. But of course we cannot overlook the fact that the Victorian domestic woman was typically seen as the repository of precisely those sympathetic or disinterested feelings that Mill is most eloquent about in *The Subjection of Women*. Indeed, part of the way the wider cultural discourse redressed the negative moral implications of self-interestedness was to allocate a redemptive sympathy to the sphere of private domesticity and to the character of femininity. In this ideology, which reflected the close connection between political economy and utilitarianism, it was predominantly economic man who was seen to be motivated by self-interest. Thus in *The Women of England, Their Social Duties, and Domestic Habits*, Sarah Stickney Ellis, the prolific theorist of women's roles and duties, argues that the women of England have "deep responsibilities" and "urgent claims" insofar as "a nation's moral wealth is in [their]

39. "It is necessary for [woman] to lay aside all her natural caprice, her love of self-indulgence, her vanity, her indolence—in short, her very *self*—and assuming a new nature, which nothing less than watchfulness and prayer can enable her constantly to maintain, to spend her mental and moral capabilities in devising means for promoting the happiness of others, while her own derives a remote and secondary existence from theirs." Mrs. [Sarah Stickney] Ellis, *The Women of England* 40.

keeping." The growth of international communication and commerce has created a situation in which men's "whole being is becoming swallowed up in efforts and calculations relating to their pecuniary success." It is women who must "counteract this evil, by calling back the attention of man to those sunnier spots in his existence, by which the growth of his moral feelings have been encouraged, and his heart approved." Women must guide the moral development of men, precisely because women cultivate faculties that extend beyond "selfish gratification," dedicating themselves to "the great end of promoting the happiness of those around them."[40]

The doctrine of the separate spheres, and of women's role as moral guide and champion of the disinterested feelings, is familiar to anyone with even a superficial knowledge of the Victorian era. It is significant to my discussion here because of its implications for an understanding of fallenness as attenuated autonomy. The question becomes, how does this doctrine affect the idea that fallenness is dominantly a negative version of the (masculine) self conceived in terms of rational control, freedom, and self-consistency? After all, the virtuous domestic woman was certainly expected to be self-consistent and, to a certain extent, self-regulating. Crucially, however, she was often not accorded the same level of rational control and deliberative consciousness that is so prominent in the construction of masculine virtue, or *character* in Mill's sense. Accounts that claim extraordinary responsibilities and duties for "the women of England" recurrently struggle against portraying feminine influence as a form of power that women wield too deliberately or instrumentally. The idea of action that is both selfless and overly reflective risks aggrandizing an agent who is supposed to be self-effacing.[41]

40. Ellis, *The Women of England* 16, 48, 49, 50, 23.

41. Although Ellis's text reflects this tension, it is also clear that she wishes to make potent claims on behalf of feminine cultural practices. In a nuanced discussion of domestic ideologues, one predicated on the notion that Victorian discourses on domesticity were multivalent and internally contested, Leonore Davidoff and Catherine Hall argue that Ellis negotiated the tension between subordination and influence by claiming that female satisfaction could be achieved through selflessness. Their discussion also points out that Harriet Martineau appropriated for women a more individualistic discourse typically associated with masculine conceptions of identity. See Davidoff and Hall, *Family Fortunes* chap. 3. Ruth Bernard Yeazell discusses similar contestations of the ideal of unconscious virtue in eighteenth-century culture, particularly focusing on Wollstonecraft's appeal for active consciousness in women. See Yeazell, *Fictions of Modesty* 51–64. For a Foucauldian discussion of how the "pleasure of self-sacrifice" operated as a positive incitement in the production of gendered

So, although the pure woman is characteristically protected from the public forces that fracture the identity of the fallen, and often symbolically shores up normative conceptions of (masculine) identity, depictions of feminine fallenness and feminine virtue can share the attribute of diminished selfhood.[42] In fact, selflessness can actually promote lapses.

Moral Statistics and Magdalenism

"We believe, upon our honour, that nine out of ten originally modest women who fall from virtue, fall from motives or feelings in which sensuality and self have no share."[43] Thus writes W. R. Greg in the *Westminster Review* in 1850, in his article reviewing four accounts of prostitution that had appeared during the previous decade or so: Alexandre Parent-Duchâtelet's *De la prostitution dans la ville de Paris*, James Beard Talbot's *Miseries of Prostitution*, Dr. Ryan's *Prostitution in London*, and Henry Mayhew's *Letters in the Morning Chronicle—Metropolitan Poor*. Greg's statement reveals three aspects of the discourse on prostitution that I take to be central to the Victorian rhetoric of fallenness. First, he participates in an empirical, scientific approach to the study of individual action and social conditions when he casts his claim in the form of a statistic, even though, within the context of the statement, it is clear that the ratio is merely a guess. His need to avow his own sincerity attests not simply to his awareness that he lacks sufficient proof, but more crucially to his conviction that a profound responsibility attends the circulation of such statistical claims.

Second, he entirely diminishes the perception of the fallen woman as a sexually desiring being. Drawing on the Victorian theory of feminine sexual passivity, Greg emphasizes the active and aggressive sexuality of men in order to exculpate the woman from the stain of licentious desire.[44] But while accentuating the role of men's lust

---

behaviors in Victorian culture, see Lynda Nead, *Myths of Sexuality* 24.

42. See my Introduction for a discussion of current critical approaches to feminine purity.

43. [W. R. Greg], "Prostitution" 460.

44. Here Greg is reproducing a prevalent conception of female sexual passivity, but it was certainly not an undisputed view. See F. Barry Smith, "Sexuality in Britain, 1800–1900."

in the fate of the fallen, Greg's account more generally works to attribute prostitution to social factors, holding up poverty as the prime determining cause. That is, Greg's dismissal of the woman's sexual agency is accompanied by a shift away from reductive understandings of prostitution and fallenness as the inevitable effect of a sexual lapse, and toward a social, even protosociological, understanding of her plight.[45] Third, and last, Greg avers that the woman is not motivated by self-interest; he goes on to say that in many cases, selfishness would have saved the woman from the negative consequences of her own generosity. Greg constructs a naturalized feminine identity constituted by "a strange and sublime unselfishness," but his statement that "self" has "no share" in the motives or feelings of the woman who falls unwittingly expresses a more fundamental assumption about the eclipsed agency of the fallen.[46]

The prostitution accounts that Greg reviews form part of a genre of social criticism that flourished in the early Victorian era. Closely allied to the rise of statistics and both state and voluntary philanthropy, early Victorian social criticism concentrated primarily on the problems of urban industrialism: public hygiene, crime, poverty, education. This work had a strong empiricist character and was also committed to political intervention and amelioration. Indeed, the statistical movement, which began in British cities in the 1830s and grew out of utilitarianism and political economy, sought to provide a factual basis on which to establish social knowledge and ultimately to base social policies. Although in their early self-descriptions the statistical societies claimed to exclude all opinion from the presentation of their data, theoretical assumptions and policy agendas nonetheless attended their researches and activities from the start.[47] Eileen Janes Yeo points out that in fact many of the

45. Ironically, when Greg insists on the primacy of poverty as a cause, he dismisses the need for statistical proof, precisely because, for him, the social fact is so obvious: "We shall not take much pains in proving that poverty is the chief determining cause which drives women into prostitution in England, as in France; partly because we have no adequate statistics, and we are not disposed to present our readers with mere fallacious estimates, but mainly because no one doubts the proposition." This sentence can be read not only as an appeal to common sense but also as a protosociological appeal to a larger structural cause that renders empirical facts about individuals and groups of individuals moot. Greg, "Prostitution" 461.

46. Greg, "Prostitution" 459.

47. Thus the Statistical Society of London: "The Statistical Society will consider it to be the first and most essential rule of its conduct to exclude carefully all Opinions

early statistical societies acted as virtual town councils, shaping the collection of social data, monitoring the poor, and influencing the development of policy.[48] The Statistical Society of London, founded in 1834, included Edwin Chadwick, who prepared the Poor Law Report of 1834 and later, as Secretary of the Poor Law Commissioners, produced the *Report on the Sanitary Condition of the Labouring Population*. These reports addressed social, moral, and medical topics; they aimed to impose some coherent understanding on the vast problems generated by industrialism and an increasingly dense urban population; and they were the basis for discussions of policy interventions.

Most analyses of early and mid-Victorian social criticism judge it against the standards suggested by a developed sociology or by the method of social survey that was employed by Charles Booth in the 1880s.[49] They acknowledge that mid-Victorian "moral statistics" introduced a broad array of social issues into statistical practice, which had hitherto been dominated by more strictly demographic questions, but they also underscore the lack of sufficiently structural understandings. The myriad practitioners of such forms of information gathering and social criticism—royal commissions, parliamentary committees, government officials, doctors, clergymen, journalists, private philanthropists—are seen as producing a hybrid

---

from its transactions and publications—to confine its attention rigorously to facts— and, as far as it may be possible, to facts which can be stated numerically and arranged in tables." Quoted in Martin Bulmer, Kevin Bales, and Kathryn Kish Sklar, "The Social Survey in Historical Perspective" 8. As Philip Abrams points out, with the rise of more developed social surveys later in the century the attempt at "pure empiricism" was explicitly abandoned. Abrams, *The Origins of British Sociology* 21.

48. Eileen Janes Yeo, "The Social Survey in Social Perspective."

49. In their account of the development of the social survey, Bulmer, Bales, and Sklar note that "it is hard to escape an implicitly Whiggish history." They then go on to claim that those who were practicing forms of the social survey previous to Booth were not engaged in "mature social surveys": "Booth conceptualised the problem differently, conducted a larger-scale inquiry, attempted to measure the phenomena with which he was concerned, and collected data from multiple observers rather than relying upon a single observer." Bulmer, Bales, and Sklar, "The Social Survey in Historical Perspective" 4. Similarly, Philip Abrams, in his discussion of the National Association for the Promotion of Social Science, writes: "The most frequently used units of social analysis in the *Transactions* of the Association are those of the state, the individual (moral or immoral) and occasionally, the classes. What is missing is any developed concept of the social system, any extended or general analysis of structured interactions between individuals or classes, any theory of the social basis of the state. Where there *is* a model of society it is typically an administrative one suffused with moral judgment." Abrams, *The Origins of British Sociology* 48–49.

genre, one that oscillates between environmental and moral explanations without clarifying the relation between the two. And insofar as the ameliorist aspect of these reports, accounts, and articles stressed reformation of character as much as or more than transformation of circumstance, the environmental and structural explanations were seen to be further diminished. Philip Abrams sees the development of the National Association for the Promotion of Social Science (founded in 1857, it was an umbrella for a wide range of reform groups, and counted John Stuart Mill among its members) as the culmination of the ameliorist approach. Not until the 1880s, as a response to deeply structural economic crises and in the face of working-class contestation, would the predominantly middle-class, paternalist understanding of social problems be significantly challenged.[50]

It is certainly true that the category of character was prominent in social reformist literature, yet to interpret this literature too exclusively from the vantage point of developed sociology is to fail to enter into the social and intellectual horizon of mid-Victorian culture. For the emphasis on the individual was in large part already a response to the threat entailed in scientistic and structural understandings of individual action and social conditions. After all, the traditions of "political arithmetic" and political economy, traditions that lay behind the development of statistics, were premised on a systemic approach to the social order, one that subordinated the individual to the larger well-being of the community, city, or nation. One of the reasons most prominently adduced for presenting aggregate data about individuals was that pervasive vicious behaviors or conditions of disease had profound, ramifying effects throughout many spheres of society. The search for causes that exceeded the individual's control was thus merely one aspect of a larger social contextualization of moral issues; and the emphasis on the individual was frequently a recuperative response to threatening reconceptualizations of character and human action.[51]

As the previous half of this chapter demonstrates, Mill's own writings on the subject of character illustrate well the tensions and

50. Abrams, *The Origins of British Sociology* 44–49.
51. In discussing the Victorian public health movement, Michael J. Cullen casts the tension between individual and social explanations as an informing ideological dialectic, thereby avoiding the anachronistic judgment of incoherence or sociological immaturity. Cullen, *The Statistical Movement in Early Victorian Britain* 62.

internal debates precipitated by a dual impulse toward scientific understandings of human action and idealist investments in autonomous virtue. Mill, who participated in the early statistical movement, saw social data as providing proof for the fundamental claim of ethology, that human actions are subject to uniform laws of causation.[52] Still, as with the doctrine of necessity, Mill also realized that the kind of reconceptualization of human conduct entailed in statistical approaches caused uneasiness: "The facts of statistics, since they have been made a subject of careful recordation and study, have yielded conclusions, some of which have been very startling to persons not accustomed to regard moral actions as subject to uniform laws."[53] I have traced the kinds of recuperations that Mill's own uneasiness produced. Significantly, his vindication of "moral freedom" and shift toward "internal culture" conform to a more general movement: from the time of the development of the statistical societies in the 1830s until the development of the National Association for the Promotion of Social Science in 1857 there was increasing emphasis on the individual as the primary site of social reformation.[54] But this shift must be interpreted within the context of, and as a response to, emergent social and scientific approaches to moral behavior. An unexamined focus on the primacy of the individual, especially from the perspective of a developed sociology, can occlude the context of this development.

My premise here is that discourses on prostitutes and representations of fallen women register Victorian culture's most extreme threats to cherished notions of private selfhood and autonomous self-control. The accounts of prostitution that flourished in Scotland and England during the early and mid-Victorian period support this view. In discussions of causes, effects, and remedies, these accounts repeatedly generate profound aporias of agency, and the entire category of character becomes highly unstable. If there is a more general move within mid-century discourses of reform to privilege individual character and moral transformation, the condition of fallenness be-

52. The "singular degree of regularity *en masse*, combined with the extreme of irregularity in the cases composing the mass, is a felicitous verification *a posteriori* of the law of causation in its application to human conduct." Mill, *Logic* 933.

53. Mill, *Logic* 932. Philip Abrams stresses that the statistical movement concentrated on the individual as the primary unit of analysis, but to aggregate data about individuals, as this quote from Mill clearly shows, is to assign a fundamentally social significance to that individual behavior. Abrams, *The Origins of British Sociology* 11.

54. See Abrams, *The Origins of British Sociology* 37–39.

comes the site for the most threatening and unassimilable ramifications of the statistical and socially scientific conceptions of character and human action. In fact, the term "the great social evil," which was frequently applied to prostitution during this period, insists on the irreducibly social aspects of what had hitherto been conceived as natural sin. In a sense, the use of this phrase indicates, to reinvoke James Martineau, a materialist perversion of traditional moral vocabularies. In forwarding this argument, I am challenging the tendency to see the prostitution accounts as clearly displaying a bias toward moralism. Certainly, a marked ethical and religious rhetoric appears in many of the accounts, but it is powerfully undermined by the protosociological and other secular concerns with the nature of individual and social identity.[55]

Moral statistics, or social statistics as they later came to be called, investigated a range of topics: crime, poverty, disease, alcohol consumption, education. Conceptions of vicious or weak character were created and partially codified in these analyses. Like other broadly defined forms of vicious or depraved behavior—stealing and gambling, for example—prostitution was beginning to be reified into a status, one brought on by repeated acts but far-reaching in its effects on character and destiny.[56] As William Tait writes in *Magdalenism: An Inquiry into the Extent, Causes, and Consequences of Prostitution in Edinburgh*, under the subheading "Definition of a Prostitute,"

There is a distinction between the terms prostitution and prostitute, besides that which exists between a certain course of conduct and the individual who follows it. By prostitution is understood merely an act; while prostitute is always employed to denote a person who habitually follows the course of conduct implied in successive acts. Prostitution may arise from various causes; but by prostitute is

55. For the claim that moralism prevails, see Judith R. Walkowitz, *Prostitution and Victorian Society* 37; Nead, *Myths of Sexuality* 101–2; Linda Mahood, *The Magdalenes* 55–56. For a more general discussion of the approach represented by Walkowitz, Nead, and Mahood, see my Introduction.

56. In claiming that "the prostitute" was a type of character defined through repeated acts, for example, Ralph Wardlaw also invokes "the thief": "A prostitute and a thief are designations of *character*; and a character can never be formed, nor the designation which expresses it merited, by a solitary act." Ralph Wardlaw, *Lectures on Female Prostitution* 14. Still, as I shall show presently, Wardlaw distinguishes the thief from the prostitute precisely in terms of their control over the situation: a thief may rise in his profession, but a prostitute will always follow a downward path.

generally meant a person who openly delivers herself up to a life of impurity and licentiousness, who is indiscriminate in the selection of her lovers, and who depends for her livelihood upon the proceeds arising from a life of prostitution.[57]

Tait's definition emphasizes habitual behavior and a way of life, and begins to suggest the same approach to identity that Foucault sees as central to the emergence of "the homosexual" as distinct from sodomy as a mere act: "The nineteenth-century homosexual became a personage, a past, a case history, and a childhood, in addition to being a type of life, a life form, and a morphology, with an indiscreet anatomy and possibly a mysterious physiology."[58] The more general category of feminine fallenness, like prostitution, was also beginning to be conceived as a status, one frequently seen as inaugurated by a discrete event and defined through temporal sequences or stages: it was determining of identity and hence not something that one could assume or slough off at will.[59] Most commentators on prostitution and fallenness were scandalized by the suggestion, inaugurated by Parent-Duchâtelet and endorsed by William Acton in England, that women entered prostitution only transiently and were perfectly capable of rescuing themselves and being reintegrated into society. By contrast, many British writers conceptualized prostitution itself as an extensive economic and social system, into which the fallen woman was entirely absorbed.[60]

In my discussion of the quote from W. R. Greg, I focused on three features of the discourse on fallenness and prostitution: the statistical or scientific approach to human action, the rejection of lust or desire as a primary determinant, and the shifting toward social factors that supercede conceptions of individual agency or control. In the ac-

57. William Tait, *Magdalenism* 1.

58. Michel Foucault, *History of Sexuality* 1:43. Mahood, citing Foucault, draws the same analogy between the constructions of the prostitute and the construction of the homosexual. Mahood, *The Magdalenes* 10.

59. Nead argues that the definition of prostitution as a repeated act cast it in moral rather than economic or social terms, but the category of repeated acts, especially when linked to discernible stages or trajectories, actually helps to constitute prostitution as a social status. See Nead, *Myths of Sexuality* 101.

60. Commentators provided tables listing the number and kinds of brothels, the number and kinds of prostitutes, and the financial costs of the aggregate system (including sums spent on drinking and money lost through robberies, which were perceived as pervasive). See for example William Logan, *An Exposure, from Personal Observation, of Female Prostitution* 20–25.

counts I am concentrating on here—accounts primarily by doctors, clergymen, and social reformers—these features reappear with some frequency, though not uniformly in the same pattern, and are accompanied by other related characteristics as well. Those that I want to draw most attention to are the appeal to underlying laws of causation, the evocation of a peculiarly modern conception of self-reflexivity, a heightened sensitivity to the influence of popular cultural forms, and an anxiety about the visibility and readability of the fallen. In all of these cases, personal autonomy becomes a charged and vexed issue, and social identity and human behavior are conceptualized in radical terms, even as older religious and moral paradigms are partly employed. As may well be apparent from the kind of taxonomy I am producing, I am not as concerned to reconstruct fully the positions within the literature on prostitution as I am to light up some crucial terms structuring and forwarding the debates as a whole. This means as well that I do not impose a chronology on the debate that followed in the wake of Parent-Duchâtelet's book in 1836. And because I am most concerned to provide context for my analyses of literary works during the same period, this discussion focuses on accounts that appeared between 1840 and 1860. I thus do not address the debate surrounding the Contagious Diseases Acts, a debate that has been carefully reconstructed in the work of Judith R. Walkowitz.[61]

Many of the titles of the prostitution accounts foreground causation: *Magdalenism: An Inquiry into the Extent, Causes, and Consequences of Prostitution* (1840; by William Tait, Surgeon), *Lectures on Female Prostitution: Its Nature, Extent, Effects, Guilt, Causes, and Remedy* (1842; by Ralph Wardlaw, Doctor of Divinity), *An Exposure, from Personal Observation, of Female Prostitution in London, Leeds, and Rochdale, and Especially in the City of Glasgow; with Remarks on the Cause, Extent, Results, and Remedy of the Evil* (1843; by William Logan, City Missionary), *Prostitution Considered in Relation to Its Cause and Cure* (1859; by James Miller, Professor of Surgery). These accounts order their presentation to follow the categories of causation, as do many accounts whose titles are more spare or less scientific, for example *The Miseries of Prostitution* (1844; by James Beard Talbot, Secretary to the London Society for the Protection of Young Females), "Prostitution" (1850; by W. R. Greg), and *Prostitution Considered in Its Moral, Social,*

61. Walkowitz, *Prostitution and Victorian Society.*

and Sanitary Aspects, in London and Other Large Cities; with Proposals for the Mitigation and Prevention of Its Attendant Evils (1857; by William Acton, Surgeon).

The actual causes presented are multiple and varied: individual, familial, social, cultural, economic. Many of the accounts unanxiously reproduce one another and list wildly incompatible explanations side by side. Among the causes of prostitution that appear are sexual desire, love of finery, irritability of temper, indolence, dishonesty and desire of property, intemperance, ignorance, men's aggressive sexuality, seduction, bad example of parents, neglect of parents, lack of proper surveillance of servants, inadequate remuneration of women's work, marriage customs, education and early habits (and sometimes women's education more specifically), overcrowded urban housing, intermingling of the sexes in factories, poverty and destitution, immoral publications, socialism, women's attire, the theater, society's countenancing of vice, and the appearance of prostitutes in public. Unquestionably, we are dealing with a lack of systematicity, yet partly motivating such extensive lists is the conviction that discrete causes of human action and social conditions can be identified, and concomitantly, that if proper measures are applied to remove or mitigate the determining causes, then a cure will be effected. Sometimes the measures must be directed at reformation of character—typically, training in self-control—and sometimes they must address external circumstances. Although I draw attention to the more extreme emphases on determined identity in these accounts, their approach generally follows from the early utilitarian and associationist traditions and is characteristic of the scientific ameliorism of the mid-Victorian period.

The appeal to laws of causation becomes most pronounced in the discussion of effects, especially effects on the prostitute herself. While all of the writers I refer to here suggest reforms and remedies, they all insist, with the notable exception of Acton, on some form of downward-path scenario.[62] Wretchedness, misery, destitution,

---

62. Bracebridge Hemyng, whose text on prostitution I do not discuss here, agreed with Acton. See Hemyng, "Prostitution in London." Acton's position was based on his medical experiences in both Paris and London, and he endorsed Parent-Duchâtelet's claim that women were involved in prostitution only temporarily. As Acton writes in his preface, his experience in Paris and London caused his "dissent from the vulgar error that early death overtakes the daughters of pleasure, as also my impression that the harlot's progress as often tends upwards as downwards. I became daily more convinced that far from perishing in hospitals, workhouses, or

loss of the affections, deadening of the mind (or, in some alternate formulations, insupportable mental anguish), disease, decay, death (often by suicide): these are among the effects that inexorably descend upon the lapsed woman. Wardlaw's text contains the classic formulation (and this is a passage quoted repeatedly by others):

> [To] this lowest grade, in all its horrors, the entire system tends. Yes:—I repeat it, and press it on your serious attention,—the tendency is all downwards. The case is, in this respect, unique. Even in thievery, there may be an advance. The boy, of the lowest grade, who, by his inferior practice, comes to be a dexterous pickpocket, or a clever abstracter of the contents of a till, may in time rise to the envied, though unenviable, celebrity of a Barrington. He who first pilfers a penny from a shop, if he gets forward in the arts of villainy, may find his way to the thousands of a bank.—But in the present case, rising is a thing unknown. It cannot be. It is all descent. . . . I am speaking at present, not of the morality, but of the misery of the case. And again I say, the tendency is all downward.[63]

Likewise, in his section "Observations Applicable to All Classes of Prostitutes," Tait writes, "The general law in regard to them [prostitutes] appears to be, like that of gravitation, always pressing downwards."[64]

It seems less that the prostitute confirms Mill's conviction that the actions of human beings are "subject to invariable laws" than that she embodies that principle. In this context, it appears no accident that a generalized category of decay, as distinct from disease, obtrudes powerfully in the accounts. Tait argues that "the great ma-

---

obscure degradation, she generally, in course of time, amalgamates with the population." Acton later debunks what he calls "three vulgar errors: 1) That once a harlot, always a harlot, 2) That there is no possible advance, moral or physical, in the condition of the actual prostitute, 3) That the harlot's progress is brief and rapid." William Acton, *Prostitution Considered in Its Moral, Social, and Sanitary Aspects* v-vi, 52. Also see Alexandre Parent-Duchâtelet, *La prostitution à Paris au XIXe siècle* (first published in 1836 with the title *De la prostitution dans la ville de Paris*).

63. Wardlaw, *Lectures on Female Prostitution* 52–53.

64. This remark in Tait's text is preceded by the following comment, which is of course very similar to Wardlaw: "A man may by industry, perseverance, and determination, raise himself from any rank of society to another; but this is not the case with a woman who forsakes the path of virtue, and prostitutes her body for the love of gain." Tait, *Magdalenism* 34. For other moments that insist upon the inevitability of the downward path see James Beard Talbot, *The Miseries of Prostitution* 26–27, and James Miller, *Prostitution Considered in Relation to Its Cause and Cure* 12.

jority of females begin to decay very soon after abandoning themselves to a life of prostitution," and revealingly distinguishes decay from disease when he claims, "Their decay is greatly *accelerated by* repeated attacks of syphilis, or other disorders to which they are subject."[65] An unmediated manifestation of the law whereby material circumstances determine character, the prostitute inevitably tends toward the most degraded condition; she is not capable, like the (masculine) thief or Mill's rational subject, of acting in such a way as to alter or improve her circumstances. Wardlaw brackets "morality" and highlights "misery" because he is invoking a law that erodes the very possibility of moral freedom.

It may be difficult to imagine how the concept of remedy or reform can be held in light of the downward-path principle. Some writers simply contradict themselves; others seem to intend extreme formulations of the prostitute's doom as the strongest argument in favor of ameliorist action. Occasionally, adopting a more critical perspective, a writer will claim that societal endorsements of the downward-path principle themselves contribute substantially to the plight of the fallen. For example, in glossing a scene between Jem and the prostitute Esther in Elizabeth Gaskell's *Mary Barton* (a text I discuss in Chapter 3), W. R. Greg both invokes and critiques the downward-path principle:

> The career of these women is a brief one; their downward path a marked and inevitable one; and they know this well. They are almost never rescued; escape themselves they cannot. *Vestigia nulla retrorsum.* The swindler may repent, the drunkard may reform; society aids and encourages them in their thorny path of repentance and atonement, and welcomes back with joy and generous forgetfulness the lost sheep and the prodigal son. But the prostitute may *not* pause—*may* NOT *recover*: at the very first halting, timid step she may make to the right or to the left, with a view to flight from her appalling doom, the whole resistless influences of the surrounding world, the good as well as the bad, close around her to hunt her back into perdition.[66]

In the Gaskell scene that Greg is glossing, Esther insists, in the face of repeated entreaties from Jem, that she cannot be saved. Greg's

---

65. Tait, *Magdalenism* 169; my emphasis.
66. Greg, "Prostitution" 454–55.

remarks begin with what looks like an unequivocal endorsement of the "marked and inevitable" downward path. But the passage shifts toward critique when Greg underscores social inequities among the vicious. By the time we reach the emphatic "may *not* pause—*may* NOT *recover*," we understand it as the potent force of opinion and social decree, and not as any natural moral law. Finally, Greg provocatively includes the climate of virtuous ("good") social opinion among the conditions that overwhelm the woman's feeble attempts to escape her doom, thereby dramatizing the power of social discourse over the prostitute's destiny.

Greg suggests not only that the principle of irretrievability be abandoned but also that a potently censorious opinion be brought to bear on men's habits of fornication, so as to relegate vicious men to their own downward path: "fornication would become vulgar by being regarded as such, and would descend to a lower and a lower class of society, till it was pushed out of existence altogether, or was confined to the ruffian and the criminal alone."[67] This statement may appear to separate the subject who fornicates from the act of fornication (thereby following a different pattern from the rhetoric of fallenness, which disallows such a separation), but on the following page Greg writes: "*Let the same measure of retributive justice be dealt to the seducer who deserts the woman who has trusted him, and allows her to come upon the town*" (Greg's emphasis). The idea of taking a more harsh and punitive stance toward seducers and other male participants appears in many of the accounts, but rarely with the same level of awareness of discursive effects as we find in Greg.[68]

Greg's article on prostitution participates in the radical tradition of social critique by invoking social and economic causes of prostitution—most centrally, poverty and inadequate availability of and remuneration for women's work—and assigning a large share of blame to society for the woman's downward path.[69] However, ele-

---

67. Greg, "Prostitution" 503.

68. For arguments that seducers be shunned rather than countenanced, see Tait, *Magdalenism* 97, 209, and Wardlaw, *Lectures on Female Prostitution*.

69. "There can be no doubt that such a rectification of social anomalies—such a general amelioration in our social condition, as should place the means of earning an ample livelihood by honourable industry within the reach of women of all classes, would at once remove one of the most prolific of those sources whence prostitutes are supplied." Greg, "Prostitution" 495. Of course an even more trenchant social critique of prostitution was represented in the writings of socialists, and in Owen

ments in his account reflect uncritical assumptions about the condition of fallenness, among them, his denial of women's sexual agency and his representation of the consciousness of the fallen. Greg presents Gaskell in the first place because he believes she so realistically evokes the *feelings* of the prostitute Esther, her utter conviction that she cannot be saved and her desperate need to obliterate this unsupportable self-knowledge: "If we did not drink, we could not stand the memory of what we have been, and the thought of what we are, for a day."[70] Greg insists on the fallen woman's self-condemnation partly to dispute the dominant view that fallen women lose their sense of shame or experience a deadening of the mind and feelings.[71] According to Greg, just as natural womanly unselfishness and generosity often lead to a woman's fall, so too do those ineradicable feminine virtues determine the anguished sense of her own degradation, the "feeling of her inevitable future pressing her down with all the hopeless weight of destiny."[72]

Ironically, however, it is just this utter conviction of her own doom that, at a crucial juncture, prevents the woman from being saved. This particular twist of fate asserts itself in a passage that begins, once again, by laying blame at society's door:

> We have seen that the great majority of these poor women fall, in the first instance, from causes in which vice and selfishness have no share. For that almost irresistible series of sequences, by which one lapse from chastity conducts ultimately to prostitution, *we*—the world—must bear the largest portion of the blame. What makes it *impossible* for them to retrace their steps?—almost impossible even to pause in the career of ruin? Clearly, that harsh, savage, unjust, unchristian public opinion which has resolved to regard a whole

---

himself, who attributed prostitution to the current system of private property and marriage. See Nead, *Myths of Sexuality* 110–18; Mahood, *The Magdalenes* 65–66.

70. Quoted in Greg, "Prostitution" 454.

71. Here's James Beard Talbot's version of the dominant view, which Greg is contesting: "The one fatal step which has brought shame upon her head, has banished shame from her heart. The first false movement leads to crime; crime blunts the feelings, and hardens the heart; and, afraid to return to the home she has forsaken—no friendly hand being extended to save, the whole moral principle speedily becomes obliterated; she plunges deeper, and still deeper, into vice and iniquity, until she is irrecoverably lost." Talbot, *The Miseries of Prostitution* 44. See also Tait, *Magdalenism* 158; Logan, *An Exposure* 29. (Tait actually maintains a somewhat contradictory attitude toward this topic.)

72. Greg, "Prostitution" 451.

life of indulgence on the part of one sex as venial and natural, and a single false step on the part of the other as irretrievable and unpardonable. How few women are there who, after the first error, do not awake to repentance, agony, and shame, and would not give all they possess to be allowed to recover and recoil! . . . Instead of helping her up, we thrust her down when endeavoring to rise; we choose to regard her, not as frail, but as depraved. Every door is shut upon her, every avenue of escape is closed. A sort of fate environs her. The more shame she feels (*i.e.* the less her *virtue* has suffered in reality), the more impossible is her recovery, because the more does she shrink from those who might have been able to redeem her. She is driven into prostitution by the weight of all society pressing upon her.[73]

This is perhaps Greg's strongest statement about the power of social discourse to enforce the woman's fall into prostitution. Yet he almost surreptitiously introduces a more powerful force preventing the woman's rescue: her own consciousness of her abasement and moral failing, a consciousness that is a function of her residual virtue. The prerequisite for her redemption, a feeling of shame, also guarantees her doom: the dilemma is profound and constitutes her distinct tragedy.

Greg is clearly trying to humanize the fallen woman in his repeated insistence that she remains fully aware of her condition. He takes pains to let her speak in her own voice: in addition to presenting the Gaskell scene, in which a prostitute tells her own story, he quotes extensively from Mayhew's interviews with prostitutes and also reproduces a poem found "among the papers of a poor penitent prostitute, who died of want in a garret in Glasgow." The poem is entitled "Verses for My Tombstone, If Ever I Should Have One," and in part reads:

> *My thoughts were racked in striving not to think;*
> Nor could rejected conscience claim the power
> To improve the respite of one serious hour.
> I durst not look to what I was before;
> My soul shrank back, and wished to be no more.[74]

73. Greg, "Prostitution" 451, 471.
74. Greg, "Prostitution" 453. It is unclear whether the italics are Greg's or the author's.

In debunking the claim of deadened or petrified feelings, Greg fixates on the image of the fallen woman acutely tortured by her own self-consciousness. Tormented by the impossibility of overcoming or transforming her situation, the prostitute vainly attempts to flee from this paralyzing self-knowledge. She is racked not so much with guilt as with the anguished knowledge of her unavoidable fate. In this sense, the fallen woman comes to carry the burden of a peculiarly modern form of self-consciousness. The anxious feeling of fatalism that Mill saw to exist "more or less obscurely in the minds of most necessitarians" is visited upon her as a distinct part of her punishment.[75] In Mill's autobiography, consciousness of being a fully determined character is figured in sexualized, feminine terms: it "[weighs] on his existence like an incubus." In Greg, conversely, the fallen woman provides a spectacle of self-consciousness: society is the primary agent of her fate ("She is driven into prostitution by the weight of all society pressing upon her"), but she is forced to watch helplessly as her fate unfolds.[76] And whereas Mill defined virtue as the freedom to participate in the regulation and cultivation of one's own character, the residual virtue of the Gregian prostitute consists merely in the minimal and paradoxical freedom of knowing that she cannot alter her character, for it is no longer her own. If Greg is humanizing the prostitute here, he is humanizing her experience as a subject in exile from the traditional moral realm.[77] As becomes clear in the following chapter, this particular form of fallen consciousness receives its most heightened representation in the novels of Dickens.

75. The attempt to obliterate an agonizing self-consciousness is also reflected in Esther's comments about drinking. And compare Tait: "A moment's reflection on the dangerous nature of their conduct so alarms and distresses them, that they hasten to drown their grief in dissipation, or by joining in the sinful conversation and merriment of the brothel." Tait, *Magdalenism* 244.

76. It is interesting that in the Mill passage, the dilemma about agency includes an attenuation of consciousness: he is anxious and obsessed, but the incubus image necessarily casts him as sleeping fitfully, that is, as not fully conscious. Perhaps this image reflects the suspicion that if we are determined, then we cannot be fully conscious, an assumption that might be seen to underlie the depiction of the "deadening" of the minds or feelings in some other accounts.

77. Greg's descriptions of the fallen woman's lack of freedom gain even more significance in light of his own famous argument against divine foreknowledge, in which he defends the concept of free will against determinism. This appears to be a clear instance in which anxieties about agency are at once heightened and displaced through a discussion of fallenness and prostitution. See William Rathbone Greg, *The Creed of Christendom*.

Greg's critique of social discourse is trenchant because he so powerfully casts the woman as a tragic victim of social forms, but this
portrayal also ultimately diminishes her. In blaming society for the
rhetoric of fallenness, that is, Greg simultaneously accentuates the
fallen woman's utter susceptibility to public opinion. On some level,
in fact, the woman's own sense of unreclaimability must be interpreted as false consciousness. For if the social discourse of unreclaimability is false, as Greg's article argues, then the woman's own
internalization of moral censure tragically reflects the constituting
power of that discourse and replicates its falseness. Thus the fallen
woman seems at times to occupy an alien subject-position, insofar
as she lacks the capacity for distance and critique that Greg's own
stance implies. Greg cannot really reconcile this view with his sup-
posedly vindicating insistence on the woman's authentic sense of
guilt, nor can he resolve the moral ambivalence manifested in such
conflicted phrases as "the *first* fatal, but pardonable error of
woman."[78]

The representation of the fallen as particularly vulnerable to the
constituting power of social forms emerges powerfully in many of
the prostitution accounts, though not always accompanied by the
kind of critique we find in Greg.[79] More commonly, writers simply
deplore the contaminating power of degraded cultural forms such
as the theater or "low" publications, especially novels. Victorian
culture generally associated actresses with prostitutes, perceiving
both as "public" and "false" women. " 'The theatre and houses of
ill-fame,' " writes Tait, quoting an unnamed author, " 'are linked
together by mutual interests and mutual pursuits. The morals of a
theatre and the morals of a brothel are identically the same.' "[80] The
perception of the moral impurity of the theater extended both to the
content of contemporary drama and the characters and modes of
life of players. For Tait, "every thing which is seen and done within

78. Greg, "Prostitution" 473; Greg's emphasis.

79. An exception is Acton, who also attributes a potent and pernicious effect to
dominant cultural perceptions: "I believe that the celebrated series of pictures entitled
'The Harlot's Progress,' and the commonplace reflections which usually accompany
engravings after them, have done much towards founding the necessity for this work.
They have been, I believe, the text for many a sermon, the substratum of a thousand
and one religious tracts, and have inspired our people from generation to generation
with the notion of a Pariah class existing within the bosom of society, whom the
world of sinners might be pardoned for stoning to death." Acton, *Prostitution* 4.

80. Tait, *Magdalenism* 137–38; see also Logan, *An Exposure* 17.

the walls of the playhouse has a demoralizing tendency." Tait also cites the negative influence of "improper works and obscene prints," which "corrupt the finer feelings of human nature, and inflame those passions which require all the efforts of a strong and well-regulated mind to conquer and subdue."[81]

Most of the writers caution that such cultural materials and events excite the passions of both sexes, and that young men should avoid the theater as much as young women.[82] In this sense, the susceptibility to these cultural forms appears not to be gendered. However, a concomitant tendency to depict the prostitute as an offensively contaminating spectacle or publication casts such seemingly non-gendered critiques in a new light. The metaleptic oscillations between casting the woman as effect and cause of cultural contaminations, that is, highlights the woman's malleability in a way entirely missing from the cautionary passages directed at men. The public woman as offensive publication appears dramatically in James Miller's *Prostitution Considered in Relation to Its Cause and Cure*. Miller spends several pages discussing the immorality of theatricals, modern fiction, opera, vaudeville, obscene advertisements, impure books and pamphlets—the pervasive "pollution of the page." He then argues, as do many other commentators, against allowing prostitutes to parade on public streets or appear at public events, lest they exert a corrupting influence on all who see them.

> The mere vagrant is taken up, as such; so is the mendicant, importuning the passer-by; why not the prostitute? Or, if it be thought too harsh to have her taken *up*, at least in the first instance, let her at all events be taken *off* the street at once; and if, after repeated warnings, her offensive publication of herself be persisted in, let her then be apprehended, and dealt with accordingly. We deem it to be a duty urgently incumbent on the magistrate, to purge our streets of these obscene and dangerous perambulators.

Miller's rhetoric is particularly offensive and unsympathetic—he is one of the harshest commentators in the field—yet his extreme formulations reveal something that occurs more generally. The ap-

---

81. Tait, *Magdalenism* 140, 144–45; see also Talbot, *The Miseries of Prostitution* 36; Miller, *Prostitution Considered* 24–28.

82. See for example Tait, *Magdalenism* 140, 144–45; Talbot, *The Miseries of Prostitution* 36.

pearance of the prostitute threatens to contaminate because the prostitute herself functions much in the manner of a powerfully affecting
representation or image. Like immoral fiction, theater, or advertis-
ing, she is both false and dangerous. Thus, even as Miller claims
that an actual prostitute is more corrupting than a represented one,
he identifies prostitution as something that is only impersonated:
"Whoredom in the abstract, dramatised, is bad enough; but the
living impersonation of it—brazen and unblushing—will this be
borne too?"[83]

For Miller, the prostitute becomes indelibly associated with false
representation and, consequently, is extremely difficult to represent.
In the preface to his account, speaking of himself in the third person,
he explains that

> his outline may be meagre, and his colouring imperfect; but both
> are believed to be true—too true—to nature, as far as they go. At
> some points, too, the pencilling may perhaps seem coarse, and the
> brush laid too broadly on; but it was feared that by no other mode
> of handling could a true or impressive representation of the stern
> facts be conveyed; and it was felt that questions of taste and style
> ought to give way to the requirements of duty and truth.

Miller's defense of an oscillation between understatement and hy-
perbole relates to his sense of the contaminating power of the prostitute and the moral urgency of his task, but also at issue is her
disturbing artificiality. Later, in fact, while arguing against corrupting forms of female attire, Miller claims that in the case of both
photography and portraiture, "it will be found that the best picture
is not of her bedecked with flounces and furbelows, gumflowers
and ribbons, of vast and varied colours, but of her who is modestly
and simply attired, in some plain garb of simple material and modest
hue."[84] In other words, the modest maiden and not the inauthentic,
artificial, self-publishing whore is the proper object for realist rendering. Miller's own need to exaggerate, then, to lay the brush "too
broadly on," corresponds to the falseness of his object of study: a
true representation of the false must be false itself. But in that case,

---

83. Miller, *Prostitution Considered* 28, 31, 25. For a discussion of the Victorian anxiety
over the public appearance of prostitutes, see Nead, *Myths of Sexuality* 114–16.
84. Miller, *Prostitution Considered* 3, 17.

of course, it risks participating in the contaminations of falseness, fictionality, and the "pollution of the page."

As I discussed in the Introduction, there are myriad ways in which fallenness figures forms of aesthetic determinism; as a publicized, false, or painted woman, the prostitute often suggests or displays the power of aesthetic forms. Frequently, the mere fact of her attenuated social agency, her inability to exert control over the circumstances that come to define her, generates the conviction that she is simply false and artificial. A link is made, in other words, between lacking freedom and being false: if one has no controlling self capable of orchestrating or influencing circumstances, then one is merely an artificial product. As a consequence, the aestheticized forms of fallenness often figure or dovetail with the more strictly social (e.g., environmental or economic) forms of fallenness.[85]

The prostitute's profound artificiality becomes most manifest when deliberate forms of falseness—cunning and lying, for example—are defined as strangely unconscious or compulsive. Tait provides a dramatic instance of this in his argument against allowing prostitutes to testify in court. "Dissimulation has become so natural to them," he writes, "that they fail to speak the truth even when it is for their own advantage." Since some of them do not even understand what kind of obligation is entailed in the swearing of an oath in court, "it becomes very painful to reflect on the wholesale perjuries that are daily thrust upon them in the police and other judicial courts."[86] The prostitute is so little the author of her own deceptions that others become culpable for them; and what Tait here categorizes as a "moral defect" functions more as a subverter of moral distinctions. This conception of the prostitute's falseness "all the way down" raises acute problems for programs of reform, which suddenly confront the task of not simply reforming but rather creating a character. Again, the following chapter, and in particular the section on Dickens's "Home for Homeless Women," addresses this issue in more detail.

The prostitution accounts reveal a particularly vexed relation to the category of sympathy. In Greg, as we saw, the prostitute's de-

85. Indeed, the category of social as opposed to "natural" causes of prostitution (the latter referring, for example, to lust and faults of temper or character) was often dubbed "artificial," as in Tait's account, which devotes separate subchapters to "natural" and "artificial" causes.

86. Tait, *Magdalenism* 38, 39.

fenselessness issues from her feminine virtue, her sympathetic self-lessness. Yet Greg also discloses, in his description of the prostitute's tortured self-awareness, the woman's subsequent inability to manifest anything other than a profoundly isolating other-directedness: in a self-policing move, she "[shrinks] from those who might have been able to redeem her."[87] Tait devotes a section of a chapter to the topic of "shrinking" and rescue and, like Greg, engenders a strange impasse. He begins the section, titled "Prostitution Deprives Its Votaries of the Enjoyment and Sympathies of Society," with a strong statement of the prostitute's instinctive and necessary self-exile: "Whenever a woman openly abandons herself to a life of licentiousness, she instinctively separates herself from respectable society. She knows she has committed an offence which excludes her from participating in the sympathies of those with whom she was formerly accustomed to associate." The company that she is in bears no resemblance to the ideal of harmonious familial community; marked by "discord and dissipation," the disturbingly "public" brothel produces only "unmingled misery and disappointment." Tait then shifts the lens, arguing that redemption is thwarted by an unjustifiable lack of compassion and forgiveness on the part of families and society at large. His discussion builds to an impassioned plea for sympathy for the fallen, questioning why the prostitute is thought to be so far beyond the pale: "Those that are so ready to vibrate in unison with the feelings of other classes of delinquents, refuse to sound one note of condolence for the poor, despised, and helpless prostitute. Why is she so far beyond the bounds of Christian compassion?"[88]

Tait chastises society for the prostitute's neglect and isolation, saying that she would be happy to be received back into "virtuous society," yet he simultaneously insists on her own instinctive and ennobling self-exile.[89] Like Greg, Tait protects against the forms of association that his reformist mode endorses. To what can we attribute this strange conjunction of positions? It is understandable that arguments for rescue and reclaimability, as well as mere attempts to gain the public ear on the topic of prostitution, would require strategies for promoting sympathy. All of these writers, even

87. For a related discussion of the prostitute as a self-policing agent in Victorian culture, see D. A. Miller, *The Novel and the Police* 20–21.
88. Tait, *Magdalenism* 159, 160.
89. Tait, *Magdalenism* 159.

those who most unreflectingly reproduce the harshest condemna-
tory rhetoric, seek to promote sympathy when they are discussing
the possibilities for reclaimability, however limited they may feel
that such prospects are. Ironically, they promote compassion by
praising the prostitute's self-condemnations, her dutiful internalization of the moral censure working upon her.

On one level, the impasse surrounding the woman's possible reintegration into virtuous communities surely reflects these writers'
inability to exorcise their own recoil from the woman's tainted and
sexualized nature. But, as mentioned earlier, the impasse also derives from the models of self and society that are informing the larger
rhetoric of fallenness. As someone who figures and draws off the
threat of multiple determinisms, the prostitute or fallen woman is
perceived as an effect of larger forces, structures, and narratives.
She is thus profoundly unlike her virtuous sister, who, in her other-
directedness and selflessness, ensures a realm of redemptive intersubjective communing. And whereas the masculine subject enters
the public realm in order to pursue his self-interest and "rise" in his
profession, returning home to the "disinterested" private sphere for
the antidote provided by his virtuous wife, the feminine "public"
subject can only, in obeisance to the laws of causation, exhibit the
spectacle of her fractured autonomy. The model of political economy
yields an atomized conception of the (masculine) subject, but the
fallen subject lacks the agency of a stable self-interest and hence is
the mere product of those larger forms and structures that were seen
to condition the interaction of more coherent selves. She is a public
self with no private ballast.

She is also a fundamentally social self with no positive social
relations. Greg stresses the sympathy shown by prostitutes to one
another, but this again is a mark of residual virtue: the tendency of
vice is away from such manifestations.[90] Ultimately, according to

90. Also compare Tait: "Duchatelet [sic] and Dr. Ryan have both briefly treated
of the good qualities of prostitutes; but have differed considerably in the account
which they have given of them. The former has represented them as kind-hearted
and affectionate towards one another in distress, which fact will be adverted to in
the following chapter; and the latter, on the authority of Mr. Talbot, observes, that
'they have very few if any good qualities.' It is the opinion of the author that there
are no good properties peculiar to prostitutes, or arising from their iniquitous calling;
and that, if they are found attentive to one another in sickness—to old and infirm
people, and to children—it is but in obedience to a powerful feeling in their nature,

Tait, the prostitute's fall destroys social relatedness because it prevents even the most basic recognizability: "The effects of sin are not more plainly and fearfully displayed on any class of human beings than on fallen and decayed prostitutes. . . . Every feature appears altered in expression, and gives frightful indication of the writhings of an agonized conscience. The friends with whom they associated only a short time before, are now unable to recognise them." Not many pages later, in a discussion of syphilis, Tait presents a truly horrific instance of the prostitute's loss of distinct identity, as though to drive home the absoluteness of a fate far worse, and far less assimilable, than actual death:

> There is one case under the author's charge at the present time, where the whole bones of the nose, external and internal—the bones which form the roof of the mouth—the bones of both cheeks—the greater part of the superior and inferior maxillary or jaw-bones, with the teeth which they contained, besides all the soft or fleshy parts connected with or covering them, have been successively separated from the body. The disease has continued for more than three years, and has set defiance to every remedy which the most celebrated medical practitioners in Edinburgh could suggest. Her face is literally rotten, and presents a large opening, into which an ordinary-sized fist may be thrust without difficulty. Exfoliation of the bones of the head is very common.[91]

The violence attending this ostensibly neutral medical description, replete with latinate appellations, is quite disturbing, and itself participates in the defacement it describes. From one who is simply unrecognizable to her former companions, the prostitute progresses to one who *has no face* and is hence exiled from communal experience, sympathetic or otherwise.

It should come as no surprise, then, that sympathy should itself be seen as the precondition, and sometimes the actual guarantee, of the fallen woman's redemption. She not only has to repent; she has to be brought back into the human community. Social reintegration and the production of a kind of self-control—these constitute the two basic prongs of those remedial efforts that value the fate of

which they share in common with their whole sex, and which no circumstances will entirely eradicate." Tait, *Magdalenism* 31–32.

91. Tait, *Magdalenism* 162, 167.

the woman. Indeed, many writers see the need for redemptive sympathy as so overriding that they suggest that "pure" women are the most appropriate rescue workers.[92] Because the fallen condition is one of supreme exclusion, only an ardent and manifest sympathy can transform that condition. This is a striking and somewhat radical suggestion given fears of moral contamination, and in D. G. Rossetti's "Jenny" we will see a powerful literary prohibition against such a redemptive ideal. I believe that we must view the insistence on sympathy *as* redemption in light of the fallen woman's multiply determined exile from social communities, an exile that is enforced by her reified status. Many of the commentators criticize society for treating the fallen woman as an outcast, but the paradigm of subjectivity more generally informing the rhetoric of fallenness itself precludes any conception of sympathetic recognition, insofar as it constructs fallenness along the model of a single subject fractured or driven by systemic forces.

Victorian fallenness served as a charged cultural site for some of the most acute anxieties about agency, character, and reform in mid-century Britain. The new scientific approach to character and social policy undermined conventional understandings of virtue and vice, responsibility and guilt; and although Mill and others compensated for the more radical implications of the new social sciences by recuperating a conception of cultivated character or inward consciousness, feminine fallenness came to figure the most extreme forms of attenuated autonomy, which, rather than being seen as deliberate viciousness, were conceived as forms of subjection to larger forces—environmental, social, cultural. In some instances, the fallen subject is assigned a conscious awareness of her determined status that lacks any transformative capacity. In these latter scenarios, she is condemned to watch her own inescapable destiny unfold, with full foreknowledge and no power to alter her fate. While most commentators believe that, through a process of rescue and redemption, some prostitutes can be trained to participate in the cultivation of character and self-control, many of their representations of fallenness militate against just such a capability. The kinds of aporias thus precipitated are discussed in more detail when I turn to Dickens in the following chapter.

92. See Tait, *Magdalenism* 247; Talbot, *The Miseries of Prostitution* 78.

2

"The Taint the Very Tale Conveyed": Self-Reading, Suspicion, and Fallenness in Dickens

Victorian representations of fallenness frequently displace new and defamiliarizing conceptions of selfhood, agency, and character, conceptions intimately related to the emergence of social science and statistics. And if any Victorian novelist is known for his power to represent new and defamiliarizing conceptions of character, surely it is Charles Dickens, whose gallery of eccentric caricatures reflects a profound fascination with the forces of social determination. Moreover, Dickens was also an active journalist and social reformer who wrote directly on problems of crime, poverty, industrialization, education, delinquency, and, not least, feminine fallenness. In this chapter, I focus on Dickens as a pivotal figure, one whose writings introduce fallenness as a broad social and aesthetic category. As we shall see, Dickens constructs the fallen woman, both in his nonliterary and literary writings, in ways strikingly similar to the prostitution accounts I examined in the previous chapter.

From 1846 to 1858, Dickens managed Urania Cottage, a refuge for fallen women that was sponsored by a prominent Victorian philanthropist and close friend of Dickens, Angela Burdett Coutts. Dickens's writings relating to this experience include an extensive correspondence with Coutts and a *Household Words* article on Urania Cottage ("Home for Homeless Women"). In light of these texts and a relevant journalistic piece titled "A Nightly Scene in London," I explore constructions of the fallen in *Dombey and Son* and *David Copperfield*, the two novels Dickens wrote contemporaneously with the management of the refuge. In focusing on both nonliterary writings and the novels, my aim is to establish conceptual and rhetorical continuities between them, to argue that during this decade the fallen woman serves as a crucial point of intersection for Dickens's concerns about the reform and representation of character.[1]

Dickens's interest in the power of social forces over character was profound and far-reaching, and was of course not restricted to his depictions of fallen women. But fallen women in Dickens focus particular predicaments of agency and are generally allotted the more spectacular ordeals associated with the modern conceptions of identity and consciousness that began to dominate Dickens's imagination during the middle decades of the century. In this way Dickens perfectly instances the rhetoric of fallenness, which concentrates more pervasive anxieties in the depiction of fallen women. For Dickens, the fallen woman displaces three primary threats: the threat of environment over character, the power of "stories" over their tellers, and the alienating effects of self-consciousness. The fallen woman herself becomes menacing, moreover, insofar as she metaleptically comes to figure those forces that determine her. In a rhetorical mimicry of the contagion so commonly attributed to tainted women, metalepis transforms the fallen woman from a victim into a threat, an effect into a cause. In these cases the feminine figures transmute into allegorical embodiments of suprasubjective forces, both social and aesthetic. And as we shall see in the case of *Dombey and Son*'s Alice Marwood, the depiction of environmental force in Dickens can sometimes serve to displace political threats associated with the urban population.

All of the threats figured by the Dickensian fallen woman imperil

1. Many earlier critics insisted on a disjunction between Dickens's literary constructions of fallen women and his approach to fallenness as a social problem. Pointing to the "unreality" of Dickens's literary prostitutes or "fallen women," they argued that Dickens "knew better," that his extended stint as manager of the "Home for Homeless Women" gave him a firsthand knowledge of prostitutes that, out of capitulation to a public attitude of censorship and a literary convention of censure, was not carried over into his art. "No one would have guessed," writes Philip Collins, "from reading *David Copperfield* or any of the other novels which contain 'fallen' or delinquent girls, that their author really knew what he was talking about." Collins, *Dickens and Crime* 115. For other criticisms of "unreal" or "melodramatic" presentation, see for example F. R. and Q. D. Leavis, *Dickens the Novelist* 24, 77. F. R. Leavis writes that Alice Marwood "holds forth on her own position and history with a finished rhetorical eloquence . . . that bears no relation to anything real" (24). Q. D. Leavis states that Martha Endell and Alice Marwood were "drastically edited for the purpose from the originals he knew and had helped in real life" (77). Also see Kathleen Tillotson, *Novels of the Eighteen-Forties* 176–82; Peter Fairclough's notes in *Dombey and Son* 988 (note to 572).

strongly held investments in autonomy and private selfhood. The "public woman," assimilated to the degrading urban milieu and figuring the constituting power of the social order, has no interior self. Likewise, the prostitute who has become a story is subjected to the perusal of all. And the self-conscious fallen woman, who as in W.R. Greg and William Tait is acutely conscious of her reified status, cannot look "inward" or keep her character to herself. In Dickens, the equation between autonomy and privacy is profound, and his fallen women are at once determined and public.[2] A heightened concern with the readability and visibility of fallenness, with what James Miller refers to as the prostitute's "offensive publication of herself," becomes linked in Dickens to deep anxieties over the possibilities for self-understanding and the constraints of self-presentation.[3]

7

"Assume a Virtue, if You Have It Not"

Charles Dickens, like other Victorian social reformers, actively sought to challenge exclusively moral and religious discourses of the fall. He did so by pushing the fall's origin back beyond the time of the actual sexual lapse, insisting that circumstances or context were to blame. Thus, even while Dickens capitulates to literary convention and describes a spiritualizing apotheosis at Alice Marwood's deathbed in *Dombey and Son*, he strongly challenges moralizing religious discourses when he stresses the environmental determinants of her fall. Dickens thereby aligns himself with those reformist etiologies that construe the fall as socially predestined, unavoidable because of poverty, a degraded environment, diminished options.[4]

2. My discussions of interiority and character in this chapter are generally indebted to D. A. Miller's *The Novel and the Police*, especially 192–220. I find Miller's readings of Dickens, and of Dickens's obsessions with privacy and autonomy, powerful and nuanced. However, as becomes clear both in this reading and in my Afterword, I do not endorse Miller's Foucauldian frame, insofar as it casts Dickens's extreme conceptions of determined subjectivity as an absolute fact about the social world.

3. James Miller, *Prostitution Considered in Relation to Its Cause and Cure* 31.

4. Dickens also actively criticizes the negative effects of religious sermonizing when he explains to Coutts the rationale for forbidding the chaplain to address the girls individually: "The extraordinary monotony of the refuges and asylums now existing, and the almost insupportable extent to which they carry the words and forms of religion, is known to no order of people so well as to these women; and

Ironically, however, like the sensational melodramas that depict innocent women falling victim to villainous seducers, reformist etiologies often deny agency to the fallen, casting them not merely as conditioned subjects but as powerfully determined ones. "It is dreadful to think," writes Dickens in a letter to Coutts, "how some of these doomed women have no chance or choice. It is impossible to disguise from one's self the horrible truth that it would have been a social marvel or miracle if some of them had been anything other than what they are."[5]

It's difficult to know exactly how the "other" women, the ones for whom "chance" or "choice" might still be operative, could possibly evade the determinist logic, since they too are already "doomed"—in Dickens's sentence as in life. And even if we allow that Dickens is careful to restrict his discussion to "some of" the women (and dismiss "doomed" as a proleptic adjective), he still forwards an extreme and oddly static conception of social determination: the women haven't *become* but always *have been* "what they are." It is no wonder that he and Coutts felt compelled to extend the field and take in women who had yet to undergo a sexual lapse. Urania Cottage thus welcomed those who "had already lost their characters" as well as those "in danger of falling into the like condition."[6]

If social context produces the fall, reforming the fallen becomes a task of decontextualization. Indeed, the policy of emigration to Australia enforced by Urania Cottage engages in a fantasy of complete severance. The refuge admits only those "who distinctly accept this condition: That they came there ultimately to be sent abroad."[7] Dickens partly justifies this policy as a necessary capitulation to a prejudicial society, but his stress lies equally on the belief that without

they have that exaggerated dread of it, and that preconceived sense of their inability to bear it, which the reports of those who have refused to stay in them, have bred in their minds. I am afraid if they were thus taken to task, and especially by a clergyman, they would be alarmed—would say, 'it's the same old story after all, and we have mistaken the sort of place.' " Charles Dickens, *Letters from Charles Dickens to Angela Burdett-Coutts 1841–1865* 102.

5. Dickens, *Letters to Burdett-Coutts* 105.

6. Charles Dickens, "Home for Homeless Women" 161. Dickens was not alone in suggesting this more interventionist approach to potential falls. William Tait, the Edinburgh physician and social reformer whom I discuss in the previous chapter, also advocated scouting for those who might be likely to fall, given their social conditions. See William Tait, *Magdalenism* 263.

7. Dickens, "Home for Homeless Women" 161.

the "effectual detaching" of the women from their "old associates," they will fall again.[8] Of course, for the British the "new world" contained in large part the refuse of the old: it was criminals who were routinely "transported" to Australia.[9] Hence ambiguities surround this new chance: for Dickens and Coutts, it may constitute a pragmatic rescue, yet it also has the appearance of a commuted sentence or a radical solution.[10]

The conception of the fallen as contextually determined emerges most forcefully in Dickens's representations of the public woman, a figure who blurs with her environment even as she testifies to its force. In "A Nightly Scene in London," this figure enables a powerful social critique yet also seems beyond the reach of any actual reform project. The article describes an act of charity performed by Dickens and a "well-known" companion when they "accidentally strayed into Whitechapel" one evening and discovered five women locked out of an overcrowded "Casual Ward."[11] Here is the initial apprehension of what will later be revealed to be unsheltered women: "Crouched against the wall of the Workhouse, in the dark street, on the muddy pavement-stones, with the rain raining upon them, were five bundles of rags. They were motionless, and had no re-

8. In referring to the potential success of his reform scheme, Dickens writes, "I think it not too sanguine to suppose that many good people [in England] would be glad to take them into situations. But the power of beginning life anew, in a world perfectly untried by them, would be so important in many cases, as an effectual detaching of them from old associates, and from the chances of recognition and challenge, that it is most desirable to be, somehow or other, attained." Old associates and judgmental challenges are equally to be feared. Dickens, *Letters to Burdett-Coutts* 82.

9. Transportation, an alternative to the death penalty, was used more and more during the period in which capital punishment was becoming less acceptable yet penitentiary systems were insufficiently developed to handle the vast number of criminal cases. Opposition from the colonies as well as internal critiques questioning whether transportation served either its punishing or deterring function caused a decrease in transportation through the 1840s and beyond, though the practice was not abolished judicially until 1857. Another important context for Dickens's policy was the contemporary bureaucratic and philanthropic effort to promote emigration of women as a way of dealing with "the surplus women problem." See Selma Barbara Kanner, "Victorian Institutional Patronage."

10. James Beard Talbot, the Secretary to the London Society for the Protection of Young Females, also advocated emigration as a policy; see Talbot, *The Miseries of Prostitution* 73. Also see William Acton, *Prostitution Considered in Its Moral, Social, and Sanitary Aspects* 185. For discussion of emigration policies as part of a process of "proletarianization," see Linda Mahood, *The Magdalenes* 98.

11. Charles Dickens, "A Nightly Scene in London." All quotations in this paragraph are taken from this source.

semblance to the human form." Dickens and his companion, themselves "rooted to the spot," see the bundles as Sphinxes crying, "Stop and guess! What is to be the end of a state of society that leaves us here?" After an encounter with a "decent workman," who also laments the condition of a country that boasts such sights, Dickens and his friend inquire at the workhouse. Ascertaining that there simply isn't room inside, that this occurs nightly, and that the women—the master of the workhouse identifies their sex—are not suspected of being thieves, Dickens goes back to give the women money for food and a night's shelter. And in dispensing the money, Dickens also dispenses with the women in a peculiar way:

> I put the money into her hand, and she feebly rose up and went away. She never thanked me, never looked at me—melted away into the miserable night, in the strangest manner I ever saw. I have seen many strange things, but not one that has left a deeper impression on my memory than the dull impassive way in which that worn-out heap of misery took that piece of money, and was lost.

The scenario is enacted with each of the "five apparitions," all of which fade away in like manner. The crowd that has gathered watches in "profound silence," impelling Dickens to write "an exact account of what we had seen" so as to move people to action. There is a strange tension in this piece: the objects of charity, already of doubtful subjectivity, melt away on contact. The street woman serves as a powerful index of a faulty society yet cannot sustain the status of subject in that society. Initially she is indistinguishable from the environment; later she dissolves as mere apparition. Dickens doesn't blame but rather "disappears" the victim. Charity for the public woman turns out to be impossible: to take the proffered coin is to be "lost" again.

In Dickens's imagination, the fallen woman is identified not only with her social context but also with the narrative that records her own devolution: the "horrible truth" of fallenness can be rewritten as the sequential events of an individual fall. At Urania Cottage Dickens ritually records each woman's official history:

> The history of every inmate, taken down from her own mouth—usually after she has been some little time in the Home—is preserved in a book. She is shown that what she relates of herself she

relates in confidence, and does not even communicate to the Superintendents. She is particularly admonished by no means to communicate her history to any of the other inmates: all of whom have in their turns received a similar admonition. And she is encouraged to tell the truth, by having it explained to her that nothing in her story but falsehood, can possibly affect her position in the Home after she has once been admitted.[12]

Telling stories of one's former exploits is no innocent pastime. It raises the possibility of actually "communicating" one's history to another inmate in the sense that one communicates a disease. As in the case of social accounts of prostitution, the fallen woman becomes not simply an instance of a familiar story but also, through metalepsis, an actively dangerous representation. Accordingly, Dickens seeks to disconnect the woman herself from her own defining history. "Preserved in a book," the woman's past is effaceable but also encrypted. Yet, as the phrase "taken down from her own mouth" hints, Dickens has some difficulty conceiving of the woman as distinct from her story: not only does this description contribute to the suggestion of bodily communications, but it assigns an embodied immediacy to the story and seems to deny the woman any mediating consciousness.[13] The policy of forbidding reference to the women's histories thus repeats the same fantasy of severance that the policy of emigration does: both attempt to separate a self from that which, at another level, constitutes it.[14]

If Dickens suggests that the woman both coincides with and spontaneously "communicates" her textualized history, the final sentence of the passage seems suddenly to change the terms of the encounter Dickens has been elaborating. *History* is replaced with

12. Dickens, "Home for Homeless Women" 170.
13. For a related discussion of Dickens's identification, in the Urania Cottage writings, of the fallen woman's story with her sexuality, see Joss Lutz Marsh, "Good Mrs. Brown's Connections." Drawing on Barthes and Foucault's theories, Marsh interprets Dickens's attempts to appropriate and suppress the women's stories as a complex imbrication of narrative, power, and sexuality.
14. This policy corresponds to a particular form of contemporary prison discipline. Advocates of what was known as the Silent System (which I discuss later in the chapter) pointed to the virtues of freeing the criminal from his or her past, though this was not the only reason silence was enforced: prison officials also sought to ensure that prisoners did not associate with, or "contaminate," one another. Dickens also partly justifies his policy by invoking the rigidity of the conventional religious narratives through which to present one's fallen past.

story, and the reliability of the narrator is thrown into question. The subjectivity of the woman suddenly assumes a troubling prominence: she is endowed with the power to deceive. As we will see, however, this is only a temporary empowerment; oddly, not even the prostitute's "falseness" remains her own.

The letters to Coutts amply demonstrate that Dickens perceived falseness or insincerity as endemic among the fallen. He fetishized and insisted on personally conducting the initial interviews of all candidates for admission to Urania Cottage. If he has high praise for those whom he considers genuine, he also exhibits great glee in being proven right in his suspicions of particularly persuasive phonies.[15] Of course we know well from the novels that Dickens was fascinated by all kinds of hypocrisy. Moreover, letters to Coutts reveal that he more generally performed the role of charity detective for her, perusing appeals to ascertain their validity. What emerges in his treatment of the prostitute, however, is a peculiar form of falseness. The anxiety about deception redefines its object later in the article, as revealed by the following tip Dickens offers other managers of the transgressive imagination:

> It has been observed, in taking the histories—especially of the more artful cases—that nothing is so likely to elicit the truth as a perfectly imperturbable face, and an avoidance of any leading question or expression of opinion. Give the narrator the least idea what tone will make her an object of interest, and she will take it directly. Give her none, and she will be driven on the truth, and in most cases will tell it. For similar reasons it is found desirable always to repress stock religious professions and religious phrases; to discourage shows of sentiment, and to make their lives practical and active. "Don't talk about it—do it!" is the motto of the place.[16]

In this scenario, falseness is a function of histrionic self-presentation; the "more artful" prostitute is actually not the author of her own deceptions. When she embellishes her story, or leaps to an alternative narrative, she is motivated merely by an other-directed, strangely short-sighted impulse to please.[17] Only by refusing to re-

15. See Dickens, *Letters to Burdett-Coutts* 104–5.
16. Dickens, "Home for Homeless Women" 172.
17. For a related discussion of the prostitute's "habit of lying" and the tendency to deny prostitutes authorship of their own fabrications, see my previous chapter and Tait, *Magdalenism* 38–41.

spond affectively, by displaying no sensations, can an auditor elicit the truth.[18] If Dickens momentarily introduces a narrator threateningly capable of deception, he later reinstates an inauthentic subject, false because utterly subject to contiguous desires. In "A Nightly Scene in London," the woman of the street is rendered inauthentic by her socially determined status, which causes her to melt away. In "Home for Homeless Women," the construction of the narrating prostitute similarly renders unreliable a subject earlier cast as determined by, and inseparable from, her own history. Perhaps, for Dickens, it is because she is unable to stand apart in any way from her history that she becomes a mere story. Her "falseness" becomes "fictionality," not deception, and the generation of narrative becomes an unreflective sexual act: for the prostitute, talking about it *is* "doing it."

Given the forms of falseness and attenuated autonomy that attach to the fallen, Dickens has difficulty in imagining the women as potential agents of their own reform, as his earliest proposal to Coutts reveals:

> It would be necessary to limit the number of inmates, but I would make the reception of them as easy as possible to themselves. I would put in the power of any Governor of a London Prison to send an unhappy creature of this kind (by her own choice of course) straight from his prison, when her term expired, to the asylum. I would put it in the power of any penitent creature to knock at the door, and say For God's sake, take me in. But I would divide the interior into two portions; and into the first portion I would put all newcomers without exception, as a place of probation, whence they should pass, by their own good-conduct and self-denial alone, into what I may call the Society of the house.[19]

Dickens may appear to emphasize the woman's choice, yet her empowered status emanates from him ("I would put it in the power of . . . "). More important, he quickly retracts: unable to conceive what to do with the woman once she's crossed the threshold, he erects another portal, to be passed only once the woman has become a self-policing agent. The structure becomes vertiginous when one

18. This interviewing technique closely foreshadows the analytic posture Freud later recommended for dealing with hysterics.
19. Dickens, *Letters to Burdett-Coutts* 78.

recalls that the entire stay in the refuge has been projected as a probationary period previous to starting life anew in the colonies. Double doors and double probation: the *mise-en-abîme* reflects the problem not of reforming but of producing a self. Indeed, Dickens stresses that before a woman can enter a program that will allow for the "formation of habits of firmness and self-restraint," she must be brought to the realization that her past life has been, above all, "destructive to *herself*." When Dickens urges this initial emphasis on the woman's own interests, insisting that society has "used her ill," he certainly means to criticize prejudicial views that the fallen cannot be saved. But he also means that the woman's past life has been destructive to her *self*. In order to earn the right to "return to any kind of Society—even to the Society of the asylum," the woman must evolve a self capable of controlling itself.[20]

To accomplish this task, Dickens proposes the adoption of an elaborate program, "Captain Maconochie's Mark System." Originally, Dickens envisioned using the system in the probationary ward; eventually, however, it was adopted for use in the refuge as a whole, structuring the women's lives there.[21] A contemporary writer on prison reform, Captain Maconochie also for a time commanded Norfolk Island and Birmingham Gaol. In his Mark System of prison discipline, a version of which was adopted in English prisons in the 1860s, one earned a certain number of marks for good conduct and lost them for bad behavior. By accumulating marks, one achieved promotion to a higher "class" within prison and eventually earned release. For Maconochie, then, one should ideally be sentenced not to time but to a specified amount of good behavior.

In the 1840s, when Maconochie publicized his ideas, the debate over prison discipline centered on two divergent methods: the Separate System and the Silent System. Both systems aimed to combat the perceived evils of association among prisoners. The former, which isolated prisoners in individual cells, sought to promote moral reflection and "authentic" reform; the latter stressed deterrence,

20. For all quotations in this paragraph see Dickens, *Letters to Burdett-Coutts* 79.
21. In a letter of August 29, 1848, Dickens includes an explanation of the Mark Table, and by late fall the system was in place. While newcomers were put on probation, in the end Urania Cottage did not have a probationary ward. Dickens, *Letters to Burdett-Coutts* 124–28. Other asylums for women employed probationary wards; see Mahood, *The Magdalenes* 77–78; also see the discussion of the London Female Penitentiary in Tait, *Magdalenism* 252.

though claims were also made for the salutary effects of enforcing self-control by imposing silence.[22] The Mark System, by promoting habits of restraint through the reward of good behavior, could be described as a positive version of the Silent System. Unlike the Separate System, which conceived of reform as a turn within the soul, the Mark System set itself the more modest and mechanical task of imposing new habits.

Dickens's own writings on prison reform are not consistent. "Pet Prisoners," "The Ruffian," and the familiar passages in *David Copperfield* and *Great Expectations* display a pessimism that Philip Collins locates as the eventual dominant stance. It is true that Dickens thought the Silent System, with its harsh accompanying versions of useless labor, superior to the Separate. On the other hand, he occasionally praised Maconochie's system, believing it should be tried in cases where reform was possible.[23] Whether reform was possible, of course, depended in large part on who the criminal was. The "hardened" adult male criminal, who has amply demonstrated his threatening agency, deserves and requires the treadmill. The juvenile, that primary candidate for reform among the Victorians, attracts attention and repays effort because his character is still in the process of formation. The prostitute, by contrast, is a vexed object of concern for the reformer. Her susceptibilities to the environment and to the desires of others carry a double edge. Her attenuated agency mitigates her guilt and means that she is not "hardened," yet it also limits her capacity for authentic self-control.[24] The easy adaptability of the fallen facilitates, yet also seems to delegitimate, the desired conversion to a stainless life. The prostitute seems at times to have

22. See Clive Emsley, *Crime and Society in England 1750–1900* 225–38; J. J. Tobias, *Crime and Police in England 1700–1900* 170–80. For a contemporary Victorian discussion, see Hepworth Dixon, *The London Prisons*.

23. For a fuller discussion of these issues, see Collins, *Dickens and Crime*, chaps. 3, 4, 7.

24. The concern with lack of control comes out, among other places, when Dickens explains the reasons why he and Coutts must anticipate an appreciable recidivism: "There is no doubt that many of them would go on well for some time, and would then be seized with a violent fit of the most extraordinary passion, apparently quite motiveless, and insist on going away. There seems to be something inherent in their course of life, which engenders and awakens a sudden restlessness and recklessness which may be long suppressed, but breaks out like madness." Dickens, *Letters to Burdett-Coutts* 81. An emphasis on instability, linked to madness, often appears in Victorian depictions of fallenness, as a distinct element of the woman's fate or destiny. For a discussion of women and madness in Victorian culture, particularly in relation to the category of self-control, see Elaine Showalter, *The Female Malady* 23–98. I take up this topic further in Chapter 4.

no self to reform; one can impose a new identity, but it might not stick.

Dickens created a "Mark Table" that had nine headings: Truthfulness, Industry, Temper, Propriety of Conduct and Conversation, Temperance, Order, Punctuality, Economy, Cleanliness. ("The word Temperance," we are cautioned, "is not used in the modern slang acceptation, but in its enlarged meaning as defined by Johnson, from the English of Spenser: 'Moderation, patience, calmness, sedateness, moderation of passion.' ") The behavior of the women was assessed daily, and they were given a duplicate table to keep and tally themselves. The standard allotment for unexceptionable conduct was three marks, except in the Truthfulness and Temperance categories, where the standard allotment was two, "the temptation to err in those particulars, being considered low under the circumstances of the life she leads in the Home." Objectionable behavior produced "a bad mark (marked in red ink, to distinguish it at a glance from the others), which destroys forty good marks." And there was an added incentive: marks carried a monetary value. "The value of the good marks is six shillings and sixpence per thousand; the earnings of each girl are withheld until she emigrates, in order to form a little fund for her first subsistence on her disembarkation." This sentence necessarily lends a skeptical edge to the claim that immediately follows: "The inmates are found, without an exception, to value their marks highly."[25] The same ironic edge occurs in the letter explaining the rationale for distributing duplicate tables to the women: "Besides the probability of its producing some moral effect upon her, it would be a lesson in arithmetic, in which she could not fail to have a personal interest."[26]

The fallen woman is transfigured from a story into a sheet of marks. More important, she is asked to read herself as a sheet of marks, but that self-reading simply duplicates a prior process undertaken by the superintendents. Does this system produce "some moral effect"? In addressing Kay Shuttleworth's criticisms of the impending adoption of the Mark System at Urania Cottage, Dickens takes pains to establish that it does:

I have considered Mr. Kay Shuttleworth's desire to introduce some greater *moral* stimulant into this system, and do not descry any

25. Dickens, "Home for Homeless Women" 171.
26. Dickens, *Letters to Burdett-Coutts* 126.

means by which it can hopefully be done. But I submit this consideration for his reflection—whether incentives to good conduct, successfully addressed to the reason and prudence of people and obviously tending to their welfare, be not likely to become, imperceptibly, the awakeners of a real moral stimulant—suggesting, in the first instance, the wisdom of virtue and the folly of vice; and, afterwards, the inherent beauty of the former, and the deformity of the latter? In this, my hope of the system as a moral influence, mainly lies.[27]

Evidence elsewhere in Dickens suggests that it would not be perverse to "misread" the final word of this passage. The shift from a structure of self-objectification to a position of moral autonomy in the novels is generally violent and never "imperceptible." Furthermore, as will become clear in my reading of *Dombey and Son*, continuous monitoring of the self defines the condition of fallenness itself: the wages of sin are not death but, as in W. R. Greg's view, excruciating self-objectification. Insofar as the Mark System also enforces a reifying mode of self-reading, it thus becomes difficult to distinguish Dickens's reform process from the unreformed state that preceded it. Indeed, there is a disturbing similarity between the Mark System and the structure of prostitution, in that the women are paid to please.[28] Likewise, the lesser allotment of marks in the Truthfulness and Temperance categories seems to express the impossibility of getting around the forms of falseness and attenuated autonomy that define these women.

In *Dombey and Son* and *David Copperfield*, fallenness serves as a critical category through which relations among self, society, and representation become articulated and gendered. In both novels, the woman of the street reappears, serving as both victim and embodiment of threatening forces in the social environment. In *Dombey and Son*, the self-objectifying character of Edith Dombey, the prostituted wife, displays powerful threats to private selfhood and magnifies Dickens's deep skepticism about the transformative self-readings

27. Dickens, *Letters to Burdett-Coutts* 127.
28. Another way in which Urania Cottage resembled a brothel was its gradually evolved policy on dress: in order to prevent escape, it was decided that the women could not keep their own clothes in the refuge. In a similar fashion, by providing and owning all their employees' clothes, brothel keepers were able to retain powerful control over their stables of women. See Talbot, *Miseries of Prostitution* 18; Tait, *Magdalenism* 49; Mahood, *The Magdalenes* 33–34.

that enable the novels' endings. In *David Copperfield*, an autobiographical novel, the masculine protagonist achieves his consolidation and recovery of self by defining himself in opposition to social and aesthetic versions of fallenness. And whereas Edith Dombey focuses concerns about character, *David Copperfield*'s depictions of Little Emily and Annie Strong display an anxiety about the contaminating power of narrative form, its capacity to distort or even eclipse the character whose "history" it attempts to order. As in the case of the illicitly circulating stories, telling a tale can set a fall in motion.

"Pale Phantoms" and Divided Selves

Raymond Williams has pointed out that *Dombey and Son* is a pivotal novel in Dickens's career, marking the turn from a more traditional form of moral analysis, "in which society is a backdrop against which the drama of personal virtues and vices is enacted," to a newer, more socially aware form, "in which society is the creator generating and controlling, or failing to control, what in the earlier analysis could be seen as faults of the soul."[29] The novel's incoherencies, according to Williams, stem from the fact that Dickens was unsuccessfully combining both forms of analysis. Of course, as I discussed in the previous chapter, Victorian social critique and emergent British sociology themselves manifested similar strains, and in many social accounts of prostitution the fallen woman was alternately excoriated as innately depraved and exculpated as social victim. *Dombey and Son* displays such tension in its presentation of feminine impurity, yet the greater emphasis lies, as in the Urania Cottage texts and in Victorian depictions of fallenness more generally, on the fallen woman's lack of an internal moral character. Dickens's depictions of Alice Marwood, the sketchy street woman, and Edith Dombey, the commodified wife, reveal how his emergent preoccupations with competing versions of character and selfhood—with moral autonomy and the forces that threatened it—are significantly gendered in the novel. As we will see, the fallen woman is endowed with a peculiarly modern form of self-consciousness.

Dombey and Son, whose title seems to insist on a certain masculine

29. Raymond Williams, Introduction, *Dombey and Son* 16.

privilege, has stimulated a significant amount of feminist criticism.[30] But this is not because the novel enacts a blatant suppression of femininity or of women's stories; rather, the novel excites interest because of its complex exploration of a thwarted patrimonial pride: for the cherished son of the title, little Paul Dombey, dies early in the novel, and the rejected and resented survivor, Dombey's daughter, Florence, becomes a primary narrative focus. As Miss Tox exclaims after the death of Paul, "To think that Dombey and Son should be a Daughter after all!"[31] The novel traces the effects of Dombey's proud dealings, both economic and familial, as well as the powerful retributions visited upon him. Dombey's pride must suffer not only the loss of his son and the rankling presence of his self-sacrificing daughter but also the scandalous revenge exacted by his second wife, Edith, who leaves Dombey in the company of his business manager, Carker. Having been tortured by her blatantly prostitutional marriage to Dombey, Edith does not think of actually committing adultery with Carker and merely uses him to accomplish her flight and to humiliate Dombey publicly. Significantly, we later learn that Carker was earlier responsible for the fall of Edith's lower-class double, the prostitute Alice Marwood.

The famous passage that introduces *Dombey and Son*'s climactic "Thunderbolt" chapter, in which Edith leaves the imperious Dombey, argues that men have worked such distortions on nature that it is now "natural to be unnatural" (737). Mr. Dombey's "master vice," pride, is attributed to his privileged isolation: "Coop any son or daughter of our mighty mother within narrow range, and bind the prisoner to one idea, and foster it by servile worship on the part of a few timid or designing people standing round," Dickens writes, and the "willing captive" will never see nature in her "comprehensive truth" (737). Rather abruptly shifting his lens to the "Vice and Fever" propagating among the poor, Dickens then threateningly invokes the contaminating miasma and "moral pestilence" that "blight the innocent and spread contagion among the pure": "Where we generate disease to strike our children down and entail itself on unknown generations, there also we breed, by the same certain

---

30. Nina Auerbach, *Romantic Imprisonment*; Robert Clark, "Riddling the Family Firm"; Lynda Zwinger, "The Fear of the Father: Dombey and Daughter"; Joss Lutz Marsh, "Good Mrs. Brown's Connections."

31. Charles Dickens, *Dombey and Son* 298. Further page references to this edition are made parenthetically in the text.

process, infancy that knows no innocence, youth without modesty or shame, maturity that is mature in nothing but in suffering and guilt, blasted old age that is a scandal on the form we bear. Unnatural humanity!" (738). The idea of an infancy without innocence might remind us of the fallen women who troubled Dickens at Urania Cottage, though here Dickens employs an organic metaphor to describe the generation of fallen selves. His lament seemingly having reached its limit, he concludes by suggesting that the human community would right itself immediately if only people could *see* "the pale phantoms rising from the scenes of our too-long neglect, and from the thick and sullen air where Vice and Fever propagate together, raining the tremendous social retributions which are ever pouring down, and ever coming thicker!" (738).

The "Thunderbolt" passage not only describes the diseased urban environment in terms evocative of illicit sexuality ("Vice and Fever propagate together"); it also generates crucial class distinctions. Mr. Dombey, the upper-class victim of vice, enjoys a unity of subject-hood: though a prisoner, he remains a stable subject insofar as he is *bound* "to one idea." As I explain later in more detail, the "contracted sympathies" that afflict him also allow him a shielded interiority (739). The vice of the lower classes, on the other hand, is a diffuse and unlocatable contaminating force. The haunting products of the urban environment are "pale phantoms" and, in another phrase from the "Thunderbolt" passage, "dark shapes" (738). The vice of the upper class has produced in Dombey an atomistic agent; the vice of the lower class produces, on the other hand, chimerical subjects. Moreover, the phrase "social retributions" and the subtle shift in perspective from "ever pouring down" to "ever coming thicker" suggest that Dickens is not only figuring victims but also warding off the threat of an imagined, and more "horizontal," attack by the lower class.[32]

If the "Thunderbolt" passage works both to deny subjectivity to potential retributive agents and to figure the "pollution" of the urban environment as the product of unnatural "propagation," then it is not surprising that Alice Marwood, the woman of the street, is employed to represent and deflect the threat of the vicious poor.

32. For a rather different reading of this passage, one that emphasizes Dickens's hope for the moral efficacy of the third-person perspective it adopts, see Jonathan Arac, *Commissioned Spirits* 111.

Alice is memorable in that she, like other vengeful women in Dickens, can seem to adopt a lucid critical perspective akin to the narrator's own stance; indeed, she seems to voice the perspective of the "Thunderbolt" passage. No mere bundle of rags or mute Sphinx, Alice recognizes the social nature of her fall and exposes the ideological function of such concepts as "duty" when applied by institutional spokesmen ("the gentlemen in the Court") to the poor (571). Yet such social awareness and self-understanding as Alice displays are profoundly undermined by other aspects of her portrayal, and I refer here not only to her ultimate religious submission. Indeed, this character poses such acute problems for Dickens that he must dispel her: despite all her eloquence, she becomes in the end a pale phantom, forced to fade.

The depiction of Alice interestingly combines the constructions of fallenness we examined in the Urania Cottage texts. She is a social product, a familiar "story," and finally an apparition that fades. Moreover, her own moments of self-reading are presented as an acute form of self-alienation. At her initial appearance, in which she insists on the force of the environment that produced her, she presents herself in the third person:

> "There was a child called Alice Marwood," said the daughter, with a laugh, and looking down at herself in terrible derision of herself, "born, among poverty and neglect, and nursed in it. Nobody taught her, nobody stepped forward to help her, nobody cared for her."
>
> "Nobody!" echoed the mother, pointing to herself, and striking her breast. (570)[33]

As in the nonliterary texts, the actual fall is ensured, prefigured, even rendered somewhat superfluous by social deprivation. It is true that in the second segment of her narrative, which treats not childhood but girlhood, Alice directs attention toward her mother as the agent of her ruin. On one level, this focus on a discrete agent works to contain what in the first segment were diffuse forces of "poverty and neglect." And yet the attempt to locate agency in the mother merely reproduces the problem it sought to solve. If Alice suggests that her mother functioned as designing procurer, it is also

33. See Marsh, "Good Mrs. Brown's Connections," for a reading of the novel that centers on the identification of the fallen women with their stories, and that draws connections between *Dombey and Son* and the Urania Cottage texts.

true that the mother tends to be coupled with the environment in such a way that they become indistinguishable from one another. The very chapter that contains Alice's narrative begins, "In an ugly and dark room, an old woman, ugly and dark too, sat listening to the wind and rain, and crouching over a meagre fire" (566). Later, as she bends over the fire, "a gigantic and distorted image of herself [is] thrown half upon the wall behind her, half upon the roof above" (566). The walls of the home thus grotesquely repeat the image of the lower-class mother: the mother *is* the environment.[34] Metonymically aligned with the agentless fallen woman, the mother doesn't naturalize the terms of the fall, she repeats them: " 'Nobody!' echoed the mother, pointing to herself."[35]

If we feel even in this first scene that Alice's independent critical powers are undercut by what appears as a compulsion to "communicate her history," it later becomes even clearer that she cannot sustain the status of a subject. The eventual erasure or forced fading of Alice occurs when, having relinquished the retributive impulse against her seducer, she visits Harriet Carker to warn her that her brother is in danger. Her ostensibly urgent mission begins with a characteristic lapse into self-absorbed narrative: she dreamily (re)tells her story "as if she were forgetful, for the moment, of having any auditor" (847). When she recalls herself to her task, she suddenly becomes obsessed with the issue of her own credibility, voicing a deep anxiety that there is a noncorrespondence between her narrative and her demeanor. "I have done this. . . . Do I speak and look as if I really had? Do you believe what I am saying?" (848). Of course Alice does have a specific credibility problem—she has previously presented herself to Harriet in a contradictory way and plausibly fears being taken as incoherently violent. But the problem reveals itself to be deeper than that: it is as though Alice realizes she is losing her power to act and think.

This effect is heightened by the fact that Alice's utterances are actually not quite true: most of the actions she claims to have per-

34. Alice has said earlier to Harriet Carker, "I think I have a mother. She's as much a mother, as her dwelling is a home" (565); and on her deathbed, Alice produces what no longer strikes us as a zeugma: "bad homes and mothers" (922).

35. I am indebted here to Mark Seltzer's reading of Stephen Crane's *Maggie: A Girl of the Streets* and to his larger argument that the production of persons in the slums is rewritten in the two figures of the "monstrous mother" and "fallen girl." Seltzer, *Bodies and Machines* 98–100.

formed were undertaken by her mother while she herself stood by. And although she herself then performs the act of submission and relenting that eventually issues in full-fledged religious conversion, the narrative itself performs a rather different action. That is, the reversion to traditional religious discourse is accompanied by a rhetorical strategy more in keeping with Alice's status as the emanation of a degraded urban environment: the narrative "disappears" her at the end of the chapter. Dickens moves into the pluperfect to describe Alice's departure as a vanishing of a powerful presence both seen and felt: "The fire ceased to be reflected in her jet black hair, uplifted face, and eager eyes; her hand was gone from Harriet's arm; and the place where she had been was empty" (849). Alice's visit, which significantly does not issue in any plot-determining action, is cast retroactively as a vision that fades. The character who testified to the determining power of the social and narrative forces that defined her next appears on her deathbed, "the shadow of a figure that had spurned the wind and rain" (918).

The shadowy Alice Marwood also serves as double and alter ego for Edith Dombey, who herself dramatizes predicaments of modern identity. With Edith in mind, however, critics often complain that *Dombey and Son* degenerates into melodrama and runs down through excesses and repetition.[36] From this perspective, the novel constitutes not so much a new form of social analysis as an embarrassing devolution, a fatal swerve into formula: it seems regressive and lamentable when the novel is derailed by the melodramatic Edith/Carker plot. Indeed, the "Thunderbolt" chapter can itself be read as reflecting, in a highly condensed manner, the supposed tendency to flee from social critique to conventional melodrama. After the initial impassioned reformist plea, the chapter mechanically generates a series of melodramatic clichés. The retribution doled out to Dombey takes the form of a theatrical domestic scandal. Edith flings down her jewels at the feet of the imperious Dombey, taking flight with the sharp-toothed, catlike Carker. Humiliated beyond endurance, Dombey lashes out and strikes the innocent Florence, who must take to the streets.

To focus on the containing effect of the Edith/Carker plot, however, is to pass over the fact that Edith's repeated theatrical displays

---

36. See Leavis and Leavis, *Dickens the Novelist* 23; Tillotson, *Novels of the Eighteen-Forties* 176–82.

operate on two important levels that transcend crude melodrama. Specifically, Edith's "melodramatic" moments constitute the most heightened display of her commodity status and, more important, establish a troubling inverse relation between self-reflexivity and interiority, between reading the self and having a self.[37] Here is Edith the night before her mercenary marriage to Dombey:

> To and fro, and to and fro, and to and fro again, five hundred times, among the splendid preparations for her adornment on the morrow; with her dark hair shaken down, her dark eyes flashing with a raging light, her broad white bosom red with the cruel grasp of the relentless hand with which she spurned it from her, pacing up and down with an averted head, as if she would avoid the sight of her own fair person, and divorce herself from its companionship. Thus, in the dead time of the night before her bridal, Edith Granger wrestled with her unquiet spirit, tearless, friendless, silent, proud, and uncomplaining. (515)

The translation into narrative of theatrical excess produces a description that seems almost designed to bewilder the reader. Edith is presented as a split self, painfully conscious of its own reification, impelled to display its struggles, disruptions, outbreaks. Melodrama here gives expression not to a stable embodiment of vice or virtue but to a form of perpetually falling selfhood. In the description of the spurned bosom, for example, Dickens freezes what must be a repeated gesture on the part of the hand described as "relentless," thereby heightening Edith's own apprehension of herself as a static spectacle. Moreover, it is not merely Edith as consciousness but also the strangely disembodied "relentless hand" that performs the action of self-rejection or, more precisely, self-division. Spurning her own bosom, averting her head from herself, seeking divorce from her own fair person, Edith here displays—before Dickens relinquishes the theatrical and closes with a distanced description of internal struggle—the impossibility of her own subject-position, the fact that her self-reflexivity seems to participate in her reification. Edith lucidly sees herself, but only as determined and false. Her

37. For a discussion of Edith's status as a fully public exhibition and spectacle within the context of the novel's approach to property and capital, see Jeff Nunokawa, "For Your Eyes Only."

self-knowledge changes nothing—it merely forces her to repeatedly exhibit a "remarkable air of opposition to herself" (369).[38]

If we read Edith against other forms of character in the novel, particularly against the two male Dombeys, we can better see how Edith as "falling" woman displays anxieties about interiority and self-reading. It is not simply that the masculine characters possess selves while Edith does not. After all, the novel's title and early chapters reveal how a masculine subject's identity can be fixed by the prior determining instances of father and firm. Yet Dickens applies forms of protection to the male Dombeys that remain unavailable to Edith, who suffers the most radical threats to identity. The masculine characters are generally protected from moments of stark self-reading, while Edith is continually subject to an enforced spectatorship of her fully public self.

To begin with, the theatrical descriptions of Edith contrast strikingly with the indirect and muted presentation of Mr. Dombey, to whose interiority the narrative has such infrequent and limited access. Contemporary critics were so hard on Dombey's conversion that Dickens added a preface to defend his character: "Mr. Dombey undergoes no violent change, either in this book, or in real life. A sense of his injustice is within him, all along." A reader's inability to intuit this hidden remorse results from a common mistake, "the not understanding that an obstinate nature exists in perpetual struggle with itself" (43). We certainly would never make this mistake about Edith, whose body speaks the struggle Dombey allegedly always experiences "within him." Indeed, it seems that the fallen woman cannot exercise the option of keeping one's character to

---

38. The disagreement between A. O. J. Cockshut and Barbara Hardy reveals the difficulty critics have had in accounting for Edith: how does one reconcile her melodrama with her self-awareness? Cockshut, for example, sees the melodrama as primary and dismisses the moments of self-reading as unbelievable. Edith's apprehension of a parallel between herself and Alice "would require exceptional qualities of detachment and self-analysis," he writes. "And Dickens is unable to persuade us that Edith possesses them. He is guilty here of a failing very common in novelists of strong convictions—he is making a character do the author's work for him by commenting (as if from above) upon her own personality." Barbara Hardy takes issue with Cockshut's claim but tends to cast the melodramatic moments as excesses in an otherwise convincing portrayal: Edith is "a character whose detachment, self-analysis, and insight are important, conscious, and fundamental." See A. O. J. Cockshut, *The Imagination of Charles Dickens* 105, and Barbara Hardy, *The Moral Art of Dickens* 60–61. By my reading, they are both right: Edith is insightful, but she is also commenting from above—this is the peculiarly modern form her self-consciousness takes.

oneself. And if the novel teaches us the necessity of acknowledging the power of context over character, as Edith must come to see that "causes" produced Dombey's character as much as hers, the treatment of Dombey's character throughout the greater part of the novel forecloses such a lesson (968).

One could argue, it is true, that Dombey's inward character is not richly rendered precisely because he is the effect of a single cause: he exists only by virtue of the position he occupies as "head" of the firm. That is why, for example, we know nothing about his own past and childhood. Yet the narrative actively shields Dombey even as it shows him to be rigidly unfeeling: it is not just other characters but the narrative itself that runs up against Dombey's solipsistic unreadability. After Paul's death, when Dombey repulses Florence's sympathetic appeal, his resentment at her surviving his son is articulated indirectly, through questions (328). The night he almost relents toward Florence, watching her through a handkerchief while pretending to sleep, we are merely told what he "may have" realized and experienced (586–87). In these instances, the tentative hypotheses and rhetorical questions that condemn Dombey by guessing at the distorted self-defenses of his inner life simultaneously defer to his sovereign inaccessibility.[39] It is interesting in this regard that Dickens himself experienced, in relation to the illustrating of this character, "a nervous dread of caricature." Demanding that his illustrator provide a wide range of models, he finally chose the one he took to be least contaminated by exaggeration.[40] This choice repeats the double-edged narrative strategy: the protection from caricature encourages the view that Dombey lacks marked individuality but it also accords him a depth, though a strangely contentless one, to be sure. The novel that judges Dombey so harshly thus respects

39. This is of course not to say that Dombey's inner life is never more directly represented, though such occasions are rare. We are given Dombey "communing with his thoughts" in chapter 40; the other prominent moments are the rendering of Dombey's thoughts during the train ride in chapter 20 and, as I discuss later, Dombey's collapse into self-reading in chapter 59.

40. John Forster writes, "Several letters now expressed his [Dickens's] anxiety about the illustrations. A nervous dread of caricature in the face of his merchant-hero, had led him to indicate by a living person the type of city-gentleman he would have had the artist select; and this is all he meant by his reiterated urgent request, 'I wish he could get a glimpse of A, for he is the very Dombey.' But as the glimpse of A was not to be had, it was resolved to send for selection by himself glimpses of other letters of the alphabet, actual heads as well as fanciful ones." John Forster, *The Life of Charles Dickens* 3:23–24.

his privacy, acknowledging an interiority so absolute as to be utterly inaccessible.[41]

Dickens's legible effort to protect Dombey—while he exposes Edith—reveals the pressure of his anxiety that no character can escape social inscription. Little Paul Dombey, as the embodiment of imperiled private imagination, offers a further perspective on this governing anxiety. In vivid contrast to Mr. Dombey, little Paul keeps his character to himself through intimate acts of the imagination which the narrative brings before us. Paul shields himself from becoming a mere instance of the family and firm, a means to an end, by choosing solitude and fostering fancy. In his private forays he sees things in the wallpaper and carpet patterns that no one else sees—"miniature tigers and lions running up the bedroom walls, and squinting faces leering in the squares and diamonds of the floor-cloth" (234). For Edith, of course, wallpaper does not enable private acts of the imagination. As a reflection of her ornamental status, it torments her: "The mimic roses on the walls and floors were set round with sharp thorns, that tore her breast; in every scrap of gold so dazzling to the eye, she saw some hateful atom of her purchase-money" (503).

To render Paul's "old-fashioned" character, Dickens employs an altogether new-fashioned "stream of consciousness" narration. The literary term, which we associate with early modernism, is oddly appropriate here, since Dickens represents that stream, to adopt the imagery of the novel, only as it ebbs out to sea. Little Paul's consciousness is brought before us only as it experiences its own fading, during the chapters devoted to his collapse and death (chapters 14 and 16). The emergence of the private or interior character in *Dombey and Son*, through the figure of Paul, thus has the appearance of a stillbirth. Despite the fact that Dickens will move in his next novel to first-person narration, the private imagination emerges here as that which can no longer survive in a society that sees individuals only in terms of the ends they will serve. If this is the novel in which Dickens is moving away from caricature, as Q. D. Leavis claims, then it is hardly an easy transition.[42] The innovative rendering of

41. Tillotson, *Novels of the Eighteen-Forties* 167, documents the indirect and telegraphic presentation of Dombey: "In Mr. Dombey Dickens achieves the remarkable feat of making us aware of the hidden depths of character, while keeping them largely hidden; his own method respects Mr. Dombey's own proud reserve."

42. Leavis and Leavis, *Dickens the Novelist* 349.

Paul's interiority is profoundly elegaic and issues in actual death; Mr. Dombey is so private that his individuality remains purely abstract. Of course, Dickens preserves Paul Dombey's "old-fashioned" character by having him die, just as he protects Mr. Dombey from being exposed. Florence, by contrast, is defined mainly by her devotion to others, and her purity largely precludes representations of her consciousness: "Nothing wandered in her thoughts but love" (326).

Dickens displaces onto Edith the fear that in reading the self, one loses the self. If we miss noticing this, that is because the Victorian fallen woman conventionally engages in tortured moments of self-reading: there is a perfect match here between a dominant convention and Dickens's own fears about self-reflexivity. The threat is also masked or deflected in Edith's case by her overdetermined falseness, which is sometimes attributed to her status as a commodity and sometimes to a more naturalized conception of feminine artifice.[43] Only by comparing the fallen with the other versions of character Dickens offers us, and by noticing what happens when those other characters do "fall" into self-reading, can we perceive the burden the feminine character is being called on to carry. Of course, the characters of Dombey, Son, and Florence are normally protected from self-reading. Things only break down toward the end. To effect the final reconciliation, Dickens must convince us that Dombey has undergone a process of transformative self-reading. Yet if Dickens dreaded Dombey's being caricatured by his illustrator, he seems equally to dread allowing Dombey to become self-aware, only allowing his hero temporarily to inhabit this nightmarish "fallen" condition. The scene demonstrates that, for Dickens, self-reading is self-obliteration; only by using the "pure" Florence as antidote is Dickens able to recast the scene as conversion.

In "Retribution," the consequences of Dombey's proud and selfish life, and above all of his emotional exiling of the perpetually devoted Florence, come home to him. Dombey's guilt produces a strangely distanced form of self-reflexivity as he looks in the mirror: "A spec-

43. "You gave birth to a woman," Edith says to her artificial, continuously posing and play-acting mother (473). "I was a woman—artful, designing, mercenary, laying snares for men—before I knew myself, or you, or even understood the base and wretched aim of every new display I learnt" (472). Like the "more artful" prostitutes at Urania Cottage, Edith is not the author of her own designs and displays; but the statement "You gave birth to a woman" temporarily naturalizes Edith's artificiality.

tral, haggard, wasted likeness of himself, brooded and brooded over the empty fireplace. Now it lifted up its head, examining the lines and hollows in its face; now hung it down again, and brooded afresh. Now it rose and walked about; now passed into the next room, and came back with something from the dressing-table in its breast" (939). As in the case of the perpetually "falling" woman, reading the self becomes a form of self-alienation: the one Dombey watches the other, and only the watched Dombey, repeatedly designated as an "it," moves or thinks. Dombey sees himself, in Edith-like fashion, as a surface, a readable text: his face is legibly "lined." The structure of moral reflection is self-obliteration, its telos, suicide (he has picked up a knife from the dressing-table). Florence must intervene so as to provide a collapse into affective immediacy that overcomes the self-destruction of self-reading. No longer compelled to look upon himself, Dombey allows Florence to lay his face "upon the breast that he had bruised" (939).

Dombey finally achieves the sanctuary of emotional immediacy, the protection of the self through the hiding of the face, that he had envied in Florence's relations with his first wife, with his son, and even, at times, with Edith. Yet fallen women are trapped in the position through which Florence enables Dombey to pass, cleansed and restored. This displaced enactment of a redemptive sympathetic encounter reflects the same assumptions as the prostitution accounts by Greg and Tait: it suggests the fallen woman's profound need of sympathy as well as her profound exile from its curative powers, caught as she is in a continuous spectral alienation. In reading herself as "fallen," the Dickensian fallen woman does not emerge into the transforming light of self-awareness but falls more profoundly into the Spinozist trap of knowing she is determined.

Nancy in *Oliver Twist* provides a succinct and early instance of the dilemma of self-reflexivity. Like many nonliterary accounts of prostitution, this early novel seems to both premise and disavow reclaimability. Nancy's impulses to save Oliver are linked to an emerging moral reflection against which the fall, and the fallen state, are originally defined. And yet, ironically, Nancy's latent purity is proven by the fact that she knows she cannot be saved. Mr. Brownlow and Rose Maylie mistakenly think that Nancy can be extricated from this trap and start life anew, but she reveals the prostitute's catch-22 in her response: "I am chained to my old life. I loathe and hate it now, but I cannot leave it. I must have gone too far to turn back,—and yet I don't know, for if you had spoken to me some time ago, I should have laughed it off."[44] It is certainly true that Nancy is partly chained by emotional loyalty to Sikes, but that is not enough to account for her self-representation here. She goes on to posit suicide as her end, revealing the extent of self-condemnation in her moral awakening. However, Sikes's brutal murder preempts the suicide. It may not be unreasonable to see that murder as an indication of the problems that Nancy's consciousness posed for Dickens. Nancy represents not so much a fall as a failed attempt to transcend social inscription. The novel both displays the force of social determination and deflects the perceived predicament of non-liberatory self-reflexivity by representing the brutal murdering of the "aware" but utterly determined subject.

The trials of Florence also indicate that self-reflexivity constitutes a fall. Dombey's senseless cruelty to his daughter culminates with the charge that she is in league with the disgraced Edith, and with an act of physical violence that causes Florence to flee the house. The memory of the blow Florence entirely represses. She is reminded of it only after taking sanctuary at the Captain's, when she approaches the mirror to "bind up her disordered hair": "Her tears burst forth afresh at the sight; she was ashamed and afraid of it; but it moved her to no anger against him. Homeless and fatherless, she forgave him everything; hardly thought that she had need to forgive him, or that she did; but she fled from the idea of him as she had fled from the reality, and he was utterly gone and lost. There was no such Being in the world" (772).

Since on one level mere positionality, or publicness, defines the prostitute, Florence's "homelessness" necessarily places her in a threatened position, as did her earlier adventure with Good Mrs. Brown.[45] Central, however, is the way her predicament is figured by and reduced to a tortured moment of self-viewing, in which the self is eclipsed by a mark. The position of the mark recalls as well Edith's own self-marked bosom, which figures static self-viewing. Indeed, Florence's mark, which first appears here, does not serve as an index of her father's blow: it causes shame, but its origin is utterly effaced. Just as there is no "him" for the already "fatherless"

44. Charles Dickens, *Oliver Twist* 415.
45. For a discussion of the sexualized nature of Florence's adventure with Good Mrs. Brown, see Marsh, "Good Mrs. Brown's Connections" 409.

Florence to forgive, so too is there no blow to which the threatening mark can be traced. Yet Dickens takes pains both to rescue Florence from her class-inflected brush with "publicness" and to exempt her from the continual self-viewing to which Edith is subject. Walter returns to the scene and offers the sanctuary of marriage; the mark, though it remains on the surface of her body, is banished from Florence's consciousness. The refuge that Walter provides, and to which Florence clings, is a refuge from the memory not only of her father's violence and neglect but also of her stark moment of self-reflexivity. Indeed, Florence is threatened only when she goes to see Edith, and they exchange a look. "On each face," we are told, "wonder and fear were *painted* vividly" (964; my emphasis).

Dickens's nightmarish fictional representations of self-reading in *Dombey and Son* are somewhat difficult to reconcile with his avowed enthusiasm for Captain Maconochie's Mark System. A suspicious reader might wonder whether the tendency in *Dombey and Son* to assign the affliction of self-objectification to fallen women might not coincide, at a deeper level, with the heralding of the Mark System as especially applicable to the fallen. The assigned task of daily duplicating the "master copy" of one's Mark Table repeats the structure in which the fallen character reads herself as already written. And the attaching of a monetary value to the marks, by duplicating the structure of prostitution, corresponds in an eerie way with Dickens's tendency to figure self-reading itself as a fall. If this is true, the supposed precondition of reclaimability simultaneously renders it impossible.

The fallen woman's dramatic display of losing the self in reading the self must be read in light of Dickens's prevailing anxiety that our actions are not fully our own but are determined by larger social forces. For Dickens, as for the rhetoric of fallenness generally, the question of agency tends to be starkly posed, producing a hypostatized opposition between utter determination (being *marked*) and full autonomy. As Dombey's conversion scene shows, to be marked is to be obliterated: in viewing the self, Dombey becomes a "marked man." Dickens's dramatic depictions of fallen states ultimately reveal a profound uneasiness with the forms of modern self-consciousness that were being suggested and enacted by the systemic perspectives of the new sociologies, perspectives that were being generated, among other places, in the social and literary discourses on prostitution. Dickens helped elaborate the new perspectives, which were of vital importance to reformist arguments seeking to establish the social nature of "moral" problems; yet he was also shoring up his own anxieties about threatened autonomy by constructing the fallen woman as hyperdetermined and as painfully aware of her own lack of inwardness.[46]

Dickens's deterministic depictions are similar to those fatalistic conceptions of necessity that Mill saw as endemic to his culture, and they ultimately prevent a sufficiently mediated understanding of the relation between subjects and the social structures they inhabit. Dickens's own tormented relation to questions of determinism becomes even clearer if we consider the depiction of fallenness in light of Dickens's fascination with caricature. As a thoroughly unreflective form of determined character, caricature may be interpreted as in some sense the flip side of fallenness, which is a thoroughly reflective form of determined character. Dickens's distorted caricatures comically reveal the limits of spontaneous, unreflective character and suggest the desirability of self-awareness; but his fallen women, and the discrete "falls" other characters undergo, figure the instability, the paralysis and self-obliteration, of an overly reflective character. The fallen women reveal a fear that the escape from caricature is no escape at all, that one cannot look inward but can only confront oneself as an already marked surface: they paradoxically see themselves as caricatures. The "protected" character, by contrast, engages in a fantasy of autonomy from the reflection that might disclose such a horror.

"The Taint the Very Tale Conveyed"

David Copperfield presents itself as a novel entirely different from the one that precedes it. A richly rendered first-person narration, it

46. Arac situates Dickens as one of those important fiction writers of the nineteenth century who were joining "the writers of journalism and social polemic in establishing a discourse crucial for the new social sciences." Arac traces through Dickens's career from *Martin Chuzzlewit* to *Our Mutual Friend* a series of engagements with new perspectives on the social world, and an eventual collapse into an atomized solitary self. Arac, *Commissioned Spirits* 7. Of course the tension between autonomy and determination is constitutive of Dickens's work and has been addressed in many critical treatments. What I am interested in showing is how distinctive anxieties about autonomy are focused on the fallen woman during the period in which Dickens managed the "Home for Homeless Women."

represents simultaneously a young man's consolidation of self in society and his recovery of self through memory. As such, it does not seem to conceive the task of self-scrutiny as a terror from which to flee; indeed, at the end of the novel, David professes a "desire to linger yet."[47] Still, the ideal mode of this novel of memory is not the observation or viewing of a past self but a collapsing of the distance between the time *of* and the time *in* the writing. Ideally, the "recollection rises fresh upon" David (128), the consciousness of the past merging into the consciousness of the present: "Here I sit at the desk again ...," "Here I am in the playground ..." (142). As the traumatic experience of the placard indicates, David fears becoming a *read* self; instead, he wants to recapture his readings of others.[48]

My discussion of *David Copperfield* focuses, however, not so much on stark self-reading as on the relation between character and narrative form, a relation central to this autobiographical novel. Three women in the novel occupy the region of fallenness: Emily, David's childhood sweetheart; Martha Endell, the peripheral street woman; and Annie Strong, the young wife of David's cherished schoolmaster, Dr. Strong. Surely it is striking that *David Copperfield* seems to require fallen women to carry the burden of plot: what are so many fallen women doing in David Copperfield's "personal history"? I argue that David achieves a consolidation and recovery of self largely by defining himself against (but also more self-consciously through) versions of fallenness. Like his double, the falsely suspected Annie Strong, David is not-a-fallen-woman.[49] And as in the discussions of *Dombey and Son*, I focus on two levels of fallenness. If Martha Endell represents the threat of falling into a low environment and losing one's powers of self-determination, Emily and Annie Strong ultimately represent the threat that coercive narrative forms are per-

47. Charles Dickens, *David Copperfield* 950. Further page references to this edition are made parenthetically in the text.

48. See D. A. Miller, *The Novel and the Police* 209.

49. Mary Poovey argues that in *David Copperfield* the domestic heroine (the pure woman) stabilizes masculine bourgeois identity; a correlative need to ward off the "stain" of transgressive desire displaces a contaminating sexuality onto certain women. I agree that the pure woman functions to ground identity but am more interested here in the complementary move to define oneself against the fallen, socially and formally. See Poovey, *Uneven Developments* 89–125; also see my Introduction for a more general discussion of Poovey's approach to the construction of gender in Victorian culture.

ceived to pose to the recovery and representation of the self. Annie in fact brings to mind the strange way in which the women at Urania Cottage became their own stories. David seems willing to grant centrality to the fallen and to render his position as hero uncertain ("Whether I shall turn out to be the hero of my life, or whether that station will be held by anybody else, these pages must show" [49]) if it will save *him* from becoming a story instead of a (personal) history. David fears being eclipsed or distorted by a narrative as much as he fears a social fall.[50]

By focusing the discussion on how the narrator uses the fallen, moreover, one can account for the odd ambivalences in this novel, its unsettling combination of sympathy and sadism. Writing to Coutts, Dickens said he hoped in *David Copperfield* to "bring people gently" to a consideration of "the sad subject," the subject of prostitution and the fallen.[51] Certainly there is much in *David Copperfield* that suggests a sympathetic approach. Steerforth is clearly blamed for his share in Emily's fall; and her own penitence earns her the narrator's approbation, reunion with her beloved uncle, and a chance to start life anew in Australia. Even Martha, the woman of the streets, earns a place on the boat through her other-directed act of penitence. But most impressive of all is the presentation of a case of misjudgment and prejudice, an erroneous casting of Annie Strong as "fallen," that infects even the narrator's vision and has extended painful consequences for those involved, until it is all set right through the joint action of Annie, the narrator, and Mr. Dick.

Nonetheless, instances of harshness, recoil, or scapegoating frequently inhabit even moments of ostensible charity and vindication. One cannot dismiss the sadistic scene in which David looks on as Rosa Dartle abuses the "found" Emily. Nor is it possible to sustain a view of Mr. Peggotty as mercifully forgiving. He may fervently hope to reinstall Emily as cherished daughter figure, but he is also obsessed with a fantasy of her utter prostration: his endlessly recurring dream comes true when Emily swoons and falls before him. Martha Endell, moreover, delivers melodramatic speeches about the necessity of her own obliteration and is descriptively assimilated to the degraded urban environment. Annie Strong's situation is more

50. Of course we realize in retrospect that the "secret" hero is Agnes. I am pressuring the line for a different reading, though in a certain way Agnes as secret hero also privileges the pure/fallen opposition central to the reading I sketch.

51. Dickens, *Letters to Burdett-Coutts* 165.

complicated, but one's uneasiness with respect to her vindication undoubtedly stems in part from the emblematic quality of the narrator's initial suspicions that she is not true to her husband. Moreover, as Q. D. Leavis has pointed out, in order to fully vindicate Annie, the reader is forced to imagine an unnarrated assault on the part of the rakish Jack Maldon; the reader, that is, must do violence to the image of Annie's innocence.[52]

The story of David Copperfield is the story of one who has wandered astray, the story of the novelistic hero who, to adopt the formulation of Theodor Adorno and Max Horkheimer, loses himself to find himself. David's biggest error, allowing his heart to wander from Agnes before he even knew that it belonged to her, is recuperated. In marrying her, he is able to "cancel the mistaken past" (890). David's relative freedom with respect to the category of past error, however, is balanced against Emily's susceptibility to it. The fall of Emily, as sympathetic as its portrayal can be at times, ultimately represents unrecuperable error; she serves as a containment of the tragic mode. Unlike the wandering David, Emily is an explicitly fated self: she is identified with a trajectory.[53]

Very early in the novel Emily's doom is foreshadowed; the narrator himself worries that such foreshadowing may be "premature" (87). During a morning walk at Yarmouth, David fears that Emily, "walking much too near the brink of a sort of old jetty or wooden causeway," will fall over. Emily says she's not afraid "in this way" though she fears for Uncle Dan and Ham sometimes, and wishes she were a "lady," so she might help and protect them:

52. Leavis and Leavis, *Dickens the Novelist* 87.

53. In an argument that appears very different from the one I am outlining here, Laurie Langbauer claims that fallen women in Dickens are associated with the unconstrained wanderings of romance and transgressive desire. Focusing primarily on *The Old Curiosity Shop* and *Bleak House*, Langbauer argues that ultimately "the figure of woman and the form of romance become scapegoats whose implication in power suggests autonomy for men and novels." That is, what looked to be outside of power, a romance coded as feminine, is revealed to be enmeshed in power. For the most part, my argument about fallen women makes a claim opposed to Langbauer's: by my reading, such figures are cast as fated, not free, even though they are also described as "restless" or unstable. Yet at another level our readings are parallel, insofar as they explore the pervasive anxiety that there is no space free of the enmeshment of power, and insofar as they see Dickens's gendering of character as largely a symptomatic attempt to negotiate that anxiety by emphatically casting women as subject to power. Likewise, Langbauer traces the complex processes of identification and distancing that attend Dickens's constructions of women as other. Laurie Langbauer, *Women and Romance* 127–156. The quote is on 127.

She started from my side, and ran along a jagged timber which protruded from the place we stood upon, and overhung the deep water at some height, without the least defence. The incident so impressed on my remembrance, that if I were a draughtsman I could draw its form here, I dare say, accurately as it was that day, and little Em'ly springing forward to her destruction (as it appeared to me), with a look that I have never forgotten, directed far out to sea. (86)

This description contrasts sharply with the narrator's usually privileged mode of remembering that which has deeply impressed him. In the description of watching Emily, David shifts from the evocation of the experience in its immediate fullness to a remembrance of it as *sketch* or *plan*, in the manner of a draughtsman. At both the level of retrospective narration and the level of event narrated, Emily is reduced to the form of a fall; she becomes an outline of her own future. Accordingly, Emily's status as a representation is highlighted, and in a double sense, because that which is doomed, or, more precisely, drawn as doomed, is both fixed (etched) and insubstantial (merely figural). Thus the following paragraph begins, "The light, bold, fluttering little figure turned and came back safe to me, and I soon laughed at my fears" (86). The "boldness" of the figure here is also the boldness of the draughtsman's outline, and the act of distancing that subjects Emily to a downward trajectory causes the child to "flutter" as she returns to David—returns, that is, to a self in time, rather than a self formally defined. Significantly different is the foreshadowing involving the seducer Steerforth, whose name itself announces his agency as unattenuated. "No veiled future," we are told, "dimly glanced upon him in the moonbeams. There was no shadowy picture of his footsteps, in the garden that I dreamed of walking in all night" (140). This passage warns us on the level of retrospective narrative, but it preserves the integrity of Steerforth's being in time. He sleeps on, undisturbed.

Emily, whose fall constitutes a central narrative interest in the novel, is repeatedly subject to a narrative determination: hers is a being perceived in advance of itself. Mr. Peggotty's fantasy of reunion with his lost "daughter" manifests this perception of Emily in an almost unassimilable way:

On'y let her see my face—on'y let her heer my voice—on'y let my stanning still afore her bring to her thoughts the home she had fled

away from, and child she had been—and if she had growed to be
a royal lady, she'd have fell down at my feet! I know'd it well! Many
a time in my sleep had I heerd her cry out, "Uncle!" and seen her
fall like death afore me. Many a time in my sleep had I raised her
up, and whispered to her, "Em'ly, my dear, I am come fur to bring
forgiveness, and to take you home." (651)

Peggotty's strange shift in tense seems almost to transpose the recognition and the fall: "On'y let her see my face . . . she'd have fell
down at my feet." In contrast to the divine Agnes, Mr. Peggotty
points downward, producing not stabilization but a fall out of the
self. And the climax of the frenzied fantasy, Emily's fall "like death,"
in turn lends a solipsism and ineffectuality to the whispered words
of forgiveness that follow. Indeed, in the actual reunion scene, Emily
falls and is carried out "motionless and unconscious," her face veiled
by the handkerchief Peggotty has placed on it (791). Mr. Peggotty
provides an exaggerated instance, I am suggesting, of the narrator's
own vexed relation to fallenness. The fantasy of reunion shows that
it is important for Peggotty to be "stanning still" before a repeatedly
falling woman (and after the "rescue," this dramatic falling will
transmute into a continuous drooping unto death). Copperfield
shares in Peggotty's fantasy as well as its transformations: standing
still behind the partition while Emily is abused; writing her out of
the narrative after she is "found"; enjoining her to droop and cling
to Mr. Peggotty in the last view of her ("Aye, Emily, beautiful and
drooping, cling to him with the utmost of thy bruised heart" [885]).

During David's return to Yarmouth in the company of Steerforth,
the two boys see Emily followed by Martha Endell, who as a fallen
woman represents Emily's telos. As we have seen, Emily is characteristically "shadowed" by her own future, yet Martha represents
a specific threat of her own. The rhetorical constructions of this
character, who will end up walking the streets of London, recall
those in "A Nightly Scene in London" and in *Dombey and Son*. There
is a repeated move, legible in this first appearance, to identify Martha's sketchy character as emerging uncertainly from a shadowy
background and disappearing in a similarly disturbing manner:

Suddenly there passed us—evidently following [Emily and Ham]—
a young woman whose approach we had not observed, but whose
face I saw as she went by, and thought I had a faint remembrance

of. She was lightly dressed, looked bold, and haggard, and flaunting, and poor; but seemed, for the time, to have given all that to
the wind which was blowing, and to have nothing in her mind but
going after them. As the dark distant level absorbing their figures
into itself, left but itself visible between us and the sea and clouds,
her figure disappeared in like manner, still no nearer to them than
before. (384)

Not only does Martha, like the couple who precede her, disappear
into the "dark distant level," but David retroactively sees her as
having emerged "from the shadow of a wall" (384).[54] The description
of Martha echoes and revises the description of Emily on the causeway ("the light, bold, fluttering little figure"; "she was lightly
dressed, looked bold, and haggard, and flaunting, and poor"). What
the description of Martha most conspicuously adds, as though finally
hitting upon the right adjective, is "poor": poverty is the essence
of the threat that Martha poses to David's powers of self-
determination. It is not that Emily isn't poor or doesn't pose a kind
of class threat, but she does not figure the force of the environment
in the way Martha does.[55]

The familiar passage leading up to Martha's "Oh the river!" speech
reveals most clearly the threat this figure evinces. Copperfield's description extends, and even more harshly inflects, the interpenetra-
tion of feminine vice and polluted environment that we saw in
Dombey and Son.

Slimy gaps and causeways, winding among old wooden piles, with
a sickly substance clinging to the latter, like green hair, and the
rags of last year's handbills offering rewards for drowned men
fluttering above high-water mark, led down through the ooze and
slush to the ebb-tide. There was a story that one of the pits dug for
the dead in the time of the Great Plague was hereabout; and a
blighting influence seemed to have proceeded from it over the

---

54. As though to heighten Martha's precarious status as a subject, her figure is
rendered invisible before the moment of its disappearance: for after the couple disappears, only "the dark distant level" is said to be visible. And in almost every
encounter with Martha, David "knows" but does not "recognize" her, thereby reinforcing the gap between her status as type or allegory and her status as a "real"
character. See 646, 783.

55. For a discussion of Emily as posing a class threat, see Poovey, *Uneven Developments* 98. For a general discussion of class in the novel, see John O. Jordan, "The
Social Sub-Text of *David Copperfield.*"

whole place. Or else it looked as if it had gradually decomposed into that nightmare condition, out of the overflowings of the polluted stream.

As if she were a part of the refuse it had cast out, and left to corruption and decay, the girl we had followed strayed down to the river's brink, and stood in the midst of this night-picture, lonely and still, looking at the water. (748)

During his phase at Murdstone and Grinby's, David is terrified of being absorbed by the kind of degraded environment that here seems to produce Martha. Feeling himself to have been "thrown away" (208), experiencing a profound degradation at the factory "abutting on the water when the tide was in, and on the mud when the tide was out" (209), David fears being slowly drained of all knowledge, memory, imagination—in effect, all interiority. What "cannot be written," we are told, is "what misery" it was "to believe that day by day what I had learned, and thought, and delighted in, and raised my fancy and my emulation up by, would pass away from me, little by little, never to be brought back any more" (210).

The river scene in *David Copperfield* culminates with a rescue in which David and Mr. Peggotty offer a suicidal Martha the redeeming task of saving one less lost than she. The irony is that the rescue occurs only after Martha's suicide would be, in a manner, superfluous: the previous description has already assimilated Martha to the "refuse" at the river's edge. Indeed, the impulse of the narrative to "cast out" Martha before redeeming her—as Mr. Peggotty wants Emily to fall "like death" before forgiving her—is indicated in an almost self-conscious way during the pursuit itself, in which Martha gains speed "as if to avoid the footsteps she heard so close behind" (747). The intervention of David and Mr. Peggotty is thus complicit in the production of Martha's "downward path" and its accompanying forms of attenuated subjectivity (incoherence, frenzy)—from which it then works to save her.

During his degrading sojourn at Murdstone and Grinby's David requires no such intervention and suffers no such lapses in control as characterize Martha's frenzy. Recognizing the power of the milieu into which he has "sunk," he "forms a resolution" and acts on it (210, 208). Appealing to Betsy Trotwood allows David to effect the transition from a situation in which he lives and works dangerously close to the malign waters to one in which he, installed in gentle-

man's rooms, has a reassuring "view" of the river, stands over and
against it, as he stands over and against Martha (413). Martha does
come to and dutifully performs the act of saving Emily; she even
starts life anew by going to Australia with Mr. Peggotty and Co.,
eventually even remarrying. Still, her central role in the novel is to
figure an unstable relation between self and environment, one from
which David must distance himself, one against which he consolidates a self.[56]

The case of Annie Strong is the most complicated of all. One is
tempted to say that here Dickens best succeeds in bringing us to
that "gentle consideration" at which he aimed, since the treatment
of this character lays bare the process of underwriting and scapegoating that constitutes David's relation to fallen women.[57] Through
the revelation that Annie is *not* a fallen woman we suddenly see lit
up the narrative strategies that have operated on the figure of the
fallen woman generally. When during her exoneration Annie voices
David's innermost, still inarticulate thoughts, for example, it is revealed that David identifies most deeply with a character who must
protest that she is not fallen. Similarly symptomatic is David's intervention during the scene, his breaking of the excruciating pause
after Annie pleads, "If I have any friend here, who can give a voice
to any suspicion that my heart has sometimes whispered to me . . .
I implore that friend to speak" (726). David's voicing of the charge
can be attributed neither solely to sympathy nor solely to sadism—
it partakes of an ambivalent admixture of the two.

Annie will be exonerated, yet it would be mistaken to say that
she does not fall. Her fall, however, is a fall not into sexuality but
into suspicion. Suspicions of Annie, and her own suspicion of those
suspicions, taint her self-perceptions and contaminate the narrator.
The threat that Annie represents, the contaminating power of suspicion, ultimately is cast as a fall into narrative; and what this fall
most seriously threatens is David's ability to recover the past, to
rescue memory from the distortions that a narrative trajectory im-

56. And in fact, one could read Martha's new start more cynically. Remarrying
in the colonies means integration into a community with a distinctly criminal cast:
Martha is reabsorbed into the malign waters.

57. The more fully achieved deconstruction of gender opposition in this novel is
reflected as well through the predominance of women surrounding David and
through the feminization of David in his relation to Steerforth. It is a subtle shift,
and does not foreclose scapegoating the feminine. Nonetheless, it would not be
farfetched to adduce a greater "gentleness" in this sphere.

poses. The link between suspicion and fallenness can be detected in the scene of Jack Maldon's departure, but only as viewed through the illuminations of the vindication scene. The departure scene suggests very strongly that Annie has compromised herself; it not only highlights her paleness, trembling, and distraction throughout the evening but culminates with two powerfully indicting emblematic moments. Directly after Maldon departs in the coach, Annie is discovered in a swoon on the hall floor, a cherry-colored ribbon missing from the bosom of her dress. A moment before, we are told, David had seen something cherry-colored in Maldon's hand as he "[rattled] past with an agitated face" (301). The second emblematic moment occurs when David returns later that same night for Agnes's missing reticule. Unseen and unnoticed, he comes upon Annie kneeling at the feet of the oblivious Doctor, her dress "disordered by the want of the lost ribbon," her face an enigma, even in retrospect: "Penitence, humiliation, shame, pride, love, and trustfulness—I see them all; and in them all, I see that horror of I don't know what" (304). This scene is choreographically identical to the scenes of Martha's and Emily's abasement: David stands on as voyeur while a woman kneels penitently.

Annie's future revelations seem to justify her: she was dishonored through Maldon's agency, not her own. It was delicacy that prevented her from revealing the truth to the unsuspecting Doctor. Maldon had spoken "words that should have found no utterance"; hence, her mind "revolted from the taint the very tale conveyed" (730). We infer that Maldon, upon leaving, made professions and snatched the ribbon from Annie's dress. As a victim thus of the de facto fallenness that follows upon sexual assault, Annie swoons, then reemerges penitently aware of her new status. Yet in recalling the extent and nature of Annie's distress throughout the evening, we might wonder if the profession didn't occur earlier, since neither a dear cousin's leavetaking nor Annie's perennial fear of being seen as mercenary would seem to account for her excesses. Yet if that were the case, Annie would not have repeatedly returned to Maldon's side at the sofa, as she does, in her distress and distraction. More important, if he had professed earlier, she would have swooned earlier.

The only way to account for the ambiguities of the scene is to posit a dawning awareness on the part of Annie. Her own presentation during the vindication scene thus must be read not as a synopsis of the effects of Maldon's professions but as a description of what preceded them. She suddenly "knew" that Maldon "had a false and thankless heart" (730). "I saw a double meaning, then," she goes on, "in Mr. Wickfield's scrutiny of me. I perceived, for the first time, the dark suspicion that shadowed my life." This in turn means that Maldon doesn't really shock Annie into a swoon; the swoon issues out of her own fall into suspicion. In other words, Annie is less a victim of fallenness per se than a victim of the fall that suspicion produces.

For David, who himself has been contaminated by doubts of Annie, suspicion itself becomes suspect; and, intimately linked to the act of foreshadowing, it comes to figure the distortions imposed by narrative exigency. Foreshadowing threatens the sanctity of memory itself, as revealed most powerfully in the passage that recaptures the dawning of David's own suspicions of Annie. Mr. Wickfield and Agnes are leaving the Strongs after an evening visit, when Mr. Wickfield suddenly interposes himself between Agnes and Annie, disallowing a parting embrace, and thereby evoking the same memorable "look" that David had witnessed on Annie's face the night he returned for Agnes's reticule:

> I cannot say what an impression this made upon me, or how impossible I found it, when I thought of her afterwards, to separate her from this look, and remember her face in its innocent loveliness again. It haunted me when I got home. I seemed to have left the Doctor's roof with a dark cloud lowering on it. The reverence that I had for his grey head, was mingled with commiseration for his faith in those who were treacherous to him, and with resentment against those who injured him. The impending shadow of a great affliction, and a great disgrace that had no distinct form in it yet, fell like a stain upon the quiet place where I had worked and played as a boy, and did it a cruel wrong. I had no pleasure in thinking, any more, of the grave old broad-leaved aloe-trees, which remained shut up in themselves a hundred years together, and of the trim smooth grass-plot, and the stone urns, and the Doctor's walk, and the congenial sound of the Cathedral bell hovering above them all. It was as if the tranquil sanctuary of my boyhood had been sacked before my face, and its peace and honour given to the winds. (339)

"I seemed to have left the Doctor's roof with a dark cloud lowering on it." We might read this qualifying "seemed" here as a hint that

David's impression is wrong; yet we are just as likely to read it as an instance in which the language of anticipation blends with the dominant performative mode of this novel of memory: "it seemed to me that . . . " This is a muted duplication of the apprehension, on the causeway, of the bold form of Emily as trajectory, "as it appeared" to David. Later, of course, Copperfield will employ the language of the lowering cloud in reference to Emily's impending fall: "A dread falls on me here. A cloud is lowering on the distant town, towards which I retraced my solitary steps" (509).

What deceives us in the case of Annie is not only the blending of the language of foreshadowing with the rhetoric of suspicion, but also the narrative that suspicion produces. Once the cloud appears, the landscape alters: there is an unequivocal reference to "those who injured him"; Annie cannot be separated from her look of guilt; her face cannot be remembered "in its innocent loveliness again" (339). What is especially interesting, however, is that the passage then registers its own activity: "The impending shadow of a great affliction, and a great disgrace that had no distinct form in it yet, fell like a stain upon the quiet place where I had worked and played as a boy, and did it a cruel wrong." An approaching affliction is here described in terms that evoke a fall, but a metalepsis occurs. Instead of the inexorable affliction that follows the contaminating fall, we here have the inexorability, the impendingness itself, cast as a fall: the "stain" here is anticipation, suspicion, narrative exigency itself. Further, the result of such a fall is the destruction of the "tranquil sanctuary" of David's boyhood, a sanctuary represented as discrete images connected not by narrative but by the "congenial sound of the Cathedral bell hovering above them all." To narrate the past, by setting it in relation to a telos, is to lose the very past one aims to recover. Perhaps this is why Copperfield deflects so much attention onto the stories of women.[58]

In relation to Annie, the "impending shadow" is recast as "mere" suspicion, and Uriah Heep is expunged as a pernicious "plotter." Annie devotedly subordinates herself to the cherished Doctor, that unsuspecting writer not of narratives but of discrete or "pure" definitions (the dictionary writer). And David, who now professes a

---

58. See Poovey, *Uneven Developments* 97, for a rather different reading of this passage, which Poovey sees as revealing the way woman serves as the site where a contaminating sexuality becomes visible.

wish to "linger," as he earlier was impelled to "meander," seemingly dispels any taint that may have communicated itself to him: he was not, and did not have, a hidden agenda. Memory is thereby "rescued" from narrative, and narrative from suspicion. But of course it is impossible for David to erect a *cordon sanitaire* around himself and the narrative. "I seemed to have left the Doctor's roof with a dark cloud lowering on it." As when it is suggested that David and Mr. Peggotty hurry Martha to her destination, here David can be seen as admitting his own complicity: it is he who leaves the cloud there, and this is what haunts him and causes his discomfort.

Annie's supposed fall is thus more profoundly David's fall. Yet for a narrator it is a necessary fall. Those who never suspect Annie are incapable of producing narrative or recovering the past: the Doctor is a writer only of atomistic dictionary entries; the suspicionless Mr. Dick, who effects the reconciliation between Annie and her estranged husband, can make no progress on his "Memorial." He only senses, he cannot narrate, the trouble between Annie and the Doctor. During the conversation in which Mr. Dick hits upon the idea of acting as mediator, Copperfield must help him past a crucial "break." Having just delivered an endearing eulogy to the Doctor, Mr. Dick turns his attention to Annie: " 'And his beautiful wife is a star,' said Mr. Dick. 'A shining star. I have seen her shine, sir. But,' bringing his chair nearer, and laying one hand upon my knee— 'clouds, sir—clouds' " (720). Once Mr. Dick utters the word *clouds*, syntax fails him, and Copperfield the narrator must take over.

The metalepsis that transforms Annie's fall into the threat of narrative distortion is a repetition in the literary register of the same kind of transformation that governs constructions of social fallenness. Just as the woman of the street comes to embody the force of the environment, Annie comes to embody the force of narrative. Yet we saw this same conversion in the *Household Words* article, when the narrating of a personal history transformed a person into a story, which then threatened to circulate or be "communicated to" others. Likewise, when Annie "falls" into narrative exigency, the threat of narrative becomes sexualized. The sanctuary of boyhood is sacked, "its peace and honour given to the winds." Many critics have complained of the blandness and passivity of this novel's narrator. Here we might recall Dickens's advice for eliciting "truth" rather than "stories" from narrating prostitutes: "It has been observed, in taking the histories—especially of the more artful cases—that nothing is so likely to elicit the truth as a perfectly imperturbable face, and an avoidance of any leading question or expression of opinion." For Dickens, there is something obscene about becoming a story, about fictionalizing one's past: it is what whores do.[59] Copperfield's "perfectly imperturbable face" is an attempt to belie the taint the very tale conveys.

Within Dickens's literary and nonliterary writings from the Urania Cottage period, the category of fallenness comprises several forms of objectified and determined character. The woman of the street, by blurring with those surroundings that alternately produce and absorb her, figures the threat of environmental determination. The self-monitoring fallen women, both those practicing the Mark System and those condemned to the horrors of self-alienation, reveal a modern model of the self generated by Dickens's increasingly systemic perspective on the social world. Last, the histrionic prostitute and the falsely accused pure woman suggest the contaminating and controlling powers of stories themselves, their capacity to communicate a fatal identity to their susceptible practitioners, auditors, and subjects. There are of course significant differences among these manifestations of fallenness. The notion of the fated self or the predetermined character, for example, includes a dimension of temporality missing from the static spectacles offered up in the scenes of self-reading. And one can distinguish the depictions of environmental determination from the delineations of narrative coercion, though they are frequently conflated, as in the case of Alice Marwood's story. In the case of both social and more distinctly literary versions of fallenness, however, Dickens inevitably makes appeal to forms of autonomy—power over one's social context, freedom from formal constraints—that his fictions ultimately reveal to be deluded and unobtainable.

In many respects Dickens provides the best introduction to the rhetoric of fallenness precisely because he offers such varied and dramatic instances of it, and because encounters with the specters of determination are constitutive of both his social and his literary writings. Yet despite the pervasiveness of Dickens's own anxiety about autonomy, there is a significant and repeated gendering of the predicaments of social constraint, one that allots to the fallen

59. See Marsh, "Good Mrs. Brown's Connections" 415.

woman spectacular ordeals: loss of identity distinct from one's immediate surroundings, enforced and nontransformative self-readings, and deficient immunity from the constraint and contagion of narrative. Dickens thus engages, though with an almost undermining legibility, in the Victorian cultural practice that wards off perceived predicaments of agency by displacing them onto a sexualized feminine figure. As I show in later chapters, however, there are alternatives to the conceptions of self and society that underlie such scapegoating mechanisms.

3

Melodrama, Morbidity, and Unthinking Sympathy: Gaskell's *Mary Barton* and *Ruth*

Like her contemporary and occasional publisher Charles Dickens, Elizabeth Gaskell was interested in the fallen woman as both a social problem and a literary topos. "Lizzie Leigh," Gaskell's first contribution to Dickens's periodical *Household Words*, treats the rescue of a fallen woman as secured through maternal resistance to the social law. Gaskell also at least once engaged in an act of "rescue" herself, appealing by letter to Dickens for help in arranging passage to Australia for a young woman she knew.[1] Gaskell's central contribution to the contemporary debate on reforming the fallen, however, was her novel *Ruth*, which argued for the possibilities of redemption in a community free of prejudice. Although readers of the novel perennially react to Ruth's exaggerated purity, attenuated agency, and seemingly gratuitous death, Gaskell's admittedly uneven novel also works to expose the way cultural conventions and dominant modes of deterministic thinking themselves promote, and may even produce, the "downward path" that follows upon error.

As her industrial novels demonstrate, Gaskell was concerned not exclusively with fallen women but with the condition of the urban poor in general. She did not, however, participate in any system of reform such as the one Dickens undertook at Urania Cottage. Throughout her life she advocated a resolutely individualistic and improvisatory charity, one in keeping with the tenets of her Unitarian milieu. Her insistence on the uniqueness of the individual case and on the transformative potential of direct contact between

1. Elizabeth Gaskell, *The Letters of Mrs. Gaskell* 98–99.

members of different classes made uniform schemes and anonymous contributions anathema to her.[2] *Mary Barton*, her first industrial novel, promotes sympathetic encounters between persons as the precondition or even site of social melioration. For Gaskell, writing at the time of the 1848 revolutions and amid Chartist agitation in England, it is the "masters' " perceived indifference to the sufferings of the workers that has dangerously alienated the latter. The central task before the middle classes, then, is to "disabuse the work-people of so miserable an apprehension."[3] Gaskell's recurrent ambivalence toward the workers she wants to help is registered here in the use of the word "miserable," which both blames the workers for a misperception and evokes their immiseration. Yet Gaskell also displays ambivalence toward her own class, which she alternately chastises and defends.

It is not that Gaskell excludes legislative change or concrete factory reform as desired ends—on the contrary, she explicitly supports them. But the call to sympathy remains fundamental, and she continually recurs to it. In appealing to a language of feeling, Gaskell's novel does not significantly depart from the industrial novels of her time, which shared the belief that rationalized reform was continuous with the utilitarian and dehumanizing spirit of industrialism itself.[4] This larger framework helps to explain why sympathy appears alternately as means and end in *Mary Barton*. In either case, however, transformative action requires a scenario of interclass recognition and response.

In this chapter I examine and contrast Gaskell's depictions of fallenness in *Mary Barton* and *Ruth*. I argue that the representation

2. These convictions come up in Gaskell's correspondence. "The numbers of people who steadily refuse Mr. Gaskell's entreaties that they will give their time to anything, but will give him or me tens & hundreds, that don't do half the good that individual intercourse, & earnest conscientious thought for others would do." Also: "It is hard work making one's idea of life dear [*sic*] and I am more and more convinced that where every possible individual circumstance varies so completely all one can do is to *judge* for oneself and take especial care *not* to judge other[s] or for others." Gaskell, *Letters* 193, 548. For an account of the links between Unitarianism and individualized charity, see Angus Easson, *Elizabeth Gaskell* 12; R. K. Webb, "The Gaskells as Unitarians" 147.

3. Elizabeth Gaskell, *Mary Barton* 38. The line is taken from Gaskell's preface. All further references to this edition are made parenthetically in the text.

4. See Arnold Kettle, "The Early Victorian Social-Problem Novel" 168–69; on the promotion of sympathy during the "social-problem decade" of the 1840s, see John Lucas, "Mrs. Gaskell and Brotherhood."

of Esther, *Mary Barton*'s frequently overlooked prostitute figure, reflects a radical conception of the social force of aesthetic conventions, showing the power of forms such as melodrama to constitute human social identities. While recent critics have focused especially on the exemplary actions undertaken by heroines such as Mary Barton and Margaret Hale, they do not sufficiently consider how the rhetoric of fallenness functions in Gaskell's work.[5] Gaskell's representation of fallenness in *Mary Barton* bears similarities to Dickens's conception of narrative constraint, but whereas he betrays a fear of a pervasive narrative fallenness that is sometimes (though not necessarily) linked to environmental determinism, Gaskell isolates melodrama and romance as the specific genres of prostitution and fallenness. Further, scenes involving the prostitute Esther heighten the tension between Gaskell's own reformist aesthetic and her conception of transformative action. For if what is important to Gaskell is the actual encounter between living persons, what does it mean for her audience merely to *read* a sympathetic literary depiction of the ostensible objects of concern? As we will see through an examination of the prostitute, whose privileged relation to the "literary" bequeaths her a special positioning within the novel, Gaskell secretly fears not only that sympathetic literary reading will preempt meliorative action but that the ideal of mutually sympathetic recognition will be derailed as reading subjects convert their perceptions of sufferers into mournful narratives that preclude any hope for change.

A rather different and more complicated problematic emerges in *Ruth*. Seduced innocent rather than inscribed victim, Ruth is both immune to and, paradoxically, rescued from the punishing social "laws" that enforce the fallen woman's downward path. For Gaskell, these laws participate in prevalent forms of thinking—both secular and religious—whose social power she acknowledges but would like to discredit. However, unlike some critics of overly deterministic understandings of selfhood and agency, Gaskell makes her primary counterposing appeal not to an autonomous self but rather to a sympathetic or fundamentally intersubjective self, one defined through its profoundly responsive orientation

5. For an excessive emphasis on Mary's agency, see Coral Lansbury, *Elizabeth Gaskell: The Novel of Social Crisis*. The best feminist approach to Gaskell's work as a whole—and a book to which my own reading is indebted—is Patsy Stoneman's *Elizabeth Gaskell*.

toward others. As I discussed in Chapter 1, utilitarians and other radical reformers were anxious to justify or develop models of sympathetic action that would harmonize with the ideal of moral betterment that underlay their doctrines, yet this aim often remained in conflict with the egoistic conceptions of the self informing their hedonistic philosophy. Gaskell avoids the problem of social atomism by privileging a sympathetic form of consciousness, one defined against the kind of moral autonomy that Dickens was so anxious to defend.

In its vindication of a "pure" woman, then, *Ruth* reflects a critical stance toward deterministic discourse and egoistic forms of selfhood. Remarkably, Gaskell's critique extends even to those forms of instrumental and calculative thinking associated with materialist, utilitarian, and deterministic philosophies; and ultimately, *Ruth*'s portrayal of purity as unthinking sympathy reflects a deeper anxiety that all reason may be instrumental. A second "fall" occurs in the novel when the spontaneously good Mr. Benson falls into calculation and "morbid" deliberation, thereby destroying his sympathetic "instincts of conscience." In her attempt to advocate a redemptive morality, Gaskell thus rescripts fallenness to encompass those very forms of selfhood—rational, autonomous, deliberative—against which fallenness is usually defined. If this redefinition presents a challenge to the dominant discourse, however, it also reinforces it, precisely by conceiving the reach of the utilitarian ethos as absolute, and by vainly seeking to shelter character and community from any form of calculation and deliberative rational interaction.

In promoting unthinking purity as the antidote to an encroaching utilitarian and industrial ethos, Gaskell generates another problem: a profoundly vulnerable heroine. For Ruth's sympathetic responsiveness, the index of her purity, is also the cause of her sexual lapse and continued physical susceptibility. As a more fortified alternative to a discredited deliberative or instrumental consciousness, accordingly, the novel elaborates through Ruth's redemption a form of sympathetic judgment rooted in maternity. Although this maternal mode clearly participates in the Victorian cult of motherhood, and as an intersubjective model is hardly dialogical, it signals Gaskell's attempt to transcend two linked problems: egocentric, instrumental conceptions of reason and alienated human relations.

Vivid Paint and Deadly Pale Faces

Mary Barton develops as the gradual convergence and then final splitting of two competing plot lines, Mary Barton's romance plot and John Barton's political tragedy. A spirited and attractive dressmaker's apprentice, Mary engages in a flirtation with the dandified son of the rich manufacturer, Mr. Carson, who employs her father. We are led to suspect that Mary will be "ruined," both because of ominous remarks made by the narrator ("Alas! poor Mary! Bitter woe did thy weakness work for thee" [80]) and by the linking of Mary temperamentally and physically to her streetwalking aunt Esther, whose mysterious disappearance forms the novel's inaugural narrative interest. Running parallel to Mary's story is that of her father, John Barton, a trade union activist who grows increasingly obsessed with economic injustice and the sufferings of the poor. After participating in an unsuccessful attempt to petition Parliament on behalf of the Charter, Barton grows increasingly bitter toward the rich and begins taking opium to assuage his hunger and misery. He finally loses all patience when, during bitter strike negotiations, the young Harry Carson, Mary's suitor, draws a callous caricature of the workers and circulates it among the masters. Barton convinces his men that it is time to respond with violence; they resolve to murder Harry Carson. Oblivious to the flirtation between Mary and Carson, Barton himself draws the fateful straw.

Meanwhile, Mary's outcast aunt Esther, monomaniacally driven to watch over the motherless Mary, has become convinced that her niece is on the verge of succumbing to Carson and thereby falling into the same nightmarish position she herself inhabits. She first attempts, unsuccessfully, to warn Mary's father. Next she decides upon Jem Wilson, an old childhood friend of Mary's, unaware that he is deeply in love with Mary, has already unsuccessfully proposed marriage, and knows nothing of Carson. Esther's warning is unnecessary, however: Mary regretted rejecting Jem the moment she had done so and is no longer susceptible to Carson. Esther's warning in fact destructively leads to Jem's being suspected for the murder of Carson, since he publicly confronts, strikes, and threatens Carson after speaking to Esther. To make matters worse, it turns out that Barton had borrowed Jem Wilson's gun. Although even Mary suspects Jem, she eventually becomes the lonely diviner of the truth of her father's guilt. She knows because Esther, in another misguided attempt to help, delivers to Mary a piece of evidence that she assumes incrimates Jem, whom she now takes to be Mary's lover. Instantly recognizing the evidence as pointing unmistakably to her father, Mary sets herself the Herculean task of proving Jem's alibi while protecting her father. Through an amazing sequence of heroics, she succeeds. The novel ends with Barton's dramatic deathbed reconciliation with Carson's father; Jem and Mary then marry and emigrate to Canada. Esther reappears at the end, but only to collapse and die; she is buried side by side with Barton, another "wanderer."

Traditionally, the tension between the two plots—more specifically, the eclipsing of the political by the romance plot—has been seen as the novel's main defect.[6] More recent readings, however, have thematized the relation between the two story lines.[7] For the purposes of my own reading, the most important reassessment of the novel is Catherine Gallagher's in *The Industrial Reformation of English Fiction*.[8] Gallagher has argued that the novel's generic discontinuities, and in particular the tension between melodrama and social tragedy, should be seen not as flaws but as the achieved effects of a formal self-consciousness. Conceding that Gaskell ultimately escapes conflicting causal explanations by retreating to the "anti-interpretative" immediacy of the domestic mode, Gallagher nonetheless argues that along the way Gaskell criticizes romantic and melodramatic perspectives on social reality. By being forced to understand that class antagonism and not romantic passion was the cause of Carson's death, Mary and other characters are weaned from melodramatic misperception, whose distortions can produce tragic effects. This lesson is meant equally for the reader: through the inaugural interest in Esther's fall and the subsequent prefiguring of Mary's, the novel signals itself as melodrama yet then increasingly requires us to attend to Barton and the political issues that concern him.[9]

6. See Raymond Williams, *Culture and Society, 1780–1950* 87–91; Margaret Ganz, *Elizabeth Gaskell: The Artist in Conflict* 69; W. A. Craik, *Elizabeth Gaskell and the English Provincial Novel* 5; Ruth Bernard Yeazell, "Why Political Novels Have Heroines" 135.

7. See especially Rosemarie Bodenheimer, "Private Grief and Public Acts in *Mary Barton*"; Stoneman, *Elizabeth Gaskell* 68–98.

8. Catherine Gallagher, *The Industrial Reformation of English Fiction* 62–87.

9. In a letter to the wife of W. R. Greg that seems itself to register the commercial pressures to privilege melodrama and romance, Gaskell writes, " 'John Barton' was the original name, as being the central figure to my mind; indeed I had so long felt

Indeed, although Gallagher does not discuss this, the entire first scene prefigures the tension between romance and politics as well as the novel's eventual resolution in the realm of domestic communion. Two lower-class Manchester families, the Bartons and the Wilsons, meet during a spring holiday outing in the fields outside the city. After a lingering description of the setting, the first spoken words of the novel announce its (and our) first narrative interest. George Wilson "was the first to speak, while a sudden look of sympathy dimmed his gladsome face. 'Well, John, how goes it with you?' and in a lower voice, he added, 'any news of Esther yet?' " (42). We learn that Esther, the sister of John's wife, Mary, has disappeared mysteriously, though signs indicate the departure was premeditated. Mary, whose sudden death later this same evening will be traced to the shock of her sister's disappearance, anxiously fears that Esther has drowned herself. John Barton is convinced otherwise. Esther's love of finery, her spirited temper, the fact that she was "puffed up," all argue that she has fallen and will end a streetwalker, as he once predicted she would. Barton blames Esther's supposed state at least partly on factory work for women: earning a little money allowed her to indulge a dangerous taste for luxury and finery that in turn produced unreasonable social ambitions.

Having invoked this socioeconomic explanation, however, Barton drops the story of Esther and enters into the first of his many impassioned speeches against economic inequity and the indifference of the rich to the plight of the poor. His speech culminates with the following:

> "We are their slaves as long as we can work; we pile up their
> fortunes with the sweat of our brows; and yet we are to live as

---

that the bewildered life of an ignorant thoughtful man of strong power of sympathy, dwelling in a town so full of striking contrasts as this is, was a tragic poem, that in writing he was [?] my 'hero'; and it was a London thought coming through the publisher that it must be called *Mary* B. So many people overlook John B. or see him merely to misunderstand him, that if you were a stranger and had only said that one thing (that the book shd have been called *John* B) I should have had pleasure in feeling that my own idea was recognized." Gaskell, *Letters* 70. Stoneman and Easson both claim, however, that this "original" title was a post-hoc creation of Gaskell's, drummed up expressly to placate reviewers, like Greg himself, who criticized her depictions of the working-class life in Manchester. Stoneman, *Elizabeth Gaskell* 23; Easson, *Elizabeth Gaskell* 73.

separate as if we were in two worlds; ay, as separate as Dives and Lazarus, with a great gulf betwixt us. . . . "

"Well, neighbor," said Wilson, "all that may be very true, but what I want to know now is about Esther—when did you last hear of her?" (45)

Wilson calls Barton back to the immediate concern of one they know and care about, yet his question also reflects a desire to shift from the oppressively "true" presentation of class inequity to a romantic "story" that might serve, appropriately enough for this holiday respite in rural fields, as a diverting alternative to a threatening economic understanding of their social world. This scene in miniature presents the larger tension between the political plot and the love plot.

For Gallagher, the power of *Mary Barton* lies in its conscious critique of culturally influential genres: sentimental romance, farce, and melodrama. The novel shows us that the perspectives promoted by these genres are dangerously false: they not only distort our view of reality but produce disastrous effects. What Gallagher leaves unexplored, and what I wish to focus on, is the most palpable effect that melodrama produces: the prostitute Esther. Gallagher reads Gaskell's novel as suggesting that a character can be weaned from what is essentially a misperception: one's vision can be corrected.[10] Insofar as Mary and other characters learn that a melodramatic reading is wrong and a political reading is right, the novel demonstrates that melodrama is false and class conflict is real. The character of Esther troubles the clarity of this initial claim on Gallagher's part, however, because she is a *real* melodramatic character: she constitutes, to put it somewhat differently, the conflation of romantic melodrama and the real.[11] Not simply someone who has seen too

10. The discredited modes "enter the narrative as the distorted literary viewpoints of a few characters." Gallagher, *Industrial Reformation* 68.

11. Gallagher sees the clarity of the opposition between melodrama and tragic realism as troubled instead by the destabilizing contradiction that inhabits the tragic story of John Barton: is he socially determined or is he a tragic hero? Bodenheimer seems to register but not pressure the problem I wish to focus on when she notes that Gaskell "denies the outer world its full reality by treating . . . 'lapses' from domesticity as the stuff of melodrama and romance." Gallagher, *Industrial Reformation* 74; Bodenheimer, "Private Grief and Public Acts" 204.

many plays and let them affect her view of things, Esther is a ghost from another genre.[12]

Esther's disturbing epistemological place in the plot would doubtless not have caused a ripple had she remained the merely discursive entity—"any news of Esther?"—she was at the novel's start. As it is, her status as a story that then comes to inhabit the landscape in the form of a character aptly indicates her anomalous position. Indeed, Barton's violent reaction to Esther when she attempts to warn him about Mary can be seen, despite its more obvious motive, as a function of her unassimilability to the more strictly economic perspective he embodies. Barton reacts to Esther's "faded finery" and painted face but he fails to intepret them as emblems of social injustice, as we would expect him to. Though we are reminded that Barton blames Esther for his wife's death, the scene also insists upon Esther's aesthetically eclipsed subjectivity: "In vain did her face grow deadly pale round the vivid circle of paint" (169).

Critics have typically dismissed or criticized Esther because she is so luridly drawn: she is seen, like Dickens's street women, as speaking in the exaggerated rhetoric of stage melodrama. My claim, instead, is that this seemingly conventional character is "tinged with falsifying colors" precisely because she has fallen into melodramatic representation.[13] In an important sense, Esther's condition is more horrifying than Jem's life-and-death situation: he is only the victim of melodramatic misperception, which can be, and in fact *is*, corrected. Esther, on the other hand, is trapped within the genres—melodrama and romance—that are otherwise being discredited. As we will see, Gaskell very explicitly heightens Esther's literary status by comparing her to two Coleridgean romance figures, the Ancient Mariner and "Christabel"'s Geraldine.

Ironically, then, Gaskell's portrayal of what looks like a highly conventional character works to reveal a mutually constitutive relation between character and aesthetic forms. In dramatizing Esther's aesthetic character, however, Gaskell also highlights the tension

12. One might ask whether the young Henry Carson and perhaps Sally Leadbitter might not also be seen as figures from melodrama. Henry Carson, however, is crucially not restricted to the romance plot; his field of action extends into the political sphere of class conflict. And Sally Leadbitter is a *reader* of romance and an *audience* of melodrama.

13. This remark about Esther appears in one of Stephen Gill's footnotes to the Penguin edition, 474 n. 9.

between literary reading and sympathetic encounter that inhabits her reformist aesthetic. By way of approaching the complex of issues raised by Gaskell's representation of the prostitute, I want to focus on two scenes involving Esther: her encounter with Jem Wilson, a scene of reading that reveals Esther's vexed status as both social victim and figure for melodrama or romance; and her encounter with Mary, which reveals how gender inflects the scene of reading, as well as the difficulties Gaskell's implicit ideology poses for a feminist reading.

Jem Wilson, like his father who was so eager to hear the story of Esther, functions within the novel as a surrogate romance reader. A principal in the Mary Barton love plot, as well as a reliable and obedient worker who betters his condition through skill and steady application, Jem cannot even attend to John Barton's political ideas. This inability is clearly illustrated when he visits the Bartons one day in the hopes of seeing Mary, to whom he has not yet declared his love. John Barton, indifferent to romantic motivations generally, sits him down and launches into a lengthy speech on union activity and economic inequities. Jem is quite literally unable to listen, so distracted is he by thoughts of Mary. Interestingly, although the scene is described from Jem's perspective and thus encourages the reader to align herself with the romance interest, the narrator, in what seems a lengthy digression, takes up the issues addressed by Barton. This digression participates in a repeated double impulse to both moderate and vindicate Barton's harshness by explaining the causes for his anger. Yet it also highlights the tension between romance and politics, and produces an effect of admonishment on the reader, who could not help, given the earlier narrative point of view, but share in Jem's distraction (chapter 8).

Thus it is not simply interest in Mary that allows Esther to captivate Jem: he is more generally susceptible to romance. Indeed, the meeting between the two is framed as a literary encounter when Jem is compared to the Ancient Mariner's captive auditor in Coleridge's poem: "The spell of her name [Mary's] was as potent as that of the mariner's glittering eye. 'He listened like a three-year child' " (208). Importantly, this allusion indirectly figures Esther as the Mariner, a comparison borne out not only by other elements of the scene but also elsewhere in the novel.[14] Some critics try to read Esther's in-

14. Similarly, Adela Pinch discusses the complex relation between sympathetic

terventions as instances of female agency and authority, yet Gaskell repeatedly scripts Esther's actions as compulsion.[15] She is "soul-compelled" to speak; the need to save Mary haunts her with "monomaniacal incessancy"; her pursuit of information about the murder continues only because she is "suddenly driven before the gusty impulses of her mind" (207, 291). And in this scene with Jem, after invoking Mary's name, Esther obsessively shifts to her own story: "You must hear it and I must tell it" (209). Like Coleridge's Mariner, then, Esther is a narratively straitjacketed character: the allusion renders explicit her peculiar status as a person become a story. Moreover, her seduction, unlike the one that threatens the young Mary, has a distinctly literary flavor: she was led astray by that standard of seduction, the army officer, and not by a manufacturer's son like Henry Carson.[16]

This is not to say that Esther's own story does not include specifically material aspects of her past choices and present condition, for Gaskell adopts contemporary reformist attitudes in stressing that poverty and maternal instinct impelled Esther into the streets after she was abandoned by her seducer. In fact, it is precisely Esther's dual status as social victim and story, and the form of response it elicits from Jem, that I wish to enlarge on here. When Esther finishes her story, Jem urges her to come with him, but Esther rejects his offers of help, insisting on the impossibility of her ever escaping her own position or overcoming her need for the obliterating effects of drink. When she finishes, Jem responds in what for Gaskell is an exemplary fashion: he evinces sympathy.

> Jem was silent from deep sympathy. Oh, could he, then, do nothing for her! She spoke again, but in a less excited tone, although it was thrillingly earnest.
> "You are grieved for me. I know it better than if you told me in words. But you can do nothing for me. I am past hope. You can yet save Mary. You must." (213)

---

response and structures of reading in Wordsworth's early poetry, the way in which a sympathetic response to another person also frequently figures a relation to representation or literary influence. The tension takes a different form in Gaskell, perhaps because of the primacy of the reformist impulse, yet it is interesting to note that Wordsworth's *Lyrical Ballads* did influence Gaskell's depictions of the poor. See Adela Pinch, "Female Chatter."

15. Stoneman, *Elizabeth Gaskell* 79; Suzann Bick, " 'Take Her Up Tenderly' " 20.
16. Bodenheimer, "Private Grief and Public Acts" 208.

To stress the literary nature of Esther's character alongside the depth of Jem's sympathy for the hopelessness of her social position raises the same question I posed earlier about the relation between reading and direct human contact in *Mary Barton*. Jem here performs the act that Gaskell's novel repeatedly calls upon the rich to perform: he communicates his sympathy for Esther's plight. Yet the intensity and wordless perfection of Jem's response derives from the hopelessness of Esther's case, the fact that it, like a tragic tale of suffering, is already written: "Oh, could he, then, do nothing for her!" Only after Esther is gone does he regret his capitulation to her own view of the case:

> Before he reached the end of the street, even in the midst of the jealous anguish that filled his heart, his conscience smote him. He had not done enough to save her. One more effort, and she might have come. Nay, twenty efforts would have been well rewarded by her yielding. He turned back, but she was gone. In the tumult of his other feelings, his self-reproach was deadened for the time. But many and many a day afterwards he bitterly regretted his omission of duty; his weariness of well-doing. (214)

Novels that exploit melodrama often present such "if only" moments, but here belatedness sheds light on the precise nature of Jem's "deep sympathy." Gaskell would doubtless contend that Jem is learning the necessity of exerting a greater effort in the future, but I suggest we read the gap between sympathetic display and tangible acts of "well-doing" as a reflection of the readerly nature of Jem's sympathy.

For in this scene of reading Esther emblematizes Gaskell's own narrative, revealing a dilemma central to her reformist aesthetic. On the one hand, Gaskell aims to represent within the novel the kinds of sympathetic encounters and acts of mutual cooperation that she believes can heal a class-divided social world. On the other, she uses her own narrative to evoke her readers' sympathy directly and to prompt her readers to do what they can to ease the sufferings of those whom the fictional characters represent.[17] Appearing to be a

17. The intended audience of the novel is predominantly middle class, judging from the preface, the various apologetic asides about the excesses of her hero, and the didactic perspective generally. Yet it is clear that Gaskell herself intended the novel for the lower classes as well, as an instance of the very sympathetic display

fictional figure even to the characters in the novel, Esther thus functions to allegorize literary reformism. Other characters are moved by her tale of suffering, her manifest misery, but they cannot save her. Fatally written, she prompts not sympathy but an act of mourning, reflecting the manner in which Gaskell's aesthetic seems to insist on a tragic inscription of the ostensible object of sympathetic activism.[18] Indeed, the ultimate sympathetic "embrace" in the novel is not between two people but between Mr. Carson and Barton's corpse. The representation of Esther as well as the yoking of Barton with Esther at the end of the novel—their shared grave—suggests that for Gaskell textual inscription and death are becoming figures for each other; it is for good reason, then, that many have wondered at the proliferation of corpses in the novel.[19]

Much has been made of the "actual basis" for Gaskell's representations of urban working-class life—her own practice of the daily personal contact that the novels valorize.[20] Yet R. K. Webb has argued that Gaskell relied heavily on reading in her depictions of the poor; and Monica Fryckstedt has shown that the famous description of the Davenport cellar borrows heavily from reports by the domestic missionary John Layhe.[21] I invoke these counterclaims not as a means of insisting too literally on a figurative basis for Gaskell's texts, but because of their pertinence to a discussion of Gaskell's own anxiety about fictionalizing the poor. This same anxiety moti-

---

the book encourages. The novel was originally published in a journal (*Howitt's Journal*) aimed at a working-class public. Moreover, certain middle-class manufacturers distributed the novel among their men as a good-will gesture. See Winfred Gerin, *Elizabeth Gaskell: A Biography* 77, 92.

18. This is a version of a dilemma that Catherine Gallagher ascribes to industrial novelists generally: the need to insist on social determinants and the need to preserve the distinct autonomy and identities of their subjects. See Gallagher, *Industrial Reformation* 33–35, as well as my discussion of this issue in Chapter 1.

19. Others have attributed the corpses to the fact that, while writing *Mary Barton*, Gaskell was in deep mourning over the death of her baby. Gaskell herself wrote to Mrs. Greg, "It is no wonder then that the whole book seems to be written in the minor key; indeed, the very design seems to me to require this treatment. I acknowledge the fault of there being too heavy a shadow over the book; but I doubt if the story could have been deeply realized without these shadows." Gaskell, *Letters* 75. Bodenheimer emphasizes this biographical fact in her reading of the novel, which sees grief as the category linking the two plots. Bodenheimer, "Private Grief and Public Acts."

20. Easson, *Elizabeth Gaskell* 37; Arthur Pollard, *Mrs. Gaskell: Novelist and Biographer* 47.

21. Webb, "The Gaskells as Unitarians" 158–59; Monica Correa Fryckstedt, *Elizabeth Gaskell's "Mary Barton" and "Ruth."*

vates the following letter to Charles Bosanquet, in which Gaskell argues against the recent practice of journal-keeping among the charitable "Bible-women":

A *very* good man in Manchester was a few years ago brought into much notice for his philanthropy, and many people were only too glad to learn something of the peculiar methods by which he certainly *had* reclaimed the erring. So he was asked about his "experiences," and told many *true* interesting histories. Lately I have observed that it was difficult to "bring him to book" as it were about his cases. He would tell one of a story that made one's heart bleed,—tell it dramatically too, whh [*sic*] faculty is always a temptation when, unwilling to let emotion die without passing into action one asked for the address &c,—it always became vague,—in different ways. For some time I have suspected that he told *old* true stories, as if they were happening *now*, or had happened *yesterday*. And just lately I have found that this temptation to excite his hearers strongly, has led to *pure invention*. So do you wonder that I am afraid lest "godly simplicity" may be injured by journal-keeping, & extracts from journals being printed. So ends my lecture.[22]

Gaskell's fear that an aestheticized relation to reform will replace actual rescue or eclipse the living sufferers emerges in *Mary Barton* in the depiction of Margaret Jennings's singing. The most angelic and finely attuned of sympathizers, Margaret Jennings displays a highly aestheticized form of sympathy through her singing, one that causes her to become abstracted and prefigures her blindness: "Margaret, with fixed eye, and earnest, dreamy look, seemed to become more and more absorbed in realizing to herself the woe she had been describing, and which she felt might at that very moment be suffering and hopeless within a short distance of their comparative comfort" (73). Margaret, whose "hidden power" is precisely not perceivable in the "outward appearance," becomes the unreadable reader of those less fortunate than she (74). Despite her supposition of actual suffering within "a short distance," the experience of "realizing" to herself the ballad's representation of suffering entails a movement in upon the self. A grammatical problem in Gaskell's sentence tellingly reflects the eclipsing of the actual sufferers: no

22. Gaskell, *Letters* 587.

subject attaches to the phrase "might . . . be suffering and hopeless" ("woe" can serve as the subject of "hopeless" but not of "suffering").

The passage registers a fear that the sympathy that is supposed to knit the community together and redress the resentment of perceived indifference might become an entirely inward experience, a precisely *indifferent* power that has no effect on "outward appearances." It is not that Margaret does not ever aim actively to help other people; yet the reader can't help but perceive a disjunction between the novel's scenes of myopic aestheticism and Gaskell's powerful descriptions of the material horrors suffered by the poor. Both Margaret and Alice Wilson, two of the most sympathetic and naturally good characters in the novel, gradually lose their senses: a blurred perception accompanies their spiritualized sympathy.

Still, the moments of retreat inward, which correspond to the structure of a solitary act of reading, do not entirely blot out the effect of the Davenport cellar scene and other passages that reveal the appalling material conditions of the poor.[23] Interestingly, Esther's reappearance at the end of the novel, her collapse outside Mary's window, insists upon her materiality: "Fallen into what appeared simply a heap of white or light-coloured clothes, fainting or dead, lay the poor crushed Butterfly—the once innocent Esther" (464). After an initial gesture toward apotheosis (in the white light of the clothes), this passage poignantly insists on the vulnerable condition of the still-living Esther, a crushed butterfly within a heap of clothes. If in the novel sympathy becomes an inward activity dulled to the material horrors that ostensibly prompt it, or distanced through a readerly perception of the object of concern, here the text insists on a material residue, even as it enforces Esther's final punishment.

Esther's encounter with Jem brings us up against the limits of sympathizing with a literary representation; Esther's encounter with Mary, by contrast, reveals the more specific problem of the female reader. Esther originally chooses to speak to Jem because she fears her "leper-sin" will contaminate a woman auditor: she does not want to "communicate" her story to her niece. Dickens feared that the

23. Critics generally praise Gaskell for her detailed description of the material lives of the poor. See Williams, *Culture and Society* 87 (who nonetheless acknowledges "a slightly distancing effect"); Craik, *Elizabeth Gaskell* 38–44. For a related discussion of the gap in *Mary Barton* between what Gaskell reveals and what she recommends, see John Lucas, *The Literature of Change* 34–56.

women at Urania Cottage would communicate their histories to one another; Gaskell fears, somewhat analogously, that once female subjects "read" cultural texts like Esther, they become imprinted, ideologically reproduced. So it is no accident that when Esther actually does contact Mary, she assumes the disguise of virtuous wife and falsifies her history.

Esther comes to Mary to deliver a piece of gun wadding that she discovered at the scene of the crime and fears will incriminate Jem Wilson. This small wad of paper has a complicated history. Originally a valentine sent from Jem to Mary, it carries on the reverse a poem by the weaver Samuel Bamford about the oppressive life of the poor. Mary had inscribed the poem for her father; he in turn has apparently used a piece of this double text to serve as gun wadding when he goes to murder Harry Carson. Since the trade union men condemned Carson in large part because of a "false" text he generated (a caricature of the earnestly petitioning workmen, accompanied by Falstaff's speech about his men in *Henry IV, Part I* [IV, ii]: "good enough to toss, food for powder"), Barton's shot fires not only a bullet but a counter-representation, a sympathetic social ballad by one of his own.[24] And it is fitting as well that Esther should find and carry this valentine/social ballad since, like the double text itself, her character conjoins romance and social realism. Indeed, the first two stanzas of Bamford's five-stanza poem are themselves uncannily applicable to Esther: the first treats an "outcast lamb," the second a desperate mother (154–56).

Disguised and hence unreadable, Esther does not contaminate Mary. Indeed, Esther unintentionally cures Mary of melodramatic misperception in delivering the evidence that incriminates not Jem but Mary's father. Yet in preventing a direct recognition in the encounter, Gaskell only intensifies the threat of mimetic contamination hovering around the two women, and the scene itself reintroduces the threat subtextually. Upon Esther's arrival, Mary faints in her arms, mistaking her for the spirit of her long-dead mother. This incident forces Esther to cross a boundary that she would otherwise police:

> She [Esther] had felt as if some holy spell would prevent her (even as the unholy Lady Geraldine was prevented, in the abode of Chris-

24. And surely it is no accident that the workers use the shredded caricature to make the straws that will determine Carson's killer.

tabel) from crossing the threshold of that home of her early innocence; and she had meant to wait for an invitation. But Mary's
helpless action did away with all reluctant feeling, and she bore or
dragged her to a seat, and looked on her bewildered eyes, as,
puzzled with the likeness, which was not identity, she gazed on
her aunt's features. (293)

Mary's bewildered response to Esther partly reflects the vexed epistemological status Esther occupies in the novel. The allusion to Coleridge is also significant, for "Christabel" is a poem centrally
concerned with interchanges of identity between women. Toward
the end of Coleridge's poem, Christabel is stricken with passive
imitation and loss of voice; she is also described as replicating directly—"with forced unconscious sympathy"—the look in Geraldine's eyes. That Esther is first likened to Geraldine yet then
performs Christabel's action in carrying Mary over the threshold
confirms that the poem's concern with feminine doubling is crucially
at issue here. Gaskell's passage likewise produces the effect of a
replicated look: Esther "looked on her bewildered eyes, as, puzzled
with the likeness, which was not identity, she gazed on her aunt's
features." At the moment when Mary gazes back upon Esther, the
passage presents us with an ambiguous pronoun: not until the end
of the phrase "she gazed on her aunt's features" do we realize "she"
necessarily refers to Mary and not to Esther.

Through this second allusion to Coleridge Esther acts yet again
as a figure for romance.[25] There is a distinct difference, however,
between the previous scene with Jem and this scene of potential
reading. Subtextually evoked here is not the reader's consoling distance from the inscribed object of sympathy but rather a subject's
"forced unconscious" relation to the cultural texts that have the
power to reproduce her as a subject. We might be tempted to privilege this evocation of the relation between subjects and cultural
conventions, but formulated through a rhetoric of fallenness it poses
problems. First, such a characterization figures a too mechanical and
consciousness-obliterating version of ideological power; and second,
to use the category of feminine fallenness to explore the force of
cultural forms is to reinforce the idea that women are somehow
more susceptible than men to ideological reproduction. This victi-

25. For a reading of Coleridge's poem based on the premise that Geraldine is a
figure for romance, see Karen Swann, " 'Christabel.' "

mological assumption can appear even in the midst of a powerful critique of the cultural determinants of gender, as we saw in the discussion of Mill's *The Subjection of Women*.

In this novel, questions of agency and victimization emerge not only in gender but in class terms. As recent readings have pointed out, the novel cannot decide whether John Barton should be considered responsible for his actions.[26] A socially concerned novelist, Gaskell wishes to reveal the conditions suffered by the urban poor and to attribute their threatening or vicious behavior to circumstances beyond their control. Yet she also wants to present her "hero" as a "visionary" who possesses a "soul" (220). In Barton's case, the issue of determination and agency does not extend into the realm of aesthetic conventions, as it does with Esther. Gaskell does, however, yoke and bury the "two wanderers" together at the end of the novel (465). This twin burial constitutes the final moment of a larger process, for Gaskell disempowers John Barton partly by bringing him closer and closer descriptively to the prostitute. His "latent, stern enthusiasm" does not so much evolve into a "visionary" class consciousness as devolve into "monomania" (41, 218), a term Gaskell uses only in relation to Barton and Esther. Esther and John also share addiction, the one to drink, the other to opium. More tellingly, Esther and John both are described as oddly collapsed and deflated figures: between the murder and the deathbed burst of conciliatory fervor, John Barton is described as a "crushed form," a "phantom likeness" of himself (414).

Gaskell's ambivalence toward her victim-hero remains unresolved at the novel's close, which allows Barton a morally elevating reconciliation but kills him off in the midst of it, leaving Carson as a privileged survivor. Interestingly, the reconciliation between Barton and Carson is propped on Gaskell's most fortified version of transformative reading: Bible reading. It is no wonder that Gaskell opposed journal-keeping on the part of the "Bible-women"; for her, the act of gospel reading should redeem the dilemmas of philanthropic fiction. Indeed, the scenes of reading involving Esther represent distorted inversions of the exemplary form of reading displayed when the elder Carson turns to the Bible, thereby initiating his conversion to sympathetic activism. This act of reading does not eclipse the object of sympathy; rather, it points toward the act of

26. Easson, *Elizabeth Gaskell* 76; Gallagher, *Industrial Reformation* 74.

reconciliation. Likewise, Carson's accumulated life experiences allow him to animate the text: no passive reader, he experiences an unforced, conscious relation to what he reads:

> Years ago, the Gospel had been his task book in learning to read. So many years ago, that he had become familiar with the events before he could comprehend the Spirit that made them life. He fell to the narrative now, afresh, with all the interest of a little child. . . .
> He shut the book and thought deeply.
> All night long, the Arch-angel combated with the Demon. (440)

In dialectical fashion, Carson works through the text, and the text works through Carson: the reading subject humanizes the text, the text humanizes the reading subject. Of course, the encounter that follows this idealized act of reading—embracing a corpse—is, as I suggested earlier, quite a different matter. The possibility of a mutual embrace is derailed as Barton falls dead into Carson's arms.

In this reading of *Mary Barton*, I have tried to suggest how the figure of the prostitute provides a key to the intersection of Gaskell's social and aesthetic concerns as an industrial novelist. As we have seen, Esther figures the social force of generic conventions as well as the tension between reading and intersubjective encounters. A character constituted by social scripts, Esther enables a critique of ideology that complements, extends, and complicates the more strictly economic and class-based account of social relations forwarded by John Barton. Yet this critique is itself problematic insofar as it articulates itself through a rhetoric of fallenness and is gender-marked. An adequate feminist reading of Gaskell must acknowledge this aspect of her work as well as the strangely attenuated forms of consciousness that characterize the domestic heroines. For Mary's saving action, however exemplary, ultimately secures the domestic sanctuary as a myopic realm of intuitive sympathy, broken sentences, and small acts of loving kindness.[27] As we will see in *Ruth*, Gaskell's investment in attenuated consciousness is intimately linked to her critique of certain forms of thinking and interaction associated with industrialism.

---

27. Bodenheimer, "Private Grief and Public Acts" 204; Gallagher, *Industrial Reformation* 67, 83.

Dangerous Doctrines

A domestic harmony secured by sympathetic communing emerges in *Ruth* as the ideal realm of recovery and redemption. An orphaned dressmaker's apprentice, Ruth falls prey to the rich Bellingham, who seduces her by playing upon her innocence, social vulnerability, and romantic susceptibilities. Ruth is in fact so innocent that only some time after the seduction does she become aware of her morally and socially compromised position, and then only through the reactions of others. Partly Gaskell wishes to emphasize that fallenness is socially constituted, yet she does not relinquish the concept of a higher moral law that judges Ruth's action as sinful. Accordingly, Ruth's sudden awakening into guilt leaves her desperate and on the verge of self-destruction. But she is fortuitously rescued by a crippled Dissenting minister, Benson, who ends up taking her into his home. Discovering that Ruth is pregnant, he and his sister Faith decide to represent Ruth as a widow in order to allow her to work out her redemption apart from the added burden of social ostracism. Ruth becomes an integral part of the community and wins the hearts even of the powerful and morally exacting Bradshaw family, who hire her as a companion for their recalcitrant daughter, Jemima. Eventually, however, her status is revealed, and Ruth, all of whose earthly desires have now transmuted into maternal and spiritual devotion, is subject to powerful excoriation from her employer. Bellingham also returns to tempt her yet again, but Ruth prevails and ends her saintly days by serving as a nurse during a cholera epidemic. She even nurses Bellingham before herself contracting the disease and paying the final wages of sin.

The salutary effect of the Benson household on the recently fallen Ruth derives from the unconscious, perfectly modulated goodness of its members: "It seemed that their lives were pure and good, not merely from a lovely and beautiful nature, but from some law, the obedience to which was, of itself, harmonious peace, and which governed them almost implicitly."[28] The gentle Dissenting minister exemplifies an instinctive morality, one that does not calculate consequences but instead intuitively performs the good: "It is better not to expect or calculate consequences. The longer I live the more fully

---

28. Elizabeth Gaskell, *Ruth* 142. All further references to this edition are made parenthetically in the text.

I see that" (128). But if what allows Ruth to redeem her sin is learning "to live faithfully and earnestly in the present," this immersion in the present, along with the sympathetic excessiveness that prompts her "to make any sacrifices for those who loved her" (248), is precisely what causes her to fall in the first place: going away with Bellingham she was "strangely forgetful of past and future" (131). In the case of Ruth's fall, then, it becomes difficult to distinguish the cure from the cause. And this conflation is exactly what enables Gaskell to insist on Ruth's enduring purity: the cause of Ruth's fall, unthinking sympathy, is also an index of her goodness.[29]

In stressing sympathy as a cause, Gaskell joins with reformist writers who aimed to vindicate fallen women by stressing that blank virtue, not depravity, often led to the fall. As one such reformer, W. R. Greg, wrote,

> Many—far more than would generally be believed—fall from pure unknowingness. Their affections are engaged, their confidence secured; thinking no evil themselves, they permit caresses which in themselves, and to them, indicate no wrong, and are led on ignorantly and thoughtlessly from one familiarity to another, not conscious where those familiarities must inevitably end, till ultimate resistance becomes almost impossible.

In terms that Gaskell's book echoes, Greg also invokes women's "sublime unselfishness," their "positive love of self-sacrifice," as a defining and dangerous virtue.[30] Gaskell follows Greg not only through a similar emphasis on the innate virtue of the fallen woman, but also through her reproduction of his trenchant critique of the power of social discourses to enforce downward-path trajectories.[31] As we shall see, in *Ruth* Gaskell acknowledges but also shelters her heroine from the forces of social inscription that constituted *Mary Barton*'s Esther. Moreover, Gaskell extends her conception of fallenness from the aesthetic realm of melodrama into the social and philosophical regions of utilitarianism and determinism.

29. For nuanced discussion of dilemmas of consciousness in depictions of feminine virtue, see Ruth Bernard Yeazell, *Fictions of Modesty* 51–64.

30. [W. R. Greg], "Prostitution" 459.

31. Aina Rubenius advances the hypothesis that Gaskell based *Ruth* specifically on Greg's article, so strikingly similar are the strategies of vindication. See Rubenius, *The Woman Question in Mrs. Gaskell's Life and Works* 207–10. For a discussion of Greg, see my Chapter 1.

From the moment of the novel's publication, critics have dismissed its presentation of an unconscious, plantlike heroine as the result of Gaskell's misconceived idea of how to contest unforgiving approaches to fallenness.[32] Certainly her "sympathetic" portrayal denies the fallen woman's agency as much as one that harshly locks transgressors into downward paths. What crucially distinguishes Gaskell from Greg, however, is that for Gaskell, unthinking sympathy is not simply a feminine virtue but rather a larger ideal asserted against flawed human relations and dominant modes of thinking. We can better interpret Ruth's attenuated consciousness, that is, if we recognize that Gaskell is using a story of fallenness to criticize utilitarian calculation and determinism. Furthermore, this approach may shed light on what much Gaskell criticism refers to as her "fear" of conclusions, generalizations, or abstractions.[33] Gaskell mainly elaborates her critique by casting Ruth as a victim of Bellingham's own calculations and as a potential victim of Bradshaw's dangerously determinist laws. Yet through the story of the Dissenting minister who lies to protect Ruth from societal prejudice, the novel also goes so far as to suggest that deliberation itself is locked within the iron cage of instrumentality. This, then, is why the novel stresses Ruth's unconsciousness and then routes her redemptive entry into judgment through maternity, which, for Gaskell, constitutes a form of heightened consciousness sympathetic at its origin, noninstrumental because self-negating.[34]

It should not surprise us that Gaskell's concern with deterministic thinking and means-end logic emerges both thematically and subtextually in the story of a woman's fall. As I elaborated in Chapter 1, the rhetoric of fallenness that Greg both extended and revised notoriously insists on discernible etiologies and predictable conse-

32. From the time of the first reviews, criticism has been leveled at Ruth's excessive innocence before the fall, especially if viewed in conjunction with her extreme guilt afterward. See G. H. Lewes, "*Ruth* and *Villette*." Ganz, *Elizabeth Gaskell* 105–31, traces the criticism surrounding this issue; also see Easson, *Elizabeth Gaskell* 118.

33. See Bodenheimer, "Private Grief and Public Acts" 200; Gerin, *Elizabeth Gaskell* 128.

34. It is not surprising in this regard to find that Stoneman, a feminist critic, employs Carol Gilligan's model of gender-differentiated moral development to read *Ruth*, locating in the novel an opposition between a "maternal, caring principle" and the "paternal rule of law." Her focus on an opposition between the somewhat psychologized categories of care and authority, however, does not adequately historicize the novel's concern with deterministic thinking and the instrumentality of reason. Stoneman, *Elizabeth Gaskell* 99–117.

quences. Although this rhetoric attended sociological accounts of crime and other social problems, the feminine fall, in dramatic ways distinct from other mid-Victorian social topoi, became a favored focus of early sociology's attempt to trace scientifically the determinants of character and the results of action. Gaskell's novel is remarkable insofar as it uses a narrative of the fall to criticize not only the models of causation that were being applied to character but also the forms of calculative reason that were associated with them. In a manner less self-reflective but as deeply felt as Mill's, she sees any conception of the human being as a mere "reasoning machine" as profoundly threatening ethical and social relations.

The Victorian rhetoric of fallenness, in focusing on scientific approaches to character, often secularizes an originally religious category, but Gaskell's critique of determinism is sounded in both the social and the religious registers. Indeed, the novel strikes readers as confused partly because it unself-consciously shifts back and forth between social and religious discourses on fallenness. Gaskell presents Ruth's fall as conditioned by her social position (an orphaned dressmaker's apprentice) and the circumstances that befall her (particularly, her meeting the manipulative Bellingham). But in having Benson's lie protect Ruth from the social stigma of her fallenness, Gaskell aims also to discredit the species of social determinism that insists on her inevitable downward-path trajectory. Like melodramatic conventions in *Mary Barton*, the destructive forms of thinking that threaten to saturate the social world are both false and dangerous: they produce effects, they determine lives. When the legislators of the social realm mechanically insist that inescapable consequences follow any error or lapse, they render redemption nearly impossible. From the social perspective, then, the novel seeks to demonstrate that sexual lapses don't destroy fallen women, discourse does.

Gaskell also faults the rhetoric of fallenness on theological grounds, insofar as its teleological certainty aims to infringe on or appropriate a providential prerogative. Gaskell allows that one can acknowledge the ways in which Providence has worked the redemption of its wanderers, but only after the fact: one shouldn't presume to be predictive, even armed with a vast number of confirming examples. This does not mean, however, that Gaskell believes Ruth needn't suffer for her sin, as several passages in the novel make abundantly clear.[35] As a Unitarian, Gaskell believed in individual redemption and moral evolution achieved precisely through suffering. Yet Gaskell assiduously avoids a mechanistic rhetoric, insisting instead on a slow, unreadable process. Thus at one point we are told of a great "external change" in Ruth, but it quickly appears that the manifest quality of this external change only renders more undecidable the issue of inner change: "Of the change which had gone on in her heart, and mind, and soul, or if there had been any, neither she nor any one around her was conscious" (208). In order to uphold the idea of a nonmechanistic reformatory suffering, not to mention a noninstrumental sympathy, Gaskell suggests a profound and cumulative, yet always elusively imperceptible, spiritual change.[36]

It is in fact tempting to see the novel's ending as an ironic extension of Gaskell's religious critique. Ruth abruptly declines and dies after years of redemptive harmony and peace, after surviving even the exposure of her past, because it is only through a delayed effect that the ascendancy of Providence over secular or social law can be demonstrated: "God alone knows when the effect is to be produced" (128). Ultimately, however, the ending of the novel must be seen as Gaskell's failure to work through her competing accounts.[37] Indeed, just prior to the novel's end, she attempts to tidy things up by suggesting that Providence uses misconceived social harshness precisely as an instrument to work the redemption of the sinner. After Ruth's exposure, Benson asks, "Can you accept all this treatment meekly, as but the reasonable and just penance God has laid upon you?" (357). Here man's wrongful appropriation of the providential prerogative devolves into a providential tool.

Mr. Bradshaw, the "keen, far-seeing man of business," embodies the misguided application of means-end logic and providential certainty to the study of human nature:

35. See especially 286, 313.

36. For an especially useful account of Gaskell's Unitarianism and its association with the anti-deterministic, somewhat mystical "second-phase" variant espoused by James Martineau and William Ellery Channing, see Easson, *Elizabeth Gaskell*. For an excellent general account of Unitarianism, see Geoffrey Rowell, *Hell and the Victorians*. Also see Gallagher, *Industrial Reformation* 62–65.

37. Stoneman also argues that the ending signals an "ideological impasse," but she attributes that impasse to the novel's contradictory attitudes toward sexuality. See Stoneman, *Elizabeth Gaskell* 116–17.

Stained by no vice himself, either in his own eyes or in that of any human being who cared to judge him, having nicely and wisely proportioned his means to his ends, he could afford to speak and act with a severity which was almost sanctimonious in its ostentation of thankfulness as to himself. Not a misfortune or a sin was brought to light but Mr. Bradshaw could trace it to its cause in some former mode of action, which he had long ago foretold would lead to shame. (210–11)

Allowing a utilitarian approach to distort his view of character, Mr. Bradshaw stands as Ruth's harshest accuser when her hidden past comes to light. Inhabiting fully the corrupt instrumental egotism of the public realm, Bradshaw refuses to honor the sanctuary of the domestic, converting his home into a political headquarters during an election campaign. At one point he even attempts to use Ruth's sympathetic mode as a tool to influence the behavior of his daughter, Jemima. Eventually brought low when his favored son falls, Bradshaw, with his insidious "practical wisdom," serves to accentuate the negative effects of mutually reinforcing social and religious determinisms (351).

Ruth, by contrast, is vindicated and redeemed through her instinctive participation in a noninstrumental, sympathetic mode of being. A noncalculating morality of sympathy forms the basis of the initial rescue scene, in which Benson manages—partly through intuition and partly, appropriately enough, through accident—to appeal to Ruth's sympathy and so divert her suicidal impulse. Ruth's instinctive response to Benson's cry for help (he falls while in pursuit of her) is described as a "consciousness" that "did not become a thought" (98). Ruth exemplifies, then, precisely what Benson more explicitly advocates. And like the therapeutic household in which Benson will shelter her, Ruth's own pastoral childhood home embodies the noninstrumental. Hers was a "house of afterthoughts," the result not of architectural planning but successive whims: "a picturesque mass of irregularity" that nonetheless "gave a full and complete idea of a 'Home' " (45). This undetermined and complete "Home" is very far indeed from Dickens's Alice Marwood and her invocation of "bad homes and mothers" as the double environment that produced her.

Readers of *Ruth* frequently criticize Gaskell's failure to represent the period of time during which the actual sexual fall occurred; they likewise find puzzling the apparent noneffect on Ruth of her entry into sexuality. In response, Rosemarie Bodenheimer rightfully argues that these omissions signal Gaskell's insistence on fallenness as a social construction.[38] I suggest, however, that the real fall in this novel *is* narrated: it occurs when the Bensons lie about Ruth's status, passing her off as a widow rather than an unwed mother. Though ostensibly the Bensons lie for the sake of the child and not Ruth, the effect is to protect the heroine and crucially alter her circumstances. Benson reveals this underlying concern when he justifies the lie to Bradshaw after the traumatic exposure. The child, Leonard, has dropped out of the picture: "I earnestly desired to place her in circumstances in which she might work out her self-redemption" (348).

A lapse as profound in its generation of "infinite consequences" as Ruth's seduction (58), the lie represents not so much an unequivocal "wrong" or "error" as a *calculation.* If it enables Ruth's redemption, it also causes Benson to lose his characteristic "instincts of conscience," his undeliberative morality. As Ruth grows strong, Benson becomes increasingly indecisive, developing "a feminine morbidness of conscience" (378):

> I have got what you call morbid just in consequence of the sophistry by which I persuaded myself that wrong could be right. I torment myself. I have lost my clear instincts of conscience. Formerly, if I believed that such or such an action was according to the will of God, I went and did it, or at least I tried to do it, without thinking of consequences. Now, I reason and weigh what will happen if I do so and so—I grope where I formerly saw. (362)

Benson's moral instincts had linked him to Ruth's enduring purity and the character of his own late mother: they were associated with a distinctly feminine purity. The fall into anxious deliberation, inaugurated by the lie, produces by contrast a feminine morbidity described in bodily terms: clear vision gives way to a more physical "groping." Indeed, the text suggests its own recasting of reasoning and weighing as a fall in the following interchange between Mr. Benson and his sister Faith, which takes place after they decide to extend their deception and allow Ruth to enter a neighbor's house as a governess:

38. Rosemarie Bodenheimer, *The Politics of Story in Victorian Social Fiction* 154.

"I have no fear," said he, decidedly. "Let the plan go on." After a minute, he added, "But I am glad it was so far arranged before I heard of it. My indecision about right and wrong—my perplexity as to how far we are to calculate consequences—grows upon me, I fear."

"You look tired and weary, dear. You should blame your body rather than your conscience at these times."

"A very dangerous doctrine." (200)

If Gaskell criticizes the rhetoric of fallenness as applied to women who experience sexual lapses, she nonetheless elaborates her own version of the fall into deliberation—marking it through distinct bodily figurations.[39] A powerful strand of contemporary feminist theory holds that heightened intellection denies or represses the material body or female sexuality. Gaskell's critique of deterministic aspects of Victorian sexual morality, through a remarkable series of associations and inversions, ends up casting reasoning itself as corrupted by the body. Indeed, Gaskell's exacting idea of moral purity—the ideal "instincts of conscience" and the "consciousness" that "[does] not become a thought"—reveals an anxiety that all deliberation is tainted. That Benson refers to a stark lie, as opposed to mere deliberation or calculation, does not really deflect but rather heightens this anxiety. For "calculating consequences" is what prompted and characterized the "original" lie; hence what is called lying threatens to engulf all modes of intentionality, any thought or action that focuses on the effect to be produced. And indeed, this absolute fear of calculation derives, I suggest, from Gaskell's associations of simple deliberation with precisely those faulty forms of teleological thinking that enforce both the social and religious discourses on fallenness.[40]

39. It is interesting in this regard that in her reading of *North and South*, Barbara Leah Harman argues that lying is an alternative name for illicit sexuality in the novel. See Harman, "In Promiscuous Company" 371.

40. John Kucich has offered a somewhat different interpretation of the way sexual difference informs the opposition between calculation and noncalculation in Gaskell's novels and within Victorian middle-class ideology generally. He argues that calculation is aligned with feminine deceit and noncalculation with masculine honesty; by contrast, feminine virtue is elaborated as a nontransgressive form of calculation (reserve) while masculine violence or aggression becomes an abnormal version of masculine noncalculation. Highly sensitive to the various permutations of the gendering of calculation produced in Gaskell's novels and in Victorian texts generally, Kucich's account accords only passing consideration to the category of sympathy, a predom-

Gaskell uses Mr. Benson's lie to criticize not only calculation but also the imagination, a category often valorized in industrial novels of the period, most notably those of Dickens. Lying contaminates fancy when Faith Benson dangerously indulges her "talent for fiction" by elaborating an unnecessarily thick account of Ruth's fictitious past. This "pains" the conscientious Benson, who impresses on his sister that all her embellishments are "so many additional lies" (150). Of course Gaskell's suspicion of imagination has a conservative as well as a progressive aspect. Her protofeminist awareness of the social effects of cultural conventions, reflected powerfully in *Mary Barton*, leads her to warn against indulgence in romantic fantasies on the part of young women. Ruth's fall derives in part from her wandering fancy: like Mary Barton, she "builds up vain castles in the air" and attempts to escape the concrete harshness of her existence by telling stories to herself (87). Beguiling the monotony of lonely Sundays spent sequestered in Mrs. Mason's unheated workroom, Ruth imagines histories for those who walk past the window. She likewise uses Bellingham's seductive stories of a "dazzling" childhood to "paint" a "scenery and background for the figure which was growing by slow degrees most prominent in her thoughts" (39).

All of this warns us that Ruth is constructing a Bellingham according to the conventions of romance: the novel records the disastrous effects, although Ruth does not fall *into* melodrama the way Esther does. Thus Gaskell demonstrates that for women imagination is not the unalloyed good other critics of industrialism hold it to be; the forms in which our imaginations play are themselves culturally produced.[41] Only as a "stage" within a boy's childhood is imagi-

---

inantly feminine virtue of paramount importance to Gaskell's social vision and agenda, and a virtue defined against calculation and instrumentality. That is, it seems erroneous to say that femininity in Gaskell is fundamentally aligned with calculation, when feminine virtue is so often cast as unthinking sympathy. Lying and calculation are certainly cast as feminine and sexualized transgressions. But they also are aligned with the masculine realm of instrumentality and utilitarianism, both of which Gaskell was concerned to "soften" through sympathy and mutual understanding. And Gaskell deifies a peculiarly myopic feminine sympathy—such as we saw with Alice Wilson and Margaret Jennings—in those novels most concerned with industrial harshness. John Kucich, "Transgression and Sexual Difference in Elizabeth Gaskell's Novels."

41. If anything falls outside the cultural in Gaskell, it is the natural beauty of the countryside (see Gerin, *Elizabeth Gaskell* 79). An examination of the protected pastoral forms the basis of Rosemarie Bodenheimer's reading of the novel. Perhaps women

nation harmless, as the episode of Leonard's storytelling makes clear (202). But if Gaskell demonstrates that the forms available to imagination are socially constructed and harmful to young women, she also participates in locating especial susceptibility in young women, who appear to lose all too easily the ability to distinguish the real from the imagined. It is Faith, after all, who is so naive as to see her storytelling as innocent, and it is her brother who must remind her of the ethical standards she transgresses.

Gaskell's conceptions of purity and fallenness, as well as their dual functioning in the sexual and cognitive realms, inevitably confront her with certain dilemmas. On the one hand, the unselfconscious sympathetic mode is perilous because it produces sexual susceptibility: Ruth's unthinking responsiveness allows her seduction.[42] On the other hand, as we have seen through the analysis of Benson, an overly reflective form of consciousness is itself a version of fallenness. Ruth's redemptive process must protect against a morbid concern with self, for such concern would produce a fall into the anxious, sexually stigmatized deliberation that afflicts Benson. In other words, a strict self-monitoring is not the goal of Gaskell's reformism: transformation and judgment must be intersubjectively grounded. Although Gaskell's model of reflective deliberation, with its links to utilitarianism and religious determinism, must be distinguished from the stark self-objectification that appears as one version of Dickensian fallenness, like Dickens Gaskell is careful to protect her "pure" heroine from a direct fall into self-scrutiny. In the "honeymoon" period after the seduction, Bellingham dresses Ruth's hair with water lilies and instructs her to look at her own reflection in the pond. Although Ruth "could not help seeing her own loveliness," she nonetheless "never thought of associating it with herself" (74).[43]

---

industrial novelists were more likely to evoke the pastoral than the imagination as refuge, as Bodenheimer suggests in *The Politics of Story* 150–65.

42. The novel further blurs the distinction between sexuality and sympathy through the character of Jemima, whose sympathy for Ruth is sexual in origin. Not only does Jemima's interest in Ruth begin as infatuation, her responses to Ruth are typically sexualized. When Jemima takes Ruth's part during the relentless confrontation scene with Mr. Bradshaw—to take the most extreme example—she is "flushed and panting" and she grasps Ruth's hand so tightly that it is "blue and discoloured for days" (338).

43. Brian Crick is the only critic to have remarked—though only to pass by—these crucial subtextual links in the novel: "A detailed psychological study of Ruth's internal

As an alternative to a susceptible sympathy and a deliberative self-scrutiny, the novel elaborates mothering as a redemptive process that ostensibly transcends the two faulty modes. Maternity dominates the story of Ruth's rescue precisely because it allows Ruth a measure of thoughtful consciousness untainted by morbid self-consciousness and sympathetic at its origin. As Benson says of the impending child, "Here is the very instrument to make her forget herself and be thoughtful for another" (119). Ruth's entry into judgment is thus crucially mediated through maternity: she reads *for* another. The night following the birth of her child, she suddenly is able to reread her seducer's character: "Slight speeches, telling of a selfish, worldly nature, unnoticed at the time, came back upon her, having a new significance" (163). This judgment comes to her only as she wonders whether she would ever wish to entrust her child to Bellingham, should anything happen to her. More important, the development of Ruth's intellectual powers is routed through the child. After Leonard's birth, Ruth assumes the task of educating herself, "to acquire the knowledge hereafter to be given to her child." We are told at this point that although "her mind was uncultivated" and "her reading scant," she "had a refined taste, and excellent sense and judgement to separate the true from the false" (177).

If this sounds like a rather sudden assertion of qualities that were distinctly absent in the pre-fallen Ruth, that's because it is. One can only surmise that maternity and judgment are, for Gaskell, mutually constitutive. Being a mother prompts Ruth to cultivate her mind; that prompting itself arises out of a refinement that motherhood seems to have given birth to, *ex nihilo*. Mr. Benson, who tutors Ruth, experiences an understandable amazement at what Gaskell describes as dormant powers, first tapped long ago at the knee of Ruth's own mother.

> Her tutor was surprised at the bounds by which she surmounted obstacles, the quick perception and ready adaptation of truths and first principles, and her immediate sense of the fitness of things . . . most of all, he admired the complete unconsciousness of uncom-

---

experience . . . is hampered by the author's evident distaste for introspection. Self-scrutiny tends to be equated with egocentricity throughout the novel, and Mrs. Gaskell attributes this habit of mind to Bradshaw's misguided utilitarian theory of human behavior." Crick, "Mrs. Gaskell's *Ruth*" 94.

mon power, or unusual progress. It was less of a wonder than he considered it to be, it is true, for she never thought of comparing what she was now with her former self, much less with another. Indeed, she did not think of herself at all, but of her boy, and what she must learn in order to teach him to be and to do as suited her hope and her prayer. (187)

Maternity allows a heightened consciousness and an ability to judge that simultaneously center and negate the self.

It is instructive to notice what occurs when Ruth does permit selfish pleasures to enter into her intellectual project. Not long after the passage cited above, Gaskell writes that Ruth soon claimed her new knowledge and power for herself:

She delighted in the exercise of her intellectual powers, and liked the idea of the infinite amount of which she was ignorant; for it was a grand pleasure to learn—to crave, and be satisfied. She strove to forget what had gone before this last twelve months. She shuddered up from contemplating it; it was like a bad, unholy dream. And yet, there was a strange yearning kind of love for the father of the child whom she pressed to her heart, which came, and she could not bid it begone as sinful, it was so pure and natural. (191)

This passage wants to convey that Ruth's entry into judgment allows her to sublimate her feeling for Bellingham, yet it also reveals the way Ruth's more egocentric relation to thinking produces desire. Once Ruth reads for herself instead of her child, she begins to appear fallen again.

In *Ruth*, Gaskell rewrites the conventionally redemptive process of mothering to accord with her own version of fallenness as self-absorbed deliberation. As an imaginary synthesis, however, it works more to reveal than to solve the novel's dilemmas. For in redeeming Ruth, Gaskell retreats to a version of intersubjectivity that eclipses not the subject read, as in *Mary Barton*, but the subject reading. The maternal monitor who thinks through sympathetic identification becomes, at bottom, a mere slave to the other: "It was beautiful to see the intuition by which she divined what was passing in every fold of her child's heart, so as to be always ready with the right words to soothe or strengthen him. Her watchfulness was unwearied, and with no thought of self tainting it" (366).

A frustrated ideal typically lurks behind the hyperbolic rhetoric of fallenness. Just as Dickens's depiction of the fall into self-reading harbors within it a dream of pure autonomy, so too do Gaskell's conceptions of the fall into deliberation or the fall through sympathy point toward an intersubjective ideal that transcends even the imaginary solution of maternity. Importantly, Gaskell's assiduous avoidance of any version of egocentric identity separates her from Dickens. As *Mary Barton* reveals, Gaskell insists on an activism grounded in local, sympathetic encounters between those occupying different, and to her mind unnecessarily antagonistic, social positions. Yet a number of problems confront her along the way. As Jem's encounter with Esther reveals, the dialogical ideal can collapse into an asymmetrical scene of reading that fatally inscribes the other precisely in order to promote "deep sympathy." And sympathetic female subjects run the risk of dangerous identification with sexualized women, as the encounter between Mary and Esther suggests, or of simply responding *into* sexuality, as in the case of Ruth's seduction. Moreover, the maternal alternative set forth in *Ruth* merely inverts the asymmetry of *Mary Barton*'s faulty reading scenario, for Ruth as sympathetic subject loses herself in reading for another.

Gaskell's failure to overcome the problem of eclipsed or attenuated consciousness—revealed through the asymmetrical scenes of reading and the dream of nondeliberative sympathy—is in many ways an honest failure, especially in light of her sympathetic dialogical ideal. The failed moments serve to remind us of the very real asymmetries of class and gender that structured her social world. No philanthropic visit could be truly reciprocal, nor could the category of sympathy remain free of its gendered associations. Yet Gaskell's refusal of the idea of moral autonomy and her insistent association of atomized self-consciousness with instrumentality keep before us an unrealized ideal of intersubjectively grounded thought and action.

There is in fact a remarkable passage at the end of *North and South*, one that articulates the idea of an always situated, endlessly adjusting, and profoundly dialogical approach to realizing the social and economic world:

"I have arrived at the conviction that no mere institutions, however wise, and however much thought may have been required to organize and arrange them, can attach class to class as they should be attached, unless the working out of such institutions bring the individuals of the different class into actual personal contact. Such intercourse is the very breath of life. A working man can hardly be made to feel and know how much his employer may have laboured in his study at plans for the benefit of his workpeople. A complete plan emerges like a piece of machinery, apparently fitted for every emergency. But the hands accept it as they do machinery, without understanding the intense mental labour and forethought required to bring it to perfection. But I would take an idea, the working out of which would necessitate personal intercourse; it might not go well at first, but at every hitch interest would be felt by an increasing number of men, and at last its success in working come to be desired by all, as all had borne a part in the formation of the plan; and even then I am sure that it would lose its vitality, cease to be living, as soon as it was no longer carried on by that sort of common interest which invariably makes people find means and ways of seeing each other's characters and persons, and even tricks of tempers and modes of speech. We should understand each other better, and I'll venture to say we should like each other more."

"And you think they may prevent the recurrence of strikes?"

"Not at all. My utmost expectation only goes so far as this—that they may render strikes not the bitter, venomous sources of hatred they have hitherto been."[44]

Spoken by the manufacturer Thornton to his wife-to-be, this speech of course emanates from an empowered subject-position and to that extent indicates Gaskell's guardedness. But it is remarkable in what it suggests: Gaskell theorizes a mean between the thoughtless continuous present of the domestic realm and the destructive instrumentality that contaminates human relations and modes of thinking. A nonteleological everydayness derived from the domestic mode here constitutes not retreat but a protection against an overly rationalized reform. Gaskell thereby articulates a model of communicative practice aimed not merely at mutual understanding but at social transformation, and mediated not only by rational discourse but by a sympathetic, continually renewed, nonreified recognition of the other.

44. Elizabeth Gaskell, *North and South* 525–26.

4

Dramatic Monologue in Crisis: Agency and Exchange in D. G. Rossetti's "Jenny"

The previous chapters have explored the extent to which encounters with the fallen woman, insofar as they focus on her "false" or dangerous status, preclude the possibility of dialogical reciprocity. My main literary object of study has been the realist novel and the predicaments of character and form that emerge within that genre. In this chapter, I examine the depiction of fallenness in relation to a rather different literary form, the dramatic monologue. The Victorian dramatic monologue, as we shall see, holds an important relation to the concerns of this study. As a genre that displays at once the situatedness of speech and the solipsism of the individual speaker, dramatic monologue often seeks to reveal the many distortions, imbalances, and manipulations, both conscious and unconscious, that attend any speech act. Dramatic monologue invites one to analyze intersubjective relations between the lines, so to speak, and here provides the opportunity to show with particular vividness the several ways projected anxieties about agency overpower encounters with fallen women.

Dante Gabriel Rossetti's monologue "Jenny" displays multiple versions of the Victorian rhetoric of fallenness. As an unspoken address to a potential auditor who herself appears to exist in varying states of semiconsciousness throughout the poem, "Jenny" has actually been described as "the first interior monologue in English literary tradition unrecognized as such."[1] I suggest, however, that

---

1. Daniel Harris, "D. G. Rossetti's 'Jenny' " 197. I am generally indebted to Harris's article, which challenges previous critical assumptions that the monologue

"Jenny" is not so much an interior monologue as the negation of dramatic monologue. The "speaker" repeatedly decides not to talk to the prostitute; and I argue that his failure to speak to her emerges precisely out of the extreme intersubjective distortions that characterize encounters with the fallen.[2] While actual speech is certainly no guarantee of mutual recognition, and while ordinary dramatic monologue itself explores imbalances of power, this poem heightens the failure of mutuality and reveals the anxiety over the prostitute's uncertain status by repeatedly negating the possibility of speech. Furthermore, insofar as this Victorian literary text focuses sustained attention on an actual prostitute figure (rather than consigning her to the margins, as do the works of Dickens and Gaskell), it accentuates the economic and sexual concerns that often take muted forms in other representations of fallenness. Dickens and Gaskell stress the extent to which prostitutes and fallen women figure the power of social environment and cultural forms over character; Rossetti's poem, by contrast, displays how the mutually imbricated forces of sexual desire and commodification also unsettle deliberative action, private identity, and sympathetic communication.

We saw in the reading of Mill that the Victorian investment in self-control focused not only on manipulating the circumstances that determine character but also on a more direct control over habits and temptations. As Mill states in *On Liberty*, "One whose desires and impulses are not his own, has no character, no more than a steam-engine has a character."[3] Autonomy and control are so fundamental to human integrity, in other words, that unrestrained "desires and impulses" effectively turn one into a machine. Vice is thus rearticulated to an amoral concept of determined or nonreflective identity and, in its undermining of deliberative action, is far more threatening than intentional evil. The fullest elaboration of the threats that desire and impulse pose to self-control is to be found in Victorian psychology, which generally constructs women as more susceptible to disruptions of desire and to the forms of madness and

---

is spoken and provides a subtle treatment of the approach to communication in the poem.

2. To be exact, *speaker* should always appear in quotation marks, since of course the protagonist is actually a nonspeaker; however, for the sake of readability, from this point it appears without marks.

3. John Stuart Mill, *On Liberty* 264. *On Liberty* was originally published in 1859.

fractured identity associated with those disruptions. Men, by contrast, are more capable of overcoming or vanquishing impulse, as evidenced succinctly in the title of an 1843 text by John Barlow: *Man's Power over Himself to Prevent or Control Insanity*.[4]

In a similar way, the idea of rational self-interest that informed Victorian political economy sought to uphold the notion that masculine agents exerted control over processes in the economic sphere, in part because there was a concomitant apprehension that such "agents" were also powerfully subject to external forces such as exchange, circulation, and commodification. In Chapter 1, we saw a similar tension animating the philosophies of social reform, which themselves shared close ties to political economy. In Rossetti's "Jenny," which treats the visit of a scholar to a prostitute, the forces of exchange and desire are perceived to fully infiltrate experience, threatening notions of stable and recognizable identity. The complex of anxieties surrounding this disturbing perception centers on the fallen figure of the prostitute and on counterposing, and continually thwarted, ideals of agency, identity, and recognition.

Furthermore, in Rossetti's poem the notion of contamination by means of exchange extends to the aesthetic register as well and can be traced through recurrent images of reading and of books. Unlike Gaskell, Rossetti does not isolate specific cultural forms such as melodrama and romance; nor does he focus, as does Dickens, on the power of narrative over character. Rather, Rossetti's poem reveals more general anxieties about communication itself and about the instabilities of any linguistic act, whether it takes place between persons or between a person and a text. As does the rhetoric of fallenness more generally, Rossetti's poem registers a profoundly modern conception of identity and social life, in this case through an arresting conception of the textual determinants of identity. And, once again like the rhetoric of fallenness more generally, the apprehension of determined identity masks a frustrated ideal: the poem harbors the possibility of an identity and a form of interaction that would somehow exist outside of language, which is itself seen as inextricably bound up in the forces of desire and exchange. The

---

4. John Barlow, *Man's Power over Himself to Prevent or Control Insanity*. For a discussion of the gendering of madness in Victorian England, see Elaine Showalter, *The Female Malady*.

prostitute, whose unsettling status traces precisely to the economic, sexual, and aesthetic determinants that haunt the speaker, provokes anxiety and suffers penalties because she constantly reminds the speaker of the illusoriness of his ideal.[5]

The question of whether Rossetti intends his poem as a critique of that which it so vividly displays through the speaker's meditations is a difficult one to answer—but this is always the interpretive dilemma posed by dramatic monologue, which characteristically generates moral ambiguities by eliciting both sympathy and judgment from the reader.[6] In many ways the poem must be seen to reproduce the rhetoric of fallenness, especially insofar as it attempts to convey this troubling speaker as sympathetic; still, through the techniques of revelation that characterize dramatic monologue, the poem at least partly disrupts the monologic vision of the speaker, indirectly insisting on Jenny's elusiveness and indeterminacy. Such moments thwart the speaker's attempt to objectify and stabilize his apperception of her, and indirectly suggest a more open-ended dialogical ideal.

Apostrophe and Agency

The speaker of this poem does not simply refuse to talk to Jenny; he has impulses to engage her that are checked by the apprehension that she is not a conscious, possibly not even an animate, being. Thus this poem does not simply foreclose the prostitute's agency, as do other constructions of fallenness; it anxiously and recurringly disavows it. In this sense, the "nonauditor" of this poem affects the "utterance" of the speaker as the auditor affects the speaker's utterance in ordinary dramatic monologue.[7] What "Jenny" distinctly foregrounds, in a manner more intense and sustained than the fic-

5. Harris similarly traces the "triangulation" of sexual, economic, and linguistic categories in the poem. However, my reading differs from Harris's in locating anxieties about agency in those categories. Harris concentrates more specifically on the issue of prostitution and on what he takes as Rossetti's indictment of "male" culture. In thinking about the way questions of agency function across different "registers" (the sexual, the economic, the aesthetic), I have found particularly useful and suggestive Mark Seltzer's "The Naturalist Machine"; see also his *Bodies and Machines*.

6. Robert Langbaum, *The Poetry of Experience*.

7. For an account of the roles played by auditors in the dramatic monologue, including their power to "resist," see Dorothy Mermin, *The Audience in the Poem*.

tional portrayals I have previously analyzed, is the local intersubjective effects and maneuvers produced by the pervasive rhetoric of
fallenness. The central instance in which the speaker's impulse to
speak is thwarted occurs nearly halfway through the poem, when
it is revealed that what precedes and what follows are unspoken
thoughts:

> Suppose I were to think aloud,—
> What if to her all this was said?
> Why, as a volume seldom read
> Being opened half-way shuts again,
> So might the pages of her brain
> Be parted at such words, and thence
> Close back upon the dusty sense.
>
> (ll. 156–72)[8]

Note the series of shifts: Jenny is posited as a potential auditor, then
figured as an (inanimate) book, open only by virtue of being spoken
to, and then finally reanimated, but only *as book*, her pages presumably closing back of their own accord. This moment, during which
we become aware that the poem is unspoken, carries the force of
revelation since the speaker has so conspicuously and so frequently
employed Jenny's name in direct address. And the best way to view
what we now recognize to have been a compensatory stream of
"addresses," I suggest, is as a form of apostrophe that both reflects
and counters a crisis in the perception of Jenny's status. On one
level, it is true, the "directness" of repeated address seems to act
as a form of recognition. But not to speak such a form of address,
and to use it solipsistically in the very presence of the subject it
"invokes," eerily implies that this subject exists only by virtue of
being addressed by the speaker, who is thereby endowed with the
power to animate.[9] In conventional apostrophe, direct address func-

8. All quotations from the poem follow William M. Rossetti's edition of *The
Collected Works of Dante Gabriel Rossetti*. Harris points out that in this passage Rossetti
altered the form of the poem from its earlier drafts, in order to indicate clearly that
it was an unspoken monologue. According to Harris, the poem is only explicitly
indicated to be spoken in the earliest draft (1848). Drafts date from 1848, 1858, and
1869 (two). The final version appeared in *Poems* (1870). Harris, "D. G. Rossetti's
'Jenny' " 197–98.

9. This discussion draws on work on apostrophe by Barbara Johnson and Jonathan Culler. See Johnson, *A World of Difference* chap. 16; Culler, *The Pursuit of Signs*
chap. 7.

tions to posit the animate existence of an otherwise dead, inanimate, or absent being. Here apostrophe works to insist that "Jenny" is in need of animation. Even more: it entails an act of deanimation that renders the act of animation both necessary and potent. The speaker wards off uncertainties about Jenny's agency by appropriating the power of life and death to himself.

That the move to apostrophize entails an act of deanimation is suggested by the very manner in which the speaker inaugurates the use of direct address. The poem begins by describing Jenny in the third person and enacts a rather sudden syntactical shift to the second person in line 6:

> Lazy laughing languid Jenny
> Fond of a kiss and fond of a guinea,
> Whose head upon my knee to-night
> Rests for a while, as if grown light
> With all our dances and the sound
> To which the wild tunes spun you round.
>
> (ll. 1–6)

The first line is ambiguous as to whether Jenny is being addressed or described, though the sequence of adjectives and the appearance of *whose* in line 3 make one initially infer the latter. But the syntactical turn of line 6 effectively spins the inert Jenny round and constitutes her as addressee. This turn is followed by the first explicit direct address in the poem (which I quote presently), but it is worth noting that when Jenny is here addressed in the second person she is cast in a passive, objectified role; she is not agent but patient, being spun round by an external force. If a condition of apostrophe is the addressee's absence or death or lack of animation, then perhaps it becomes crucial to see Jenny's being spun round as something more absolute than merely following a dance; rather, Jenny is spun round more in the fashion that Lucy is "rolled round" in "A Slumber Did My Spirit Seal."[10]

The lines that follow encourage and extend such a reading, in that they evoke two moments that frame the act of murder in Browning's

10. Not only is Jenny being "spun" round, as Lucy is "rolled round," but the first two lines of Wordsworth's second stanza also constitute an apt description of Jenny's condition in the poem: "No motion has she now, no force; / She neither hears nor sees."

"Porphyria's Lover." In that poem, the woman addressed by the speaker is not simply dead or inert but actively rendered so. The apprehension that enacts the lover's shift from indecision to action ("That moment she was mine, mine, fair") and the uncanny reanimation of the corpse that occurs when he ceases to strangle her ("And I untightened next the tress / About her neck; her cheek once more / Blushed bright beneath her burning kiss") are both evoked in the speaker's first address to Jenny:

> Fair Jenny mine, the thoughtless queen
> Of kisses which the blush between
> Could hardly make much daintier.
>
> (ll. 7–9)

The evocation of "Porphyria's Lover" suggests an unsettling indexical function for the otherwise vaguely pejorative *thoughtless*: it stands in as the effect of an unrepresented act of deanimation. These correspondences, moreover, merely extend an already implicit reference to Browning's poem: the static quality of the scene in "Jenny," along with the position of the pair, reflects the pose orchestrated and then sustained throughout the night by Porphyria's murderer. The presupposition of the speaker's apostrophes—that Jenny is in need of animation—is secured through the encrypted violence of these allusive devices. And through repeated apostrophic address, the poem then works to compensate for the very conditions that it creates through its own inauguration of apostrophe.

"Countless Gold Incomparable"

In *Myths of Sexuality: Representations of Women in Victorian Britain*, Lynda Nead argues that the prostitute "occupies a unique place" in the economic system: "She is able to represent all the terms within capitalist production; she is the human labour, the object of exchange, and the seller at once. She stands as worker, commodity and capitalist and blurs the categories of bourgeois economics in the same way that she tests the boundaries of bourgeois morality."[11] Nead goes on to say that the prostitute's ability to blur bourgeois

11. Lynda Nead, *Myths of Sexuality* 99.

categories and appropriate male economic prerogatives is the source of her threatening stature and the cause of a pervasive scapegoating. In "Jenny," the blurring of categories is extreme: indeed, the prostitute is not exactly cast as *both* object of exchange and economic actor; instead, she is demonstrated to be *neither*. This portrayal is in keeping with the negative mode of the poem and serves to heighten the anxiety about agency. To the extent that she acts, Jenny is cast as an object; to the extent that she is an object, the poem fetishizes and animates her. It is not surprising that the prostitute should serve as a heightened instance of both reification and commodity fetishism: she sells herself or, what amounts to the same thing, she sells a part of herself that is taken to be inalienable. This paradox produces a clear tension in Rossetti's poem. The imperfect end-rhyme of the first couplet (*Jenny/guinea*), for example, both suggests and unbalances an equation between Jenny and a piece of money. The metaphorical substitution of gold for Jenny's hair ("whose hair is countless gold incomparable") follows the more artificial form of comparison (simile) used to describe her eyes ("Whose eyes are as blue skies"), but there is a tension internal to the metaphor itself (ll. 10–11). *Countless* obeys the logic of the commodity, if negatively; *incomparable* resists that logic (since nothing, necessarily, is incomparable to the abstract form of the commodity).

The poem thus displays an uneasiness with Jenny's commodification, revealing and resisting it. However, the correlations between Jenny and the object of exchange function not only to display commodity fetishism but also to shore up the poem's systematic disavowal of Jenny's status as an economic agent. This foreclosure of Jenny's agency is motivated, my reading suggests, not so much by the prostitute's appropriation of male economic prerogatives as by the speaker's investment in an ideal purity free from the realm of desire, exchange, and, ultimately, the instabilities of communication. Crucially relevant here is the speaker's anxiety about the nature of his own aesthetic "work."

In the "child's tale" describing the prostitute's rise and fall, Jenny is subjected to the kind of conventional narrative containment we have seen before: the "tale" serves as a condensed version of the way narrative constitutes subjectivity. Not only is Jenny fully assimilated to a narrative of which she is a mere instance, but she is indicated, to the extent that she acts, only metonymically: her "lifted silken skirt / Advertise[s] dainties" and her "coach-wheels splash rebuke / On virtue" (ll. 145–49). Metonymical figuration here actually serves double duty: it registers Jenny's wealth, figuring that wealth as productive of movement and activity, yet it also eclipses Jenny as agent. Only when wealth and health are irretrievable does the prostitute appear to project—as vision—her subjectivity, but then she immovably stares "along the streets alone," incapable of responding to, or even apprehending, the children who thus identify her (ll. 149–50). The prostitute's stare is only an allusion to subjectivity and is analogous to the pathos of amnesiacs, whose eyes seem to project a saddened awareness they are incapable of feeling. An image of redemption does appear, it is true—the "fiery serpent" of Numbers 21: 8–9. But whereas in Numbers, the act of *beholding* the brass serpent effects redemption, *this* serpent is significantly beyond the range of Jenny's vision, "round the long park, across the bridge" (l. 151).[12] The hiatus between the prostitute's stare and a redemptive act of beholding is then duplicated in the lines that follow. The speaker justifies his silence by describing Jenny's "desecrated mind" as utterly unable to comprehend the (potentially redeeming?) narrative he has just recited.

At the only moment in the poem when Jenny might perform a discrete, motivated action, her threatening economic status is again registered and counteracted. The speaker appears to be handing her a glass of wine:

> But that the weariness may pass
> And leave you merry, take this glass.
> Ah! lazy lily hand, more bless'd
> If ne'er in rings it had been dress'd
> Nor ever by a glove conceal'd!
> Behold the lilies of the field,
> They toil not neither do they spin.
>
> (ll. 95–101)

It seems that some kind of overt gesture, if not explicit utterance, is made by the speaker here. However, the apprehension of Jenny's

---

12. "And the Lord said unto Moses, Make thee a fiery serpent, and set it upon a pole; and it shall come to pass, that every one that is bitten, when he looketh upon it, shall live.

"And Moses made a serpent of brass, and put it upon a pole, and it came to pass, that if a serpent had bitten any man, when he beheld the serpent of brass, he lived." Numbers 21: 8, King James version.

hand as disinclined to action and the (not uncharacteristic) rapidity with which the speaker becomes distracted might act rather to forestall any *actual* attempt to hand Jenny the glass. The "Ah!" followed directly by "lazy" suggests that here the speaker is experiencing the inert hand as a check to his advance. This positing of inherent nonactivity is then extended in the evocation of the lilies of the field. Jenny's wealth is registered again indexically, in the "rings" and "gloves," and cast, at least in relation to the glove, as deceptive, concealing. If to be *dressed* is to be *concealed*, as the alignment of the two words implies, the "lazy lily hand" synecdochally suggests that the "real" Jenny is Jenny's body. Recall too that *lazy* is the first word used to describe Jenny and the first word of the poem. Yet, as we saw earlier, activity adheres not in that body but in the commodities that attach, deceptively, to it. The speaker's strategy is thus to (literally) divest Jenny of the power of agency, revealing her as incommensurable with a projected wealth.

It is interesting to view Jenny's threatening appearance of wealth in light of the description of the virtuous working girl. Jenny is allegedly glad to evade "the pale girl's dumb rebuke, / Whose ill-clad grace and toil-worn look / Proclaim the strength that keeps her weak" (ll. 73–75). Like Jenny, the working girl is dumb, but her virtuous identity proclaims itself and is immediately legible— her "look" does not deceive or conceal, her grace is not covered over but "ill-clad." This passage clarifies the anxiety that Jenny's (otherwise "mere") appearance of wealth can induce: the appearance also conceals and, like her silence, renders her disturbingly illegible.

Toward the end of the poem, the speaker projects Jenny's dream and then interprets it as a desire for recognition through luxury and dress. Jenny is curiously absent from the dream itself; more precisely, she constitutes the absent center of an environment characterized by constant motion and animate force:

> Or like a palpitating star
> Thrilled into song, the opera-night
> Breathes faint in the quick pulse of light;
> Or at the carriage window shine
> Rich wares for choice; or, free to dine,
> Whirls through its hour of health (divine
> For her) the concourse of the Park.
>
> (ll. 352–58)

It is not Jenny who "breathes faint" or "whirls" or is "thrilled." No center of motion or experience herself, the dreamer merely produces images associated with wealth. That the only indication of her own satisfaction as well as her possible presence within the dream itself is interpolated parenthetically merely reinforces Jenny's exclusion from the surrounding syntax, which itself thwarts any actual insertion of the dreaming subject into the coveted context. The speaker's interpretation of Jenny's dream—that it gives her a satisfying sense of distinction—is thus undercut by his representation of the dreaming itself. It is hard to see how this dream constitutes Jenny as "the acknowledged belle / apparelled beyond parallel" (ll. 362–64), since there doesn't seem to be any actual scene of recognition in the dream itself.

To the extent that the poem does resist commodifying Jenny, it casts her as essentially nonquantifiable but not as an acting, conscious subject. That is, Jenny's essence can be protected or appealed to, but her consciousness cannot. Moreover, the nature of the essence itself furnishes the explanation for the denial of economic agency. The act that Jenny would perform, in economic terms, is that of selling, but the product that she sells is, for the speaker, an original purity that not only constitutes her ideal identity but also remains definitively inaccessible to any economic or sexual contaminations: as such, it cannot be given any communicative form and must remain ineffable and unread. Purity, in the poem, is thereby accorded the status of pure anteriority or pure otherness. It is no accident that in the figural sequence directly following the phrase "countless gold incomparable" a temporal predicament is played out:

> Fresh flower, scarce touched with signs that tell
> Of Love's exuberant hotbed:—Nay,
> Poor flower left torn since yesterday
> Until tomorrow leave you bare;
> Poor handful of bright spring-water
> Flung in the whirlpool's shrieking face.
>
> (ll. 12–17)

As a fresh flower, Jenny is already "touched with signs that tell" of impurity: this image necessitates a revision that evokes a more explicit notion of original purity. As a flower "left torn" since yesterday, Jenny is poised between purity and corruption, poignantly at the mercy of time. The third figure extends the implication of an identity that is purely anterior: the "handful of bright spring-water" is substantially equivalent to, and effectively absorbed by, a malign environment that now, in its "shrieking face," grotesquely mocks subjectivity. The loss of purity *is* the loss of identity.

Jenny's purity is also cast as pure anteriority just previous to the "child's tale," whose point of origin postdates the fall. Her pastoral innocence, "When she would lie in fields and look / Along the ground through the blown grass," constitutes a pre-narrative: "the old days which seem to be / Much older than any history / That is written in any book" (ll. 127–31). Fundamentally incommunicable, allowed no textual instantiation, purity for the speaker remains outside narrative and hence cannot be passed along through textual interchanges. But the word *seem* is crucial here: purity or identity is constituted after the fact, in the manner of an *après-coup*, accessible only through memory. The predicament of fallenness as inescapably public identity simply cannot be eluded, as is again displayed toward the end of the poem when the speaker showers golden coins in Jenny's hair. What has been posing a profound threat, and what in one sense constitutes the fall, is the possibility of giving original identity an exchange value, but here the speaker himself undergoes this transformation. When he translates himself into coin, in the hope of being distinctly remembered, he dooms his desire, for he loses all individual identity in leaving the coins.

Precisely because purity is constituted as inaccessibly anterior or definitively nonembodied, distinctions between Jenny and the speaker collapse. The extreme investment in private and protected identity here reveals its delusions, as the condition of the prostitute thus cannot help but be the condition of all. In the period in which Rossetti was writing, there was profound anxiety not only about women taking their private bodily wares to market but also about the market-oriented forms that ostensibly private intellectual and aesthetic practices were taking. The rise of serial publication and the professionalization of writing invited comparison between authors and prostitutes: a man's text, like a woman's sex, was seen as something that one should not parcel out for pay.[13] The fact that the

13. For a discussion of the prevalence of the metaphor of the author as whore in Victorian culture, see Catherine Gallagher, "George Eliot and *Daniel Deronda*." On

speaker refers to his "work" only once, and then only in relation to the elusive activity of "reading," reinforces the possibility that he wishes to think of his own intellectual and aesthetic practices in distinctly noneconomic terms. Jenny thus can be seen to function as a double for the speaker, who himself never succeeds in fully disavowing the extent to which his identity, both as a scholar and as Jenny's client, is bound up in networks of exchange.

Dormant Desires

As the above discussion of purity suggests, the question of whether or to what extent Jenny is a conscious being emerges in sexual as well as economic terms. To discuss the sexual register, then, requires a certain double awareness: in general the anxiety deriving from Jenny's vexed economic status cannot be separated from anxieties about sexual desire. Indeed, the economic and the sexual categories are blurred in the poem's opening verse paragraph, first when Jenny is described as "Fond of a kiss and fond of a guinea," and then some lines later, when the speaker wonders, "Whose person or whose purse may be / The lodestar of your reverie?" (ll. 2, 20–21). The shift from *and* (in the first pairing) to *or* might be said to enact and perhaps prefigure a shift from a logic of mutual implication to one of mutual exclusion, but the phonetic near-equivalence of *person* and *purse* seems to suggest an identity under-lying, or inhabiting, the opposition. What this complex of formulae indicates is that the relation between the sexual and economic remains fluid in the poem, and one category cannot be said to take precedence over the other, nor are they equated with one another in any simple way.

On one level, the relation between the speaker and Jenny, and in particular their pose, emblematize the unequal balance of desire that attends an act of prostitution. But the relation between the two also represents a conception of sexual difference that was current during the years Rossetti worked on the poem, particularly in reformist accounts of prostitution by writers such as Greg and Acton.[14] This

connections between feminine purity and an ideal of literary labor as safe from the contaminations of the market, see Mary Poovey, *Uneven Developments* 89–125.

14. See [W. R. Greg], "Prostitution"; William Acton, *Prostitution Considered in Its*

view stressed feminine sexual passivity, claiming that women were devoid of sexual appetite or, alternately, unconscious of any desire until it was excited by the sexual initiations of men. Male lust, on the other hand, was primary and active. Though by no means the only or indisputably "official" view of sexual difference in the period, it did prove especially useful to reformers who sought to absolve prostitutes of responsibility for their fall and to deny any inherent corruption on their part.[15] As we saw in the previous chapter, Gaskell's vindication of Ruth draws directly from this general view of sexual difference and from Greg more specifically.

The theory of sexual passivity allowed for an (at least locally) enabling confusion between feminine sexual purity and feminine sexual corruption. Greg, for example, argues that "a vast proportion" of kept mistresses who later became street prostitutes "fell in the first instance from a mere exaggeration and perversion of one of the best qualities of a woman's heart":

> There is in the warm fond heart of a woman a strange and sublime unselfishness, which men too commonly discover only to profit by,—a positive love of self-sacrifice,—an active, so to speak, an *aggressive* desire to show their affection, by giving up to those who have won it something they hold very dear. . . . This is no romantic or over-coloured picture; those who deem it so have not known the better portion of the sex, or do not deserve to have known them.[16]

This passage, which Acton cites approvingly, essentially argues that many fall because of virtue; more important, like those Victorian domestic ideologues who stressed the potency of selfless activity, Greg grants to women a compensatory, magnified activity (if nonetheless qualified by a "so to speak") only insofar as it is the index

---

Moral, Social, and Sanitary Aspects. Also see Chapter 1 for a related discussion of Greg, Acton, and other writers on prostitution.

15. F. Barry Smith argues that Acton, who has often been taken as representative of the official Victorian view of sexual difference, is not only not representative but was actively refuted by many contemporaries. See Smith, "Sexuality in Britain, 1800–1900." It is certainly true that a more active, threatening form of female sexuality was registered in contemporary psychology. For the purposes of my reading, it does seem significant, however, that the rather extreme and counter-intuitive theory of "sexual anaesthesia" crops up in writers specifically concerned with prostitution.

16. Greg, "Prostitution" 459.

of a self-denying instinct, only insofar as they are precluded from being sexual agents in their own right.

Ultimately, however, the figure of the passive woman displaces a predicament of agency that attends not merely feminine desire but desire in general. This displacement occurs both in Greg and in Rossetti, and in both instances it destabilizes what appears to be a founding distinction between masculine and feminine desire. Take, for example, the following passage from Greg's article:

> Women's *desires* scarcely ever lead to their fall; for (save in a class of whom we shall speak presently) the desire scarcely exists in a definite and conscious form, till they *have* fallen. In this point there is a radical and essential difference between the sexes: the arrangements of nature and customs of society would be even more unequal than they are, were it not so. In men, in general, the sexual desire is inherent and spontaneous, and belongs to the condition of puberty. In the other sex, the desire is dormant, if not non-existent, till excited; always till excited by undue familiarities; almost always till excited by actual intercourse. Those feelings which coarse and licentious minds are so ready to attribute to girls, are almost invariably *consequences*.[17]

The "radical and essential difference between the sexes" is here marked by an asymmetry: female desire is "unconscious" and "dormant" while male desire is "inherent and spontaneous." The emergence of female desire depends on an external stimulus; until then, it is unconscious. Male desire does not depend on an external stimulus; but it is not exactly conscious, it is *spontaneous*. The word has an odd double meaning: it denotes the voluntary as well as the impulsive. A man may have an active sexuality but it is not clear that he has a controlled one; his agency is protected, but not his capacity to, as Mill puts it, "make [his] desires and impulses . . . his own." The issue of consciousness in or of desire is thus unresolved in the case of the man; this irresolution is partly masked by the fact that the woman is more emphatically defined against the possibility of conscious desire, even if time and events can alter her condition.

Distinctions between purity and fallenness, and between masculine and feminine desire, are similarly dislodged in Rossetti's poem, in which the speaker fears, not exactly becoming a steam

17. Greg, "Prostitution" 456–57.

engine, but in any event a too-close identification with the spinning Jenny. As in Greg, the ostensibly more stable opposition is between masculine and feminine desire, and the upsetting of the distinction between pure and fallen seems a more studied, achieved effect, an attempt at partial vindication. This instability between fallenness and conventional purity, however, does not contradict my earlier interpretation of purity as absolute otherness; quite the contrary, for in these inscriptions of gender, the status of purity is protected only to the extent that it is never given present instantiation. Once given a form, as in the case of cousin Nell, it will inevitably devolve, of itself, into fallenness.

The identification between the "fallen" Jenny and the "pure" Nell is effected largely through resonances in the economic register. Initially, what produces the speaker's bewilderment in comparing the two women is that the pure and the fallen can, in sleep, appear to be substantially the same (ll. 177–84). The ensuing description of Nell, which seems to delimit an entirely different character and destiny, also, mainly through echoes and puns, suggests an underlying equivalence: "My cousin Nell is fond of fun, / And fond of dress, and change, and praise" (ll. 185–86). The pun on *change* brings this phrase into alignment with its counterpart, "fond of a guinea." Later, *change* and *dear* function doubly, reinforcing this effect and essentially casting marriage as a form of prostitution: "The love of change, in cousin Nell / Shall find the best and hold it dear." The counterpart to "fond of a kiss" also appears: cousin Nell is "fond of love." What seems to set Nell apart from Jenny most centrally is, to borrow Greg's terms, her "sublime unselfishness": "The unconquered mirth turn quieter / Not through her own, through others' woe." However, the proliferation of the word *fond*, and of the objects it takes, seems to transform its meaning from mere affection into restless, if muted, desire.

In his more explicitly polemical or philosophical moments, the speaker continues to naturalize gender identity, accounting for Jenny, and for prostitution in general, by citing the primacy and violence of male lust. An entire verse paragraph, distinguished by a highly impersonal tone, is devoted to a description of lust as "a toad within a stone / Seated while Time crumbles on"(ll. 282–83). That the referent in this paragraph is not humankind but men in general is supported by the speaker's earlier assertion that Jenny— silent, inactive—is most powerfully victimized by the "hatefulness of man," "whose acts are ill and his speech ill" (ll. 83, 85). The static, transhistorical account is reproduced in the relation between the voluble speaker and the inert, "dormant" Jenny. But even though we are far from the sociological reformist perspective here, the account of gender difference and desire is not entirely stable. The nature of its instability is displayed most tellingly in the functioning of the figure of the book, a figure that ultimately links the issues of sexual desire, uncertain agency, and intersubjective recognition.

The book in Rossetti's poem acts as a device that mediates between the activity of reading and the apprehension of concrete subjects in the world. For this speaker not only experiences threats to identity in economic and sexual exchange but also fears the instabilities of any communicative exchange, which he associates with the undecidability of reading in general. However, to the extent that the concrete delimited entity of the book—and not sheer language or text—figures the concrete other, the potentially precarious activity of reading and even distinguishing the other can be stabilized. Moreover, in this poem desire emerges from, and is in part a response to, a breakdown in the reading of actual texts. Hence, the figuring of people as books serves to indicate and, again, stabilize a distinctly eroticized unreadability. For the speaker, in other words, the figuring of people as books tames the textuality of otherness as well as figures the eroticization of reading. We know that the speaker's visit to the prostitute is occasioned by a certain breakdown of the (literal) reading process. He describes the "cloud" that made his brain "turn and swim / While hour by hour the books grew dim" (ll. 44–45). In explaining how he came to meet Jenny, he at once describes and displays the emergence of cognitive destabilization:

> . . . I vowed that since my brain
> And eyes of dancing seemed so fain,
> My feet should have some dancing too:—
> And thus it was I met with you.
> Well, I suppose 'twas hard to part,
> For here I am.
>
> (ll. 30–35)

Metonymical association supplants motive (figural dancing evokes literal dancing); the stop-and-start quality of the lines seems to expose meaning as a tautological process of positing. But to describe this experience merely as a "breakdown" is to cloud over the erotic play signified by "dancing." As the site of the emergence of the erotic, the breakdown of readability is not an unpleasurable predicament.

This account of the emergence or structure of desire must be viewed against the eroticized apprehension of Jenny as book. On one level, the latter certainly evokes associations between pornography and prostitution and obliquely alludes to the attitude of censorship that the poem defies.[18] But, in terms of the argument I am sketching, what is more important is the way it works to deanimate and reify Jenny as well as, ultimately, to subvert the distinction between her and the speaker:

> Why, Jenny, as I watch you there,—
> For all your wealth of loosened hair,
> Your silk ungirdled and unlac'd
> And warm sweets open to the waist,
> All golden in the lamplight's gleam,—
> You know not what a book you seem,
> Half-read by lightning in a dream!
> How should you know, my Jenny? Nay,
> And I should be ashamed to say:—
> Poor beauty, so well worth a kiss!
> But while my thought runs on like this
> With wasteful whims more than enough,
> I wonder what you're thinking of.
>
> If of myself you think at all,
> What is the thought?—conjectural
> On sorry matters best unsolved?—
> Or inly is each grace revolved
> To fit me with a lure?—
>
> (ll. 46–63)

Part of the strangeness in the first lines of this passage derives from an ambiguity surrounding the intensity of the speaker's response: is his experience of satisfaction occasioned by Jenny's deshabille or by his perception, or rather hallucination, of her as book? These two

18. For a discussion of the relation between Rossetti's poem and pornography, see Robin Sheets, "Pornography and Art."

things do not appear to be mutually reinforcing. It is true that a highly eroticized Jenny evokes *reading*, and this association is mediated by the figure of the book. But this mediating figure is also what prevents a real erotic exchange between Jenny and the speaker, since on one level the book is defined against erotic accessibility: Jenny is a book *despite* ("for all") her inviting accessibility. Here one might also recall, in particular, the "serried ranks" the speaker left behind in his room as he went in search of "real" dancing. The telos of the erotic impulse, which in this poem originates with an act of reading, is an intersubjective encounter, yet here the inability *not* to see Jenny as a book throws the speaker back into himself.

As soon as Jenny is seen as a book, in fact, the speaker becomes languid and self-incriminating. And what the speaker is "ashamed" of here seems to be the lapse into the masturbatory mode, which, for the Victorians, was associated with excessive reading.[19] In the ideology of the period, masturbation was seen as a useless and depletionary expenditure, one that led ultimately to impotence. As Steven Marcus points out, semen was seen along the model of money in an economy of scarcity.[20] The sequence here seems not insignificant: the woman is figured as a book; the speaker characterizes his thoughts as running on with "wasteful whims more than enough"; lodged between is the lament, "Poor beauty, so well worth a kiss"—not accompaniment to a kiss but apology for his own autoerotic mode.

The speaker then wonders at Jenny's thoughts, and his first projection as to their drift alludes, one might assume, to the question of his sexual potency ("sorry matters best unsolved"). The second projection evokes the question of the extent to which Jenny designs or consciously seduces: "Or inly is each grace revolved / To fit me with a lure?" Jenny's uncertain status here carries a new edge to it:

19. Similarly, at least one commentator on prostitution saw scholars as particularly susceptible: "Literature, like wealth, is inadequate to secure its possessor against the consequences of prostitution. Perhaps the baneful effects of licentiousness are not more painfully exemplified in any class of citizens, than among those who pursue the paths of literature and science. In order to relieve the dull hours of study, they resort for recreation to the tavern and brothel, till the habit becomes inveterate and irresistible." Ironically, however, he later suggests that reading will serve to diminish sexual excesses among servants: "Let a habit of reading, instead of a habit of drinking, be introduced and encouraged amongst household servants, and a different state of things will soon appear." William Tait, *Magdalenism* 184, 213.

20. See Steven Marcus, *The Other Victorians* 12–25.

the speaker imagines her as poised midway between design and action. Jenny's inertness becomes the very index for agency, since it casts her as the embodiment of pure deliberation, the threshold of action. Moreover, if you hear "a lure" also as "allure," then the apprehension of Jenny's latent agency is conflated with the possibility that the speaker cannot answer her desire: she is revolving *his* graces in an attempt to fit him with "allure." Here feminine desire threateningly exceeds, rather than is subordinated to, masculine desire. This moment of empowerment—and it is but a moment, for the speaker moves on to cast his own activity as a form of benefaction—seems to be prompted by the evocation of the "sorry matters best unsolved." But it would be inaccurate to say that this "reversal" reveals that Jenny is truly potent while the speaker is impotent; rather, it is one among several moments in the poem showing that desire severely attenuates one's pretension to agency. To cede *or* to deny agency to Jenny, depending on its context, can be an attempt, on the speaker's part, to ward off the instabilities of desire itself.

"Like a Rose Shut in a Book"

To follow the vicissitudes of the figure of the book is to gain some insight into Rossetti's conception of the possible forms of intersubjective experience. The interventions performed by this figure work generally, though never manage fully, to stabilize perceptions of the other as well as to foreclose mutual perception or dialogical intercourse.

There are two "closed" books in the poem, both of which function as images for Jenny. In one instance, which I have already discussed, the figure of the book emerges as the speaker contemplates the effects his words would have if spoken aloud. What is explicitly at issue here is the possibility of a spoken exchange; this is moreover the moment at which the form of the poem, as the negation of dramatic monologue, is revealed:

> Suppose I were to think aloud,—
> What if to her all this were said?
> Why, as a volume seldom read
> Being opened half-way shuts again,
> So might the pages of her brain

Be parted at such words, and thence
Close back upon the dusty sense.
For is there hue or shape defin'd
In Jenny's desecrated mind,
Where all contagious currents meet,
A Lethe of the middle street?
Nay, it reflects not any face,
Nor sound is in its sluggish pace,
But as they coil those eddies clot,
And night and day remember not.

Why, Jenny, you're asleep at last!
(ll. 156–71)

An objectified model of reading eclipses the possibility for dialogue and conditions the encounter. Jenny, like the book, is brought alive, and made legible, only through the consciousness of the speaker; apart from that, she is not *non*existent, but rather the embodiment of uninterpretability, utter confusion, meaningless marks (with no "hue or shape defin'd"). The effect of being read will not extend beyond the phase of reading—Jenny will not be altered by the activity of the speaker's consciousness as (speaking) reader. She has no memory; her mind "reflects not any face," that is, she herself projects no face, nor can she recognize the face of the other. Thus she herself cannot distinguish any intersubjective encounter within the meaningless flux.

The only possible mode of consciousness for the speaker is that of a distinctly monological reading; other subjects exist only insofar as they are read. And yet here the reading process suffers disruptions: the figure of the book does not quite succeed in managing what for the speaker remains to some extent an inaccessible, resistant, unreadable subjectivity. If Jenny is a closed book, open only by virtue of the speaker's words, she is also perceived to *close herself*. Note the shift from passive (if he spoke, her pages would be parted) to active (they then "close back upon the dusty sense"). As an animate book, then, Jenny cannot be in any simple way inscribed or delimited or read, though the speaker repeatedly tries to do so. The threat that she poses on this count is dramatically registered by the fact that what immediately follows is the most intense vilification of Jenny in the poem, and then the dispelling of any doubt as to whether she sleeps.[21] The imagery employed in the vilification, moreover, retroactively refigures the motion of resistance, the closing back, as a movement of waters in upon themselves: it rewrites Jenny's hypothetical action as the mere motion of the elements.

There are other moments in which Jenny's non-response seems active, producing a kind of refutation effect against the many disavowals of her agency. These refutations tend to occur precisely at those moments when the speaker is providing universal justifications for prostitution, as for example in the passage that culminates by indicting the "hatefulness of man." The speaker's thoughts here produce his impulse to move out of reflection on prostitution and into its physical act. One might see Jenny's failure to rise to the occasion, then, as that which forces the self-interrogation to continue; she is of course not resisting the precise nature of the speaker's account, but her perceived noncompliance after his "sympathetic" account of her victimization has the effect of refutation. These are moments when Rossetti seems to encourage us to see through the speaker's superficiality as well as his defensive maneuvers. A similar effect is produced after the toad-within-a-stone account. Many point to this passage as the record of Rossetti's view on prostitution, without paying attention to the lines that follow. Again, the speaker moves to engage Jenny ("Jenny, wake up . . . "), yet he is then immediately distracted by the apprehension of dawn and an evocation of the market. The noise associated with the move toward the marketplace (the "bleating" sheep and "barking dog") breaks the hermetic silence of the speaker's discourse and, like the later ring of the coins, speaks the economic realities underlying his mystified meditations (ll. 303–6).

The other occurrence of the figure of the closed book centers on its contaminating power, a quality that also appeared in the description of Jenny as a self-shutting book: there her mind is a place "where all contagious currents meet, / A Lethe of the middle street." Here Jenny, as representative fallen woman, is cast as a "rose shut in a

21. It has been argued (Harris), as well as assumed (Auerbach), that Jenny sleeps throughout the poem. Harris argues that, in line with the conventions of dramatic monologue, the speaker's self-absorption is signaled in his inability to properly perceive Jenny's sleep. However, the uncertainty of Jenny's state, the difficulty in distinguishing rest from sleep in the other, is a crucial aspect of the problems in agency that the poem displays. And of course this moment of perceiving that Jenny finally sleeps—i.e., is really unconscious—is importantly placed. See Harris, "D. G. Rossetti's 'Jenny' " 202 n. 7, and Nina Auerbach, Woman and the Demon 155.

book": the rose represents the crushed "flower within the soul"; the book, at least initially, is the corrupting medium. As in the previous instance, the intersubjective scenario is important: the speaker is lamenting that an act of ideal reading—of the fallen by the pure—is necessarily impossible:

> If but a woman's heart might see
> Such erring heart unerringly
> For once! But that can never be.
> Like a rose shut in a book
> In which pure women may not look,
> For its base pages claim control
> To crush the flower within the soul;
> Where through each dead rose-leaf that clings,
> Pale as transparent psyche-wings,
> To the vile text, are traced such things
> As might make lady's cheek indeed
> More than a living rose to read;
> So nought save foolish foulness may
> Watch with hard eyes the sure decay.
>
> (ll. 250–63)

It becomes impossible to read directly (from the heart, to the heart, as the speaker conceives it) because the rose clings to the page, thereby becoming, from one perspective, imprinted—"traced"—by the contaminating or "vile" text. But one can also read the pure woman rather than the impersonal text as the agent who traces. In this act of reading, however, it is as though the text supplants the rose as object of the pure woman's consciousness. The placement of the phrase "to the vile text" invites such a reading: less that the rose leaf "clings" to the vile text than that the blush-inducing images are, by the woman, *traced* to it. These lines further suggest the possibility that the rose, despite its near-transparency, is itself the corrupting medium, that which colors and makes necessarily "erring" the act of reading: the woman traces the vile text "*through* each dead rose-leaf." Moreover, some lines later, the rose produces a "sanguine stain" (l. 270), which contradicts its earlier paleness. The preserved rose, as emblem of the now irretrievable purity, is corruption itself.

It is perhaps no accident that the corrupting of the rose occurs simultaneously with the possibility that, in reading the text instead of the rose, the pure woman is evincing a desire that she shouldn't have. The ambiguity of "More than a living rose to read" participates in this conflation: it is uncertain whether the woman's blush issues out of her act of reading or is at that moment being read. It becomes impossible to apprehend the pure woman as reader without reading her as compromised. Here, it is reading itself that corrupts, and the pure woman is defined against such a possibility only through the defensive gesture of prohibition.

In one sense the speaker is defining an ideal encounter even as he disallows it. This passage reveals the speaker's frustrated sense of the impossibility of any kind of direct perception: any apperception of the other also becomes an act of reading that forecloses the redemptive comprehension of an original purity. It is symptomatic, then, that the entire verse paragraph begins with an untethered simile: we never know exactly what is "like a rose shut in a book." The (fallen) woman here becomes the scapegoated figure for Rossetti's fear that the "contaminations" of an erotic textuality will always upset a posited ideal human encounter—the "unerring" reading of one heart by another. Like Gaskell, then, Rossetti opposes an idealized form of intersubjectivity to his many versions of fallenness.

There is another moment in which an idealized intersubjective structure is posited and thwarted; it is also the moment when the speaker most fully reveals himself to be subject to the problems in identity that he has projected onto Jenny. This moment occurs when he performs the spectacular and compensatory act of laying golden coins in her hair, in a blatant conflation of financial and sexual potency.[22] What is clearly at stake here, for the speaker, is the need not merely to project his power but also, as we saw earlier, to con-

22. Steven Marcus describes the way Victorian pornography compensated for the economy-of-scarcity ideology surrounding male ejaculation: "The model on which the notion of semen is formed is clearly that of money.... Furthermore, the economy envisaged in this idea is based on scarcity and has as its aim the accumulation of its own product. And the fantasy of pornography ... is this idea's complement, for the world of pornography is a world of plenty. In it all men are infinitely rich in substance, all men are limitlessly endowed with that universal fluid currency which can be spent without loss. Just as in the myth Zeus descends upon Danae in a shower of gold, so in pornography the world is bathed, floated, flooded, inundated in this magical produce of the body. No one need ever worry again about husbanding nature's riches from expense." Marcus, *The Other Victorians* 22.

stitute himself as a distinct and above all *recognizable* being. He attempts to ensure the latter by imagining that he meets Jenny's dreams in leaving the gold. Jenny dreams images of wealth; the speaker leaves her what constitutes both the representation as well as the material of wealth. But the speaker wants the gold to represent *him*, and he believes that this disembodied erotic nonencounter, this signature in coin, will somehow render him distinct, constituting him as the sole memory in the Lethe that is her mind.

As I mentioned earlier, the logic is faulty, since the self-objectification into a medium of exchange renders identity indistinct. As the abstract representation of wealth, he might be meeting in a pure, unmediated way what he perceives as Jenny's desire, but he himself loses all specificity. Moreover, there is lodged in the speaker's logic a metonymical slide (from semen to self) that ensures the metaphorical substitution of gold for self. In a striking final reversal, Jenny becomes the desiring subject and the speaker is evacuated, leaving only a token of himself. He has thus become what he earlier names Jenny as being, "a cipher of man's changeless sum / Of lust" (ll. 278–79). What haunts the entire passage, and ultimately the poem itself, is a thwarted desire for recognition. The structure that governs apostrophe is reversed: now it is Jenny who must animate the speaker.[23]

In general terms, then, "Jenny" is a poem about uncertain agency, thwarted recognition, and the profound unreadability of otherness. To center such concerns on the figure of the prostitute at once heightens and deflects the anxieties that attend these epistemological and intersubjective predicaments. For in the case of the Victorian prostitute, the problems in readability that attend the intersubjective moment are part of a complex configuration; as this chapter is designed to show, these problems are inextricably linked to economic and sexual anxieties about agency. The speaker's metonymic association of the prostitute with false representations is a means of disavowing her economic agency; this act is in turn predicated on an investment in an essential identity uncontaminated by (any kind of) exchange. This speaker fears indeterminacy as much as determinacy, however, and hence also uses the prostitute to disavow the

23. Barbara Johnson discusses a similar apostrophic reversal in Shelley's "Ode to the West Wind." Johnson, *A World of Difference* 188.

fact that representations as well as other people are not as fixed and legible as the stained page that figures a lost purity. As we have seen throughout this book, the Victorian prostitute is closely identified with representation and ornamentation—with "paint," finery, narrative, melodrama, stories, and, in this case, books. "Jenny" dramatizes with extraordinary power that such associations both correspond to and enable the Victorian prostitute's multiple functions as synecdoche and scapegoat for anxieties about agency and selfhood.

Yet, as I suggested at the beginning of this chapter, we can read the poem also as a partial critique of the rhetoric of fallenness and in particular that rhetoric's tendency to thwart mutuality and recognition. Indeed, the form of the poem—its allusion to the dramatic monologue that Jenny's "figurality" renders impossible—critically inflects and frames the scenes of thwarted recognition in the poem, the laying of the golden coins as well as the rose shut in a book. These two passages reveal an objectifying stance toward self or other both in their initial idealizing impulse and in their eventual collapses into misrecognition (in the rose-shut-in-a-book passage) and nonspecificity (in the laying of the golden coins). However, not only within these very passages but also at other moments in the poem, such moves to *fix* the other are unbalanced by reversals that locate agency in Jenny or the woman, moments when a certain desire or resistance is perceived, registered, or located in the other. The form of the poem, which constitutes an insistence on a continuous intersubjective context, shows how the presence or fact of another consciousness not only produces moves to stabilize or foreclose the other but also continually unsettles such moves. Jenny's undecidable agency thus can assume a positive dimension, evoking the open-endedness of intersubjective experience and the continuous *appeal* of the other.

5

Reproduced in Finer Motions: Encountering the Fallen in Barrett Browning's *Aurora Leigh*

All of the texts so far treated in this book employ the category of feminine fallenness to focus but also displace a series of radical threats to identity and self-representation. For Dickens, whose approach is certainly not devoid of sympathy, the fallen woman nonetheless comes to figure extreme conceptions of social determination, narrative inscription, and nonliberatory self-understanding. One might be tempted to attribute to Dickens an idiosyncratic fascination with victimization and systemic forces, yet even a writer such as Gaskell, who sets out to challenge harsh and unforgiving responses to sexual lapses, still uses fallenness to express deep-rooted anxieties about the subject-constituting power of cultural forms such as melodrama and romance (*Mary Barton*) and the dominance and reach of instrumental reason within industrial society (*Ruth*). Both Dickens and Gaskell render problematic the very notion of feminine autonomy or self-knowledge, elaborating ideals of femininity based on selflessness.

Moreover, precisely because the Victorian fallen woman is seen as hopelessly subject to structural forces that do not so powerfully determine more privileged subjects, it becomes difficult for writers to imagine or dramatize scenes in which any form of dialogical reciprocity can occur between fallen and unfallen characters. Eclipsed by a "vivid circle of paint," the fallen woman fails to make herself understood; she becomes an object of condescending sympathy or violent inscription; she droops or swoons, unequal to the tasks or pleasures of reciprocal recognition.[1] It is certainly true that such

---

1. The quote is from Elizabeth Gaskell, *Mary Barton* 169.

moments can insist, sometimes in startling and memorable ways, on the forces, narratives, and structures that condition the social world and mediate human action. Yet the overarching rhetoric that informs such moments tends to cast the fallen woman as a mere systems effect, thereby generating a stark determinism that forecloses any understanding of subjectivity as fundamentally participatory. As we saw in the previous chapter, D. G. Rossetti's poem "Jenny" displays in a particularly heightened manner the forms of distortion that attend encounters with the prostitute, revealing the powerful interpersonal effects generated by a reifying discourse of otherness.

In contrast to "Jenny," Elizabeth Barrett Browning's novel-in-verse *Aurora Leigh* more actively confronts and challenges the distortions that afflict encounters with women supposed to be "fallen," "lost," or "ruined." Although primarily the story of a poet's development, just as *David Copperfield* is primarily the story of a writer's development, *Aurora Leigh* employs a subplot tracing the fall and redemption of Marian Erle, a lower-class sempstress. It is even somewhat misleading to call the Marian Erle story a subplot, since it becomes so prominently woven into the story of Aurora's own development. If one imagines David Copperfield marrying Emily or taking her into his household after she is "found," or imagines Jane Eyre setting up house with Bertha Rochester, one gets a sense of the highly unorthodox nature of the Marian Erle story.[2] One of the most remarkable aspects of *Aurora Leigh* is precisely the significance accorded the intimate and sustained relationship between the pure Aurora and the fallen Marian. This relationship indicates that, for Barrett Browning, there was a need for the woman artist to come to terms with the prevalent literary staging of fallenness. And the fact that Barrett Browning actively struggled not only with the de-

---

2. Doris Lessing, in *The Four-Gated City*, writes just such an imaginative revision of the *Jane Eyre* plot, but she does so within a cultural climate very different from Elizabeth Barrett Browning's. See Elaine Showalter, *A Literature of Their Own* 124. Among the works treated in this book, *Ruth* comes closest to *Aurora Leigh* insofar as the fallen Ruth is brought into the Benson household, though *Aurora Leigh* is more bold in its dramatization of a relation between two women (there is no adult male member of their ménage in Florence). Barrett Browning had read and liked *Ruth*, and it is clearly a source for *Aurora Leigh*. For an excellent discussion of *Aurora Leigh* as a debate with works by other women writers (such as *Corinne, Jane Eyre*, and *Ruth*), see Cora Kaplan, Introduction, *Aurora Leigh and Other Poems*. (In this chapter, all quotations from *Aurora Leigh* follow Kaplan's edition.)

piction of women in art but also with the possibilities for mediating between aesthetic isolation and intersubjective experience made the thematization of the fallen an important site of anxiety and interrogation.

Aurora Leigh is a first-person novel-in-verse that recreates the development of a woman artist and attempts, in epic fashion, to take on the largest problems of its own age. It shares affinities with *The Prelude* and *Don Juan*, the epic and the bildungsroman, the courtship novel and the "social problem" novel. Aurora Leigh, born in Italy to an Englishman and an Italian woman, loses both her parents when young (her mother dies when she is four, her father when she is thirteen). After her father's death, she is taken to England to be raised by her father's sister, a severe woman with conservative ideas about the education of women. Her cousin and friend Romney Leigh, who has espoused social reform as a vocation, proposes to Aurora on her twentieth birthday, asking that she join him in his endeavors to ease the sufferings of the poor. Aurora forcefully declines, asserting her independence and her own vocation as a poet, and criticizing Romney for his utilitarian approach to love and to the world. The confrontation between Aurora and Romney during the proposal scene introduces the larger thematic tension between philanthropy and poetry, materiality and spirituality, one that the eventual reconciliation and marriage of Romney and Aurora attempts to resolve. It also introduces the conflict between Aurora's claims to autonomy and more conventional expectations of women's roles, natures, and limitations (as represented not only by Romney but also by Aurora's aunt, who upbraids and then resents her niece for declining Romney's offer). For many readers, the marriage at the end of the book represents a lamentable capitulation to conventionality, one that dilutes the challenge of the proposal scene. The marriage is long deferred, however, and it takes place only after Aurora's significant relationship with Marian Erle.

Shortly after the proposal, the aunt dies, leaving Aurora a very modest sum to live upon. Through indirect means, Romney attempts to add to this amount the vast sum of 30,000 pounds, but Aurora discovers the ruse, tears up the check, and departs for London to write and live on her own. The next Aurora hears of Romney, he is engaged to marry the sempstress Marian Erle, who also selflessly ministers to the unfortunate. Romney conceives the upcoming marriage as a symbolic healing of a class-divided society and so invites both rich and poor, St. James and St. Giles, to the ceremony. But as a result of the machinations of the evil Lady Waldemar, herself in love with Romney, the wedding never takes place. Having convinced Marian that the marriage threatens Romney's own interests, Lady Waldemar persuades her to emigrate to Australia in the custody of one of her former servants. The servant, a designing procuress, instead leads Marian to a brothel in Paris, where she is drugged and raped.

Meanwhile Aurora's poetic career and aesthetic philosophy advance steadily as she works through various lesser forms (the ballad, the pastoral) on her way to the larger epic that will stand as her most mature poetic creation. *Aurora Leigh* is in this respect the story of an artist developing to the point of being able to write *Aurora Leigh*. Yet Aurora repeatedly experiences emotional isolation, which is rendered even more acute when she receives news that Romney is soon to wed Lady Waldemar (although this wedding never takes place either). Aurora decides to return to Italy, the site of her early affections. Stopping over in Paris, she discovers Marian Erle living with her illegitimate baby and takes the two of them along to set up house in Italy. Romney eventually seeks them out, intending to make amends to Marian by marrying her. We discover that Romney's latest philanthropic endeavor, a phalanstery at his ancestral home, has literally blown up in his face, leaving him blind, chastened, and duly reverential of the spiritual life represented by Aurora. Marian, claiming an exclusive attachment to her child and insisting on the impurity of marriage for one like her, declines Romney's offer. The poem then ends with a drawn-out reconciliation between Romney and Aurora, both of whom admit earlier blindnesses and excesses, though poetry and the inner life of the spirit clearly win out over philanthropy and the world of "external" reform.

Barrett Browning's innovative formal synthesis of epic poetry and realist fiction corresponds to Aurora's attempt to forge thematic links between art and philanthropy, the literary and the social, spirit and utility.[3] That is, the attempt to reconcile the poetic and the novelistic

3. Upon its publication in 1857, *Aurora Leigh* was immediately recognized for its formal innovativeness. Barrett Browning herself initially conceived the work as a synthesis transcending the supposed incompatibility between poetry and prose fiction: "But my chief *intention* just now is the writing of a sort of novel-poem—a poem as completely modern as 'Geraldine's Courtship,' running into the midst of our

loosely parallels, and is expressive of, the attempt to reconcile literary work and transformative social action—thematic tensions dramatized in the relationship between Aurora and Romney. I say "loosely parallels" because I don't mean to suggest that the novel, or novel writing, can be compared with "transformative social action" in any direct sense. Novelistic form corresponds to the thematic pole of social action or philanthropy only insofar as it attempts to convey "realistically" the material conditions of the age and to particularize and locate social actors within a "realistic" setting. As we shall see, Barrett Browning actually makes claims for the socially transformative power of poetry itself, but she can properly do so only within a work of poetry that integrates novelistic technique, a work that dramatizes the spiritualizing effect of poetry on character and the failure of other forms of engagement with the social realm.[4]

This chapter explores the significance of Marian Erle to the text's formal and thematic tensions. The flexible figure of Marian Erle in large part enables the text's formal and thematic mediations, insofar as she is seen to be continuous with the category of the poetic as well as symbolic of the social other. As in the case of *David Copperfield*, the artist's enabling self-definition emerges out of a relation to fallenness, though the fact that the artist is in this case a woman produces a considerably more vexed and revisionist depiction of fallenness. And the conception of fallenness as attenuated autonomy takes a very different form than it does in the other works I have examined, connecting expressly to the idea of women's status as "relative creatures." Moreover, even as Aurora assigns Marian a privileged relation to poetry and thereby risks aestheticizing her, she uses the occasion not to reproduce but to interrogate and revise the distorting relation to the other that typifies Victorian inscriptions of impure femininity. By revising her relation to Marian, Aurora at least temporarily moves beyond the stark opposition between aesthetic and intersubjective experience, an opposition that inhabits not only her own conceptions but also the dominant rhetoric of fallen-

---

conventions, & rushing into drawing-rooms & the like 'where angels fear to tread'; & so, meeting face to face & without mask the Humanity of the age, & speaking the truth as I conceive of it, out plainly." Letter from Elizabeth Barrett Barrett to Robert Browning, February 27, 1845, in *The Letters of Robert Browning and Elizabeth Barrett Barrett, 1845–1846* 1:31. Also see letter from Elizabeth Barrett Browning to Mary Russell Mitford, December 30, 1844, in *The Letters of Elizabeth Barrett Browning to Mary Russell Mitford 1836–1854* 3:49.

4. See Dorothy Mermin, *Elizabeth Barrett Browning* 183–224.

ness. But if Aurora confronts the reifying tendencies of the rhetoric of fallenness, she nonetheless fails to address adequately the larger tension between art and philanthropy, even though she is sharply critical of what she construes as Romney's deindividualizing philanthropic relation to Marian and other members of the lower classes. The problem, as we shall see, is that Aurora's concept of intersubjectivity remains restrictively dyadic and hence cannot generate a larger understanding of social plurality and social hierarchy.

Autonomy and Fallenness

In *Aurora Leigh*, Barrett Browning ends up arguing that poetry is the best form of philanthropy: the problem with Romney's view of the world, as he dutifully admits to Aurora upon their reconciliation in Florence, is its subordination of the spiritual to the material. During their twilight interview, Romney recalls and endorses lines Aurora spoke at the age of twenty, when she forcefully declined his marriage proposal:

> "You will not compass your poor ends
> "Of barley-feeding and material ease,
> "Without the poet's individualism
> "To work your universal. It takes a soul
> "To move a body,—it takes a high-souled man
> "To move the masses, even to a cleaner stye:
> "It takes the ideal, to blow an inch inside
> "The dust of the actual: and your Fouriers failed,
> "Because not poets enough to understand
> "That life develops from within."
>   (VIII, 427–36; also see II, 476–85)

Aurora Leigh joins with many industrial novels and other antiutilitarian texts of Victorian social criticism by promoting the transformative power of art itself. Philanthropy, in its attendance merely on the physical and external, remains impotent to work any real change: the cultivation of spirit, not the rearrangement of matter, elevates a degraded humanity. Barrett Browning thus directly engages the materialist/idealist debate that conditioned Victorian discussions of social reform, making appeal to the primacy of the individual soul and extending a romantic emphasis on spirituality deriving from Coleridge and Carlyle. The poem's ending finesses the problem of reconciling philanthropy and art by making art at least the precondition, if not the actual means, of social transformation. And at the very end of the poem, both terms, art and philanthropy, are sublated into a higher form: God's love.

There is another major obstacle to Aurora's acknowledging the virtues of the philanthropic attitude as represented by Romney: it not only subordinates the spiritual to the material but also, precisely as an extension of women's relative status, threatens an already precariously held autonomy. In the poem, both these aspects of philanthropy are linked to prostitution, the first literally, the second figuratively. First of all, *Aurora Leigh* actually suggests that a transformed relation to the material would cure the epidemic of urban prostitution, which for Barrett Browning was a tragedy in and of itself as well as a particularly telling symptom of the age.[5] In a rather startling passage, one that dares to envision an undegraded form of sexual passion, Aurora Leigh attributes prostitution to a rampant materialism that prevents a properly spiritual relation to the body itself. Barrett Browning's text thus reflects the larger connection between materialist thinking and the construction of fallenness by making materialism literally responsible for prostitution. For Aurora, art magnifies a truth "which, fully recognised, would change the world / And shift its morals":

> If man could feel,
> Not one day, in the artist's ecstasy,
> But every day, feast, fast, or working-day,
> The spiritual significance burn through
> The hieroglyphic of material shows,
> Henceforward he would paint the globe with wings,
> And reverence fish and fowl, the bull, the tree,
> And even his very body as a man—
> Which now he counts so vile, that all the towns
> Make offal of their daughters for its use.
>
> (VII, 856–66)

---

5. In a letter to Mrs. Martin during the Crimean War, Barrett Browning wrote, "There are worse plagues, deeper griefs, dreader wounds than the physical. What of the forty thousand wretched women in this city? The silent writhing of them is to me more appalling than the roar of cannons." *The Letters of Elizabeth Barrett Browning* 2:213; see also Mermin, *Elizabeth Barrett Browning* 213.

The converted Romney expresses a more extreme version of this same view, virtually equating a materialist philanthropy with prostitution. When the rich and the poor alike care only to satisfy their "gross needs,"

> "Why that's so far from virtue, only vice
> Can find excuse for't that makes libertines,
> And slurs our cruel streets from end to end
> With eighty thousand women in one smile,
> Who only smile at night beneath the gas."
>   (VIII, 411–15)[6]

Although Marian Erle does not become a prostitute, we must view her story in light of Barrett Browning's idea that materialist philanthropy actively promotes an epidemic of prostitution. That is, even though Marian's overdetermined fate can be variously attributed to a degraded background, poverty, or the malevolence of bad women (her mother, Lady Waldemar), it remains the case that her ultimate victimization in the brothel of Paris traces in part to Romney's misconceived philanthropy. And of course, as Dorothy Mermin has pointed out, Romney's failure as a reformer implicitly extends to his own efforts to help actual prostitutes.[7]

The figurative form of fallenness as compromised autonomy, however, assumes a greater prominence in the poem than does the concern with urban prostitution. A disavowal of dependence inaugurates the poem itself: Aurora Leigh announces in the first lines that she will no longer be writing for "others' uses" but instead for her own "better self" (I, 3, 4). The rejection of Romney's proposal issues in part out of the conviction that marriage *is* prostitution: "If I married him, / I should not dare to call my soul my own / Which so he had bought and paid for" (II, 785–87). And in the long interlude on aesthetics in Book V, Aurora describes other-directed acts of writing as a form of feminine vice. After initially lamenting that her art must fail if it fails to move one man (Romney), Aurora in a

6. Ironically, Romney proves his point by using one of the statistics circulating through the prostitution accounts, which were themselves part of the scientific approach to social and moral life that Romney here decries. And the statistic he provides is by far the largest one that appears in those accounts; it was in fact frequently disputed, others holding the number to be far closer to 8,000. For a different statistic cited by Barrett Browning herself, see n. 5.

7. Mermin, *Elizabeth Barrett Browning* 203. Also see *Aurora Leigh* III, 550–52.

characteristic recoil asserts that the need to commend oneself to a chosen audience of one "proves a certain impotence in art": "This vile woman's way / Of trailing garments shall not trip me up: / I'll have no traffic with the personal thought / In Art's pure temple" (V, 44, 59–62).

In a similar vein, though without the same imagery of feminine seduction, she denigrates contemporary drama and decides not to write in that genre, precisely because it must adapt itself to "the standard of the public taste" and learn "to carry and fetch / The fashions of the day to please the day" (V, 270, 272–73). Actually the shift in imagery signals an important distinction between two kinds of compromised autonomy: the first version of "fallen" art caters to an audience of one, the second to the whole degraded "public." The woman artist, that is, must not only avoid a general tendency within contemporary art to lower itself to the public taste, but also guard against a peculiarly feminine tendency, "the vile woman's way" of subordinating her art to the judgment of "some one friend" (V, 49).

Aurora Leigh's emphasis on feminine artistic autonomy stems from Barrett Browning's awareness of the obstacles facing women writers within a culture and a literary tradition that defined womanhood precisely in terms of its other-directedness. Aurora's claim to self-sufficiency when she rejects Romney's proposal of marriage rests on the conviction that in order to become an artist she must not subordinate herself to the needs and desires of another: "I too have my vocation,—work to do" (II, 455). According to Aurora, Romney cannot acknowledge this conviction because he, like the masculine culture at large, does not accord full moral agency to women:

> "You misconceive the question like a man,
> Who sees a woman as the complement
> Of his sex merely. You forget too much
> That every creature, female as the male,
> Stands single in responsible act and thought
> As also in birth and death."
>
> (II, 434–39)

As in the other works I examine in this book, fallenness signifies attenuated autonomy, but the terms of the model have shifted to accommodate a specifically feminist critique and aspiration. Barrett Browning does perceive certain nongendered contemporary threats to human autonomy, particularly the threat that materialism poses to the purity and freedom of the individual soul. Indeed, she apprehends the negative effects of modern industrial society in fundamentally Christian and romantic terms. Ideally, she would like to see the soul released from, transformed out of, its material fetters; and she believes the artist is especially equipped to minister to the spiritual needs of a fallen, materialistic age. This release of the soul will be a release into a kind of freedom, a finding of one's full powers, even though it will entail submission to God. For Barrett Browning, this essentially Christian and humanist vision of the self is not gender-specific. However, it is also clear that women must guard against particular threats to autonomy, ones that jeopardize this potential empowerment of the soul. As Aurora's statements to Romney emphasize, women must claim their right to vocation and discrete moral selfhood. Thus a gender-specific struggle for autonomy accompanies the more general call for spiritual rejuvenation.

The gender-specific claim to autonomy bases itself not simply on a critique of women's "relative" or "complementary" status but also on the perception that in both art and the everyday practical world women are frequently objectified by means of a distinctly aestheticizing gaze. As critics have amply shown, the problem of woman's objectification appears in poems from all phases of Barrett Browning's career, from the early ballads to *Sonnets from the Portuguese*, *Aurora Leigh*, and beyond.[8] Within the ideology of Victorian culture, women are typically objects for rather than creators of poetry: they are assimilated, in all manner of ways, to the work of art itself, and if they are poets, to their own works of art. One can read *Aurora Leigh* as a long struggle on the part of the poet heroine to become, in Dorothy Mermin's words, "a subject rather than object in relation to Romney"—and indeed, such a reading provides a clearer explanation for what many consider an excessive treatment of Romney at the end.[9] Blind, he can no longer treat Aurora as mere object, ornament, or spectacle. In a sense, for Barrett Browning the woman's tendency to prostitute herself to a single other involves a kind of self-objectification; this realization is what provokes Aurora Leigh's

8. This is a central issue in Mermin's book as well as in Helen Cooper, *Elizabeth Barrett Browning: Woman and Artist*.
9. Mermin, *Elizabeth Barrett Browning* 188.

rejection of her own self-chastisement for not properly "moving" her audience.

Yet despite the manifold ways in which autonomy emerges as an imperative for the woman artist, throughout the story Aurora also struggles *against* isolation and autonomy, partly out of a deep-seated desire for romantic and familial affections but also because of the pretensions to social action lodged within Barrett Browning's project. To remain outside of love means failing to achieve the human connection necessary to an art that wants to appropriate the role of philanthropy, which is founded on the proper recognition of, and concern for, others. The crucial book of the poem in this regard is Book VI, in which Aurora undergoes the experience—reencountering Marian—that brings her out of an isolation that is both emotionally and aesthetically debilitating. This encounter constitutes a thinking-through of the tension between aesthetic isolation and social responsiveness. Aurora generates a dialectical interplay between aesthetic and intersubjective experience, and she does so precisely through a reconceptualization of the relation between herself, as a woman artist, and Marian, as a fallen woman. In doing so, she significantly revises the dominant rhetoric of fallenness.

Poetry and Philanthropy

In retrieving Marian Erle from a fate whose obscurity is defined through its typicality (the police of Paris cannot find her because there are so many like her), Aurora Leigh addresses within the story what Barrett Browning's depiction of Marian Erle seeks to do in larger terms: she insists on particularizing the fallen woman, on rescuing her from a set of conventions that obscure the perception of her as an individual. At the same time, Aurora's relation to Marian serves as a comment on Romney's previous relation to Marian and in effect revises the terms of interclass encounter that his marriage proposal expresses. Thus two concerns come to focus on Marian Erle: the problem of the depiction of women in art (and by extension, the aestheticizing objectification of women that finds its most extreme manifestation in the fallen woman) and the problem of one's proper relation to the living subjects of philanthropy.

For Romney, Marian serves as the symbolic representative of the lower class. His proposal to her conceives of their marriage as a symbolic healing of the division between the classes:

> "Marian, I being born
> What men call noble, and you, issued from
> The noble people,—though the tyrannous sword,
> Which pierced Christ's heart, has cleft the world in twain
> 'Twixt class and class, opposing rich to poor,
> Shall *we* keep parted? Not so. Let us lean
> And strain together rather, each to each,
> Compress the red lips of this gaping wound
> As far as two souls can."
>
> (IV, 120–28)

Aurora Leigh, on the other hand, approves the impending marriage between her cousin and the sempstress because she honors the particularity of the love relation, not its attempt at symbolic recon-ciliation. It pleases her to suppose Romney "fanatical in love"; she honors his "right in choosing" a wife from the lower class because she perceives Marian as "good, true, noble" (IV, 296, 320, 313). Aurora wishes to uphold a position that is at once romantic and meritocratic: she focuses on Marian's individual worthiness rather than her affiliation with Romney's "noble people." Of course this focus entails separating Marian from her class and elevating her to the status of the Leighs or the "sublime Vandykes" (IV, 309). If Romney sees Marian as representative, Aurora sees her as excep-tional: the one brackets individuality, the other abstracts the indi-vidual from her surroundings.

Romney's position to a certain extent recalls the proposal he made to Aurora, as well as Aurora's subsequent anger at his conceiving her simply as "a wife to help [his] ends,—in her no end" (II, 403). During her own proposal scene, Aurora's complaint is that Romney dangerously neglects the individual soul in his privileging of social "diagrams" and "formal universals" (III, 744, 747). Romney's com-plaint against Aurora, on the other hand, is that, as a woman, she can "generalise / Oh, nothing,— not even grief!" (II, 183–84). Women remain impotent to comprehend or influence the world, according to Romney, because they cannot think of misery in the aggregate; unable to perceive systemic suffering, they cannot properly work for social change. Their model for charity demands proximity and generates a dangerous empathy, one that ironically obliterates any proper understanding of the actual social condition of others:

> "The human race
> To you means, such a child, or such a man,
> You saw one morning waiting in the cold,
> Beside that gate, perhaps. You gather up
> A few such cases, and when strong sometimes
> Will write of factories and of slaves, as if
> Your father were a negro, and your son
> A spinner in the mills. All's yours and you,
> All, coloured with your blood, or otherwise
> Just nothing to you. Why, I call you hard
> To general suffering."
>
> (II, 189–99)

In Romney's account, the woman's relation to suffering humanity either reduces to a sympathetic response to a single other or takes the form of an imaginative act in which the familial analogy gives life to, or "colours," the ostensible object of concern, in this case the negro or the spinner. Women require the actual presence of the sufferers, but only that they may revise them into familiar or familial presences. Romney's description thus implies that Aurora will remain incapable of any true recognition of those outside her immediate context because, paradoxically, she will inevitably respond to strangers only insofar as she can familiarize them out of their social particularity. As we will see, Aurora's experience with Marian in Paris in fact emerges out of a need to come to terms with Romney's accusations of her distance from "the human race."

Aurora first seeks out Marian Erle when she hears from Lady Waldemar of Romney's engagement to the sempstress. The poet's journey to the working-class neighborhood of Saint Margaret's Court is depicted as bold and dangerous; indeed, the description of Aurora's initial approach, alone and "close-veiled," casts the urban environment, and the lower-class individuals who people it, as threatening, vicious, and demonic. A sick child jeers at Aurora as she passes. She encounters a frightening, abusive, painted woman: "a woman, rouged / Upon the angular cheek-bones, kerchief torn, / Thin dangling locks, and flat lascivious mouth, / Cursed at a window both ways, in and out, / By turns some bed-rid creature and myself" (III, 764–65, 768). And when Aurora, from uncertain motives, responds to the curses by emptying her purse upon the stones, "the whole court / Went boiling, bubbling up, from all its doors / And windows" (III, 784–86).

In response to this threat of engulfment, Aurora plunges into Marian's house, gropes her way up a dark, dilapidated stair, knocks on an attic door, and is met on the threshold by Marian's "ineffable face" (III, 798). The elevated refuge provides immediate relief, and Marian contrasts vividly with the phantasms of the lower court:

> She touched me with her face and with her voice,
> This daughter of the people. Such soft flowers
> From such rough roots? The people, under there,
> Can sin so, curse so, look so, smell so . . . faugh!
> Yet have such daughters?
>
> (III, 805–9)

The encounter with the "pure" Marian is set off against the experience of a threatening, indistinguishable otherness (the court "bubbling up") and a painted Janus face that provocatively positions itself on the boundary between home and street. Marian provides refuge because she is at once distinct (a discernible "face") and "ineffable" (not painted or otherwise eclipsed by representation). The two aspects of Marian's protected status reveal her dual function here: she is the antidote to the faceless threat of the lower class as well as the counterpoint to the distortions of femininity as spectacle or aestheticized object (here demonized through the figure of the vicious painted woman).

Constituting Marian as the antidote to a faceless lower class involves a powerful negation—as the "faugh!" makes blatantly clear. In fleeing to Marian, that is, Aurora escapes rather than revises her objectifying and fantasmatic relation to the lower class. This fantasmatic relation in fact reappears with even greater intensity in Book IV, when Aurora recounts the coming together of rich and poor at the ill-fated wedding ceremony. Barrett Browning's heightened rhetoric reflects conventional middle-class fears about the working classes and participates in a common compensatory move to obliterate the distinct subjectivity of the poor whenever they are apprehended as a potential force or threatening crowd.[10] We encountered this not atypical Victorian rhetoric in *Dombey and Son*, where Dickens cast potentially retributive agents as mere chimerical subjects. Barrett Browning's rhetoric is quite extreme: the "people" become "the humours of the peccant social wound," descriptively assimilated to death, decay, and disease: "You'd suppose / A finished generation, dead of plague, / Swept outward from their graves into the sun" (IV, 544, 547–50). Barrett Browning accords distinct embodiment to the poor urban dwellers, but only as animate corpses. Even then, she quickly revises them into a seething, inhuman mass ("They clogged the streets, they oozed into the church / In a dark slow stream, like blood" [IV, 553–54]). This strategy of defacement becomes strikingly explicit some lines later, when "an ugly crest of faces" seemingly erupts out of the "crammed mass":

> Faces? . . . phew,
> We'll call them vices, festering to despairs,
> Or sorrows, petrifying to vices: not
> A finger-touch of God left whole on them,
> All ruined, lost—the countenance worn out
> As the garment, the will dissolute as the act,
> The passions loose and draggling in the dirt
> To trip a foot up at the first free step!
> Those, faces? 'twas as if you had stirred up hell
> To heave its lowest dreg-fiends uppermost
> In fiery swirls of slime. . . .
>
> (IV, 579–89)

Given Aurora's investment in the face-to-face encounter, this explicit defacement of the poor is extreme and reactive indeed. The association with the rhetoric of fallenness is clear. Vice is defacement, obliteration of identity ("ruined" and "lost," the faces of the poor are as the faded finery of the streetwalker, "worn out"). Purity, on the other hand, manifests itself in the protected identity of the "ineffable" or distinct face. Opposed to the terrifying facelessness of

10. Cora Kaplan argues that Elizabeth Barrett Browning's descriptions of the poor are based not on actual experience but on reading; she in particular notes the way Barrett Browning reworks scenes from Charles Kingsley's *Alton Locke*. Kaplan, Introduction 32–33. Deirdre David similarly argues that Barrett Browning's descriptions of the poor in *Aurora Leigh* are "the hellish distillation of her readings in the Victorian discourse of the poor." Deirdre David, *Intellectual Women and Victorian Patriarchy* 125.

the threatening crowd, here we find not, as before, the "ineffable" face of the unsullied Marian, but rather the protected and prevailing identity of the upper-class man. As elsewhere in Victorian literature and culture, fallenness is constructed in opposition not only to feminine purity but also to normative masculinity, which is characterized by mastery and control. When the crowd erupts on Marian's behalf, assuming her failure to appear means that Rommey has ruined her, Aurora seeks salvation and self-stabilization precisely through the finding of Romney's "masterful pale face": "I struggled to precipitate myself / Head-foremost to the rescue of my soul / In that white face" (IV, 850, 874–76). Whereas elsewhere concrete intersubjective recognition serves as an imperative and ideal, here Aurora negotiates class anxiety through violent strategies of defacement and selective acts of self-serving recognition.

As we shall see, Aurora's use of Marian to challenge the depiction of women in art and to revise conventional literary fallenness manifests a politics more progressive and reconstructive than that expressed in the reactive rhetoric of class, perhaps because she is more sensitive to those objectifying tendencies to which she herself, as a woman, has fallen victim. Romney treats Aurora as a muse, a spectacle; her aunt subjects her to a form of scrutiny that is cold, distant, scientific. As Aurora writes of the tense days after Romney's proposal, when her aunt watches every move she makes, "Being observed, / When observation is not sympathy, / Is just being tortured" (II, 866–68). As this quote implies, the ultimate aim is never entirely to avoid being seen, but rather to suggest how concrete intersubjective relations get distorted through objectification. Ideally, one is observed with the sympathy of a nonobjectifying gaze.[11] We first encounter such a gaze in Aurora's mother: the very first allusion to the mother in fact construes her gaze as a contradiction of the admonitions and interdictions she voices:

> But still I catch my mother at her post
> Beside the nursery door, with finger up,

11. It's interesting that Barrett Browning often evokes a nonvisual sense when describing an ideal encountering of another's face. Hence the description of Aurora's father's first sight of Aurora's mother: "A face flashed like a cymbal on his face / And shook with silent clanguor brain and heart, / Transfiguring him to music" (I, 87–89). Or Marian on Romney: "When he looked / It was as if he spoke, and when he spoke / He sang perhaps" (III, 1170–72).

"Hush, hush—here's too much noise!" while her sweet eyes
Leap forward, taking part against her word
In the child's riot.

(I, 15–19)

And the loss of the mother marks the loss of her "rare" gaze, a loss
exemplified further in the replacement of the mother's living face
by the haunting, uncanny portrait of her corpse (I, 30).

Marian's "ineffable face" becomes the antithesis of the portrait of
the dead mother, which as a painted corpse associates aestheticization with death. That the painter took his likeness from an already
dead model suggests that, for Barrett Browning, even ostensibly
"realist" representations of women, such as portraiture, employ a
dead iconography, one that forecloses the possibility of representing
a living individual.[12] But the portrait of the mother, a dense symbolic
field comprising every feminine type from angel to fiend, does more
than convey a negative or reifying mode of representing women. It
comes to inhabit, strangely, all of Aurora's own imaginative acts,
serving as the hovering referent for every aesthetic experience: "And
as I grew / In years, I mixed, confused, unconsciously, / Whatever
I last read or heard or dreamed, / Abhorrent, admirable, beautiful,
/ Pathetical, or ghastly, or grotesque, / With still that face" (I, 146–
51). Acts of the imagination conjure up, play upon, the image of
the fantasmatic painted face; the living encounter remains unrepre-
sentable, protected, "ineffable." While elsewhere Aurora conceives
poetry and art as spiritualizing forces that speak to and transform
the human soul, here the aestheticization of women leaves painted
corpses in its wake and generates a stark opposition between representation and life.

The apprehension of a deanimating power of representation is,
in the case of *Aurora Leigh*, profoundly overdetermined. It traces not
only to Barrett Browning's critique of feminine objectification in art
but also to anxieties about the isolating effects of artistic activity and
a perceived tension between aesthetic experience and intersubjec-

---

12. I don't mean here to suggest in any way that one could produce an unmediated
representation but simply to show that, for Barrett Browning, conventional representations of women are dead types, that representations of women need revision
so as to better portray a living individuality.

tivity, between reading texts and encountering people.[13] (As we shall see, this tension is related but by no means identical to the tension between art and philanthropy.) Like other texts I have analyzed, *Aurora Leigh* expresses fears that intersubjectivity itself will collapse into a model of reading, that representation will obscure, eclipse, or fix the self. Part of this fear stems from Barrett Browning's Carlylean stance on the need to break free of, or transcend, the encrustations of the literal and the material: the soul must be rescued from the falsifying texts that layer it. It has become a "palimpsest," an "obscene text" that only dimly reveals traces of "the old Scripture" (I, 826, 829, 832). Barrett Browning also actively denigrates a readerly model of intersubjectivity when Aurora complains that Lady Waldemar treats her like a book:

> Sweet heaven, she takes me up
> As if she had fingered me and dog-eared me
> And spelled me by the fireside half a life!
> She knows my turns, my feeble points.—What then?
> The knowledge of a thing implies the thing;
> Of course, she found *that* in me, she saw *that*,
> Her pencil underscored *this* for a fault,
> And I, still ignorant. Shut the book up,—close!
> And crush that beetle in the leaves.
>
> (V, 1053–61)

Reading Aurora like a book is presented as an underhanded and malevolent act on Lady Waldemar's part, a surreptitious attempt to discover and underscore hidden weaknesses. Moreover, in reading Aurora's weaknesses, she more deeply inscribes them: her act of reading fixes them, while Aurora remains "still ignorant."

Barrett Browning thus criticizes what the speaker in "Jenny" for the most part uncritically enacts: the aspects of violent inscription involved in objectifying acts of reading others. Still, *Aurora Leigh* joins "Jenny" in ascribing this negative readerly attitude to women

---

13. Of course there are aspects of Barrett Browning's own life that might have rendered acute the gap between reading and social intercourse. Her years spent as an isolated invalid at Wimpole Street caused her to refer to herself as a "blind poet": "How willingly I would as a poet exchange some of this lumbering, ponderous, helpless knowledge of books, for some experience of life & man." Letter from Elizabeth Barrett Barrett to Robert Browning, March 10, 1845, in *The Letters of Robert Browning and Elizabeth Barrett Barrett* 1:41.

of dubious respectability. Marian, for example, claims to be a "worthier mate" for Romney than ladies who are "wooed in silk among their learned books": "I shall set myself to read his eyes, / Till such grow plainer to me than the French / To wisest ladies" (IV, 230, 231–34). Reading here is metonymically indicated by reading French, an activity of questionable virtue, evoking the forbidden delights of the scandalous novel and the amorous epistle. Illiteracy becomes the guarantee of a "plain" reading of the eyes and face, one not corrupted by the distractions and seductions of textual reading.

But if Marian serves as counterpoint to what is construed as the distorting and deanimating power of representation, then why does Aurora insist on revising and translating the story Marian tells her during their first meeting? Why does Aurora deprive Marian of her voice and transform her into a story of her own making, announcing that she will retell Marian's narrative "with fuller utterance, / As coloured and confirmed in after times / By others and herself too" (III, 828–30)? Aurora retells Marian's story, we soon learn, so as to incorporate not only details gathered later but also, strangely, the refinements that Marian's facial expressions add to her imperfectly narrated tale:

> She told the tale with simple, rustic turns,—
> Strong leaps of meaning in her sudden eyes
> That took the gaps of any imperfect phrase
> Of the unschooled speaker: I have rather writ
> The thing I understood so, than the thing
> I heard so.
>
> (IV, 151–56)

This is no attempt at sterile transcription, such as we saw in Dickens's ritual recordings of the women's stories at Urania Cottage. Here the eyes communicate "leaps of meaning"; the "fuller utterance" originates with Marian's face; the look completes the text. Ironically, Aurora's appropriation of Marian's voice aims to preserve a spoken narrative, whose mere transcription would empty out the meaningfulness embodied in the expressive face. What this retelling implies, however, in vivid contrast to the apprehension of "dead" representation and distorted readings, is that poetry is an appropriate analogue for the expressiveness of the face, that poetic language can itself convey the elusive and nonlinguistic aspects of embodied subjectivity.

And yet we soon discover that the "ineffable face" can itself be attributed to the power of poetry. As Aurora tells it, Marian's own curiously unmediated form of early reading— snatching fragments of books from an itinerant pedlar and folding them within her breast to pore over later—literally produced the contours and motions of her face:

> And thus she had grown, this Marian Erle of ours,
> To no book-learning,—she was ignorant
> Of authors,—not in the earshot of the things
> Outspoken o'er the heads of common men
> By men who are uncommon,—but within
> The cadenced hum of such, and capable
> Of catching from the fringes of the wing
> Some fragmentary phrases, here and there,
> Of that fine music,—which, being carried in
> To her soul, had reproduced itself afresh
> In finer motions of the lips and lids.
>
> (III, 998–1008)

This passage, like the previous one, foregrounds the phenomenology of the face, though in a very different way. In the first passage, the expressiveness of the eyes represents the fact that subjectivity exceeds the limits of any linguistic utterance (and it implies the importance of the other's presence, or a poetic version of that presence, to render communication complete). In the second quote, however, Marian Erle's face is itself a paradoxically "fresh reproduction" of the literary fragments that have, through no conscious act of her own, passed through the smithy of her soul. Does this mean that she has, like the painted corpse, been reduced to the status of aesthetic object? This is one of the poem's thorniest points. The depiction of Marian's peculiar aesthetic education exemplifies Barrett Browning's conception of the potentially formative power of poetry over the living soul, her conviction that this power is more lifesustaining than any material satisfactions. Yet by creating Marian's own face as a literary reproduction, Barrett Browning recapitulates the assimilation of women to works of art and in fact participates in the tendency to cast the fallen woman as a written text. In this passage, Barrett Browning's poetic philanthropy runs up against her critique of lifeless aestheticization and feminine objectification.

Still, it is here that we see the beginnings of an attempt to set the living encounter and aesthetic experience in dialogue with one another. Written poetry can animate, rather than fix or obscure, the living face and the spoken narrative. What here emerges only fleetingly will achieve fuller elaboration in the section set in Paris, when Aurora reexperiences and more directly confronts her anxiety that intersubjectivity and aesthetic experience—people and texts—are at odds with one another, that the one always negates the other.

Faces and Fantasies

During her stay in Paris en route from London to Italy, Aurora suddenly acknowledges a need to study more closely the humanity to which she has had such a fantasmatic relation. Walking the streets of Paris, she vows to remain among the urban crowd and not retreat to the poetic pastoral: "I would be bold and bear / To look into the swarthiest face of things, / For God's sake who has made them" (VI, 147–49). Aurora's insistence on the importance of looking steadily on urban humanity leads her to propose art and philanthropy as parallel vocations:

> Let us pray
> God's grace to keep God's image in repute
> That so, the poet and philanthropist
> (Even I and Romney) may stand side by side,
> Because we both stand face to face with men,
> Contemplating the people in the rough,
> Yet each so follow a vocation, his
> And mine.
>
> (VI, 197–204)

Standing "face to face" emerges as equally a poetic and a philanthropic ideal. But what precisely is meant by standing "face to face"? Oddly, it is not a reciprocal activity: the ensuing line defines it exclusively from the perspective of the poet and the philanthropist, as a removed act of contemplation. Moreover, what is being contemplated is not discrete individuals, but "the people in the rough."

And when Aurora does ostensibly concretize "the people," through the figure of the "hungry beggar boy," she does not respond to his material situation but rather endows his inner soul with poetry, "both flowers and firmaments, / And surging seas and aspectable stars" (VI, 194–95). To acknowledge the individual soul one must see past the material; for Aurora, this visionary act is itself philanthropic. Not surprisingly, then, she shifts away from the idea that Romney's vocation parallels her own in form and importance, wondering instead whether "A larger metaphysics might not help / Our physics, a completer poetry / Adjust our daily life and vulgar wants" (VI, 206–8). Speaking on behalf of poets and prophets, she "thunder[s] down" that "Virtue's in the *word!*" (VI, 218).

Just at this point, as she elaborates yet again on the need to transcend material lack in the name of the spirit, Marian's long-lost face intervenes ("God! what face is that?" [VI, 226]), interrupting her thought and hitting her own face like a physical blow ("What a face, what a look, what a likeness! Full on mine / The sudden blow of it came down" [VI, 232–33]).

> It was as if a meditative man
> Were dreaming out a summer afternoon
> And watching gnats a-prick upon a pond,
> When something floats up suddenly, out there,
> Turns over . . . a dead face, known once alive . . .
> So old, so new! it would be dreadful now
> To lose the sight and keep the doubt of this:
> He plunges—ha! he has lost it in the splash.
>
> I plunged—I tore the crowd up, either side,
> And rushed on, forward, forward, after her.
> Her? whom?
>
> (VI, 235–45)

This interesting reworking of Wordsworth's drowned man episode in Book V of *The Prelude* registers a deep anxiety over the privileging of metaphysics over physics, poetry over social interaction. Aurora has been meditating specifically on the virtue of the word, the spiritualizing powers of language and of art. The meditation, which completes the flight from "the swarthiest face of things," is then interrupted by a corpselike face. What do we make of this? If we look to the passage in Wordsworth, which recounts the poet's view-

ing of the drowned man retrieved out of Esthwaite Lake, we can
begin to get some handle on what is going on here.

> Seeking I knew not what, I chanced to cross
> One of those open fields, which, shaped like ears,
> Make green peninsulas on Esthwaite's Lake.
> Twilight was coming on, yet through the gloom
> I saw distinctly on the opposite shore
> A heap of garments, left as I supposed
> By one who there was bathing. Long I watched,
> But no one owned them; meanwhile the calm lake
> Grew dark, with all the shadows on its breast,
> And now and then a fish up-leaping snapped
> The breathless stillness. The succeeding day—
> Those unclaimed garments telling a plain tale—
> Went there a company, and in their boat
> Sounded with grappling-irons and long poles:
> At length, the dead man, 'mid that beauteous scene
> Of trees and hills and water, bolt upright
> Rose with his ghastly face, a spectre shape—
> Of terror even. And yet no vulgar fear,
> Young as I was, a child not nine years old,
> Possessed me, for my inner eye had seen
> Such sights before among the shining streams
> Of fairyland, the forests of romance—
> Thence came a spirit hallowing what I saw
> With decoration and ideal grace,
> A dignity, a smoothness, like the works
> Of Grecian art and purest poetry.
>   (1805, V, 456–81)[14]

For Wordsworth, the encounter with the "ghastly face" of the corpse
occurs within a pastoral calmness and follows on an uncertain "seeking." This "ghastly face," whose manner of appearance seems oddly
animate (the corpse rises "bolt upright"), causes a shock that is then
swiftly recuperated into the terms of romance, art, and "purest poetry." The corpse need cause no fear once transmuted into, hallowed
by, art. The shock of death, materiality, and otherness is thus contained within a spiritualizing aesthetics.

14. William Wordsworth, *The Prelude 1798, 1805, 1850* 174–176.

Things take shape differently in Barrett Browning's poem. Aurora comes upon the face of a living person in the midst of a crowded city street, but she compares it to coming upon the face of a drowned person in a pastoral setting. We must interpret this passage in light of Aurora's earlier vow not to retreat to the poetic pastoral. In casting her own meditativeness as pastoral ("dreaming out a summer afternoon," the imagined man watches "gnats a-prick upon a pond"), Aurora acknowledges that she has abstracted herself from the earlier felt demand to recognize and confront social otherness. She has moved from the intention to "be bold and bear / To look into the swarthiest face of things" to a position in which she "thunder[s] down" as poet and prophet. The flight to a distanced vantage point recalls not only the scramble from Saint Margaret's boiling court to Marian's attic refuge in Book III but also Aurora's own London home, where the power to write emanated from, was enabled by, the evening ritual of watching "the city perish in the mist / Like Pharaoh's armaments in the deep Red Sea" (III, 196–97).

If in the analogy of the meditative man Aurora is somehow acknowledging her flight into the safe retreat of the pastoral, how then do we read the sudden intervention of Marian's corpselike face? Is Marian's face jolting Aurora back into a more direct perception of otherness, one that forces a more considered understanding of those material conditions Aurora speaks so lightly of in her privileging of the spiritual? After all, Marian has been raped, borne the child of that rape, and now lives in poverty, feeling "dead" in every respect save her maternal role. Or, alternately, is Marian's reappearance at this particular juncture, and Aurora's swift and single-minded pursuit of her, repeating the earlier flight, in Saint Margaret's Court, from a lower class perceived as threatening and all too proximate?

To answer these questions we need to consider the several issues that come together both in the depiction of Marian and in this pivotal passage. For, as I mentioned earlier, Barrett Browning uses Marian not only to explore the dilemmas that attend the philanthropic attitude but also to expose problems in mediating between aesthetic and intersubjective experience, particularly as these problems affect encounters with the fallen. It is for this latter reason, I suggest, that Aurora figures the encounter with Marian as a scene of reading. The meditative man is interrupted suddenly by a face that not only "floats up" but "turns over," like the page of a book. And as if to carry through this sense of the figure, Aurora writes, "I plunged—

I *tore* the crowd up, either side, / and rushed on, forward, forward, after her" (VI, 243–44; my emphasis). Unlike Wordsworth, Aurora does not naturalize and transmute the shock of the encounter through an appeal to romance and reading; rather, she breaks past the readerly attitude and rushes in pursuit of the living face. That Aurora likens this living face to a corpse's face is less a reflection of Marian's new status than it is a symptom of Aurora's own anxious guilt. For Aurora fears that the retreat into poetic meditation involves the negation of the living encounter, turning live faces into corpses, or mere pages. The appearance of Marian's face thus functions differently here than it does in the Saint Margaret's Court scene. No longer the site of refuge, Marian's face actively disrupts Aurora's retreat into the aesthetic. Indeed, in this scene Aurora is reconfronting her own unsatisfactory "use" of Marian as a story that needs to be retold and as the product of literary fragments she (Marian) only half understands.[15]

Aurora's pursuit of Marian fails. Losing her in the crowd, she stops and wildly looks in all directions. Only when someone bumps into her is she jolted out of her frantic state. Dazed, she wonders whether she might not have imagined seeing Marian in the first place. For a second time, then, an act of the imagination (in this case "fantasy"; in the first, "contemplation") is interrupted by the actual, experienced here as the undeniable facticity of another person:

> We shape a figure of our fantasy,
> Call nothing something, and run after it
> And lose it, lose ourselves too in the search,
> Till clash against us comes a somebody.
>
> (VI, 285–88)

Perhaps, then, the face that seemed to hit her own was only imagined. But, after continued reflection, Aurora rejects this possibility:

> those eyes,
> To-day, I do remember, saw me too,
> As I saw them, with conscious lids astrain
> In recognition. Now a fantasy,

15. Interestingly, Marian was the product of *torn* pages (*torn* appears twice in the depiction of the pedlar). See III, 975, 980.

> A simple shade of image of the brain,
> Is merely passive, does not retro-act,
> Is seen, but sees not.
>
> (VI, 325–31)

The living face is opposed to the subjective fancy. The other's recognition of the self, the act of looking back, cannot be assimilated into fantasy or ever fully appropriated. Moreover, the disruption of solipsistic fantasy through intersubjective recognition then in turn disrupts the act of writing itself. Aurora imagines that, Marian being found, she ought to write to Romney, but a fuller remembrance of what she saw in seeing Marian stops her short:

> My pen fell,
> My hands struck sharp together, as hands do
> Which hold at nothing. Can I write to *him*
> A half-truth? can I keep my own soul blind
> To the other half, . . . the worse?
>
> (VI, 334–38)

We learn that Aurora has suppressed something she saw peripherally, "not hid so well beneath the scanty shawl" (VI, 345). It is a child, an indicting emblem of Marian's impurity.

When Aurora writes, "My pen fell," she clearly refers to the act of letter writing; but at a deeper level the act of writing out her own story is being affected. Indeed, reencountering Marian in Paris coincides with *Aurora Leigh*'s important shift from retrospective narration to the diary form of installments. The first five books of the poem are written by Aurora on the verge of her departure for Italy, and they recount her life up to that point. The next four books, beginning with her arrival in Paris, are written in installments, as an ongoing account. But a total collapse of the text into the present act of writing occurs precisely at the moment that Marian is encountered. Indeed, when Aurora actually finds Marian, she experiences difficulty writing: "I'll write about her, presently. / My hand's a-tremble, as I had just caught up / My heart to write with, in the place of it" (VI, 415–17).

The encounter with Marian in Paris works toward a complicated dialectical act. The foregrounding of the process of writing makes it clear that Barrett Browning does not want to rest with some simple

opposition of imaginative acts of reading and writing to actual encounters with other people. Ultimately, the appeal of the other both
checks and prompts the aesthetic attitude. When Aurora actually
locates Marian, it happens unexpectedly: she is wandering through
the flower market, "musing, with the artist's eye, / That keeps the
shade-side of the thing it loves, / Half-absent, whole-observing" (VI,
427–29). Aurora has entered a mood of aesthetic watchfulness, one
more open than her earlier isolating contemplation (though this
openness is doubtless enabled by the fact that she is observing flowers, not people). As before, the encounter occurs with suddenness
and a powerful immediacy: Marian's face turns round "so close upon
[Aurora] that [she] felt the sigh / It turned with" (VI, 440–41). The
strategy of interruption and surprise that Barrett Browning employs
at this juncture is significantly dialectic. The "half absent" aesthetic
attitude cannot sustain itself and is importantly superseded by the
scenario of recognition and recovery; this scenario then serves to
prompt, becomes the occasion for, a renewed and heightened act
of writing.

This model revises the one in which the portrait of the dead mother
serves as dense symbolic field drawing in everything Aurora reads,
hears, or imagines.[16] Yet the productive interplay suggested by this
sequence does not hold, precisely because of Marian's own status
as a mother figure. The dialectical approach to intersubjectivity and
aesthetic experience gives way to an idealized version of the intersubjective sublime, the perfect communion of two ineffable faces,
exemplified in Marian's relation to her child:

> Self-forgot, cast out of self,
> And drowning in the transport of the sight,
> Her whole pale passionate face, mouth, forehead, eyes,
> One gaze, she stood: then, slowly as he smiled
> She smiled too, slowly, smiling unaware,
> And drawing from his countenance to hers
> A fainter red, as if she watched a flame
> And stood in it a-glow.
>
> (VI, 604–11)

16. It also can be set against the important passage in which poetic inspiration is
depicted as sexual subjugation by a male muse. See III, 121–43.

Through Marian, Aurora is herself able to experience the ecstatic encounter: the "dewy kiss" in which "the whole child's face at once / [dissolves] on [hers]" (VII, 948, 949–50). In its ultimate form, as the celebration of privatized merging based on the model of the mother-child dyad, Aurora's relation to Marian transmutes into another flight from the rigors of social interaction and the demands of aesthetic mediation. In this respect, it is telling that at Florence Aurora buys a house on a hill, "a tower which keeps / A post of double observation" over both the valley of the Arno and Mount Morello (VII, 516–17). More important still, Aurora stops writing and even reading, lapsing into a passivity broken only by the reappearance of Romney. What was originally an insistence on Marian's particularity gives way to a conventionalized view of Marian as a representation of divine motherhood, and to a mystical view of intersubjective fusion.[17] As in Gaskell's *Ruth*, the romanticized maternal ideal fails to allow for reciprocal recognition and individuated identity.

During the sequence in Paris, however, Barrett Browning goes beyond the rhetoric of fallenness, reconceiving the relation between art and intersubjectivity and redressing the reifying distortions attending depictions of fallen women. Yet one must keep in mind that Barrett Browning appears to accomplish this reconceptualization at the expense of the lower class. Aurora never gets back to "the swarthiest face of things," never contemplates the people "in the rough": her encounter at the flower market is only with the "flower" of the slums. Moreover, the entire conclusion of the poem subordinates philanthropy to art, casting philanthropy as the imposition of masks onto the conrete particularity of lower-class persons. According to

17. Delores Rosenblum argues in different terms for the centrality of the encounter with Marian to Aurora's development, stressing that the encounter allows for the recovery of the maternal face. Rosenblum focuses primarily on the poem's concern with women's depiction in art: "In *Aurora Leigh*, Barrett Browning confronts the distorting projections—pictures and ghosts—before which women and men fall silent, replacing them with the schema of the apperceptive maternal face that women can reclaim as an authentic face, as they recover an authentic language." Rosenblum, "Face to Face" 327. What lends particular force to Rosenblum's argument about the recognition scene having everything to do with recognizing oneself in the maternal face is the fact that when writing to Romney, Aurora realizes that she saw not only a face but also, peripherally, a child. For a discussion that centers on the regressive quality of Aurora's attempt to retrieve the mother through the rescue of Marian, see Virgina V. Steinmetz, "Images of 'Mother-Want' in Elizabeth Barrett Browning's *Aurora Leigh*."

Romney's account of the revolt at Leigh Hall, the subjects of charity "broke up those waxen masks [he] made them wear, / With fierce contortions of the natural face" (VIII, 891–92). Ultimately, a version of Romney's original complaint against Aurora—that she can't generalize grief—can be leveled against Barrett Browning, who simply cannot imagine the poor as a plurality. She wishes only to retrieve the singular individual from objectification: her conception of intersubjectivity remains exclusionary and dyadic. The love that reconciles all at the end of the poem is primarily "God's love" and "the love of wedded souls" (IX, 881, 882). Romney attempts to include, though only secondarily, filial, fraternal, neighborly, and civic love. Yet when Aurora responds skeptically to these inclusions, he admits that filial love is "thankless," fraternal love is "hard," and, ominously, "the rest is lost" (IX, 894–95).[18]

Nevertheless, Barrett Browning's revisions of the conventional apprehensions of otherness that characterize literary depictions of the fallen are arresting and significant, despite both the class elitism and the regressive appeal to a mystified maternal ideal. Surely it is crucial that after her rape and the redemptive birth of her child, Marian emerges strong enough to narrate her own story; indeed, if Aurora seemed to speak for Marian when she first told her story in Book III, that incident only sets further into relief Marian's appropriation of voice at precisely that juncture when a woman is conventionally perceived to be "lost." In vindicating herself to the suspicious Aurora, Marian emerges as intensely self-reliant and utterly convinced of her own innocence. She was not "seduced," she asserts, but rather "murdered" (VI, 770, 771). She powerfully elaborates the story of her own victimization and claims her right of innocence and her right to motherhood, thereby bringing Aurora to the point of utter contrition for her earlier accusations and admonishments. And since her story spans the division between Books VI and VII, she appears to have taken over the story herself, to have appropriated the artist's function, evolving from object of storytelling to storyteller herself.

By the end of the poem, the empowered Marian serves as a double for Aurora; and her actions constitute a sort of alternate ending that

18. For a discussion of the "painful contradictions" in Barrett Browning's "liberal feminist position," in particular as it is expressed in the "vicious picture of the rural and urban poor," see Kaplan, Introduction 11.

preserves the claim to independence represented by Aurora the aspiring artist. This explains why, when Marian rejects Romney's renewed offer of marriage in Book IX, she is described by Aurora "as one who had authority to speak / And not as Marian" (IX, 250–51). The poet-heroine thus writes in two voices, producing a doubled ending to her story, one in which the exiled woman claims her exile, and the other in which she capitulates to the conventional consolations of the marriage plot. This use of Marian significantly revises conceptions of fallen women and allows a subversive ending to accompany the more recuperative one. As in *David Copperfield*, the fallen woman is being used to define the artist, but Aurora significantly identifies herself with, and not against, the fallen woman.[19]

I began my literary readings with an interpretation of Dickens that argued for the importance of Victorian fallenness as both a social and an aesthetic category. I tried to show that for Dickens, fallenness always figures a form of determinism; and while his women of the street are depicted as environmentally determined, he also perceives fallenness in distinctly literary terms—as the threat of narrative forms over the autonomy or recovery of the self, for example, or as the fear that we cannot escape from caricature because we are always already written. Gaskell, by contrast, in *Mary Barton* is expressly interested to show how literary or cultural forms are themselves powerful social forces; and she uses the prostitute, specifically, to exhibit the power of melodrama to actually constitute or determine character. Precisely because of the prostitute's generic status, Gaskellian encounters with the fallen threaten to collapse into scenes of reading, thereby losing the quality of interactive face-to-face encounters. This tendency to confuse the fallen woman with a book or a story emerges across the texts I discuss in this book, nowhere more vividly or suggestively than in Rossetti's "Jenny."

Aurora Leigh is distinct, however, in its elaboration of a dialectical interplay between aesthetic and intersubjective experience. I conclude with it in order to stress the possibilities for reconceiving or transcending the rhetoric of fallenness that existed within Victorian culture itself. But I don't mean to disregard the limits of Barrett Browning's vision, its exclusively dyadic structure and its inattention to the material life of the lower class; nor do I mean, by concluding

19. For a related discussion, see Cooper, *Elizabeth Barrett Browning* 173, 177.

with Barrett Browning, to cover over the revisionist moments in Dickens, Gaskell, or Rossetti. On the contrary, I have stressed revisionist moments in all the writers so as to argue that ideals of reciprocal recognition and response are not inaccessible or nonexistent simply because the objectifying stance of the rhetoric of fallenness is dominant in the discourse of the period.

Afterword:
Intersubjectivity and the Politics
of Poststructuralism

The rhetoric of fallenness, as I have traced it in selected social and literary texts from the mid-Victorian period, expresses anxieties about what constitutes human agency and selfhood. As we have seen, there was a pervasive tendency to protect cherished conceptions of moral autonomy and stable identity by creating a category of feminine fallenness. Through depictions of fallenness, the many perceived threats to the self— to its coherence, freedom, and distinct recognizability— could be both exaggerated and displaced, and also eventually diminished and dismissed, ushered off the scene, as were so many fallen figures in Victorian literature. I have argued that encounters with the prostitute falter or miscarry because she is perceived, distortedly, as the mere effect of systemic forces—environmental, economic, sexual, and aesthetic. As I demonstrate in Chapter 1, such distortions derive from the models of selfhood and agency that informed emergent scientific and sociological approaches to character. A powerful materialist approach to the self, deriving from associationism, utilitarianism, and reformist thought more generally, supported the elaboration of fallenness, which frequently took on the most extreme and threatening aspects of the new social understandings, particularly the tendencies toward atomism and mechanism. The figure of the fallen woman thus typically appeared as a profoundly isolated and determined subject, exiled from social relations and lacking the autonomy and coherence of the self-determining masculine self.

The Victorian depiction of fallenness also lights up a more general impasse in Victorian social thought, the tension between the scientific explanation of character and society, and the commitment to ethical and political transformation, both at the individual and social levels. This tension between fact and value takes on various guises in Victorian culture and is negotiated in different ways by those who broadly accept the doctrine of necessity, or the idea that human actions conform to uniform laws. In the *Logic*, John Stuart Mill insists that it is possible to reconcile a scientific explanation of character with a principle of moral freedom (which in turn allows an understanding of character as self-crafted). Likewise, Robert Owen subscribes to a principle of external character formation and, concurrently, to a principle of rational autonomy. In other instances, followers of the doctrine of necessity stress that sympathetic or disinterested feelings, which would form the basis for rejuvenated communities, are either as primary as hedonistic impulses, or will naturally evolve through the lessons of experience (which will teach us that what promotes happiness for others ultimately promotes happiness for us).[1]

Of course the literary writers I have examined did not forward explicitly philosophical positions on the disjunction between fact and value. Still, like the philosophers and cultural critics I examined in Chapter 1, these writers attempted to preserve notions of moral autonomy and redemptive sympathy even as they insisted on the pervasive power of larger social and aesthetic forces and structures. And sometimes these writers even challenged the dominant tendency to use figures of fallenness to draw off the more troubling aspects of Victorian conceptions of selfhood. Either by partly exposing dominant scapegoating mechanisms or by recasting the very notion of fallenness, writers were able to point toward the forms of social interaction that were being systematically foreclosed by the dominant discourse.

I have stressed such moments of critique and revision precisely because they either reveal or redress the deeper problems of atomism and mechanism in the rhetoric of fallenness and, by extension, in some influential Victorian approaches to individual and social identity. Dickens exhibits some self-consciousness about the scapegoating mechanisms directed toward the fallen, and he certainly uses their plight to focus social criticisms; but he does not significantly

---

1. As I discuss in Chapter 1, Mill also forwarded versions of these latter arguments.

transform the dominant paradigms through which fallen subjectivity was conceived, and his moments of sympathy often remain senti-mental, reinforcing a view of fallen women as fated to a perpetual, and profoundly isolating, self-condemnation. Gaskell suggests a deep complicity between instrumental reason and conventional views of fallenness, though her stress on the transformative powers of sympathetic communing, if greater than Dickens's, is still marred by asymmetries of power. Her elaboration of a more reciprocal and far-reaching model of class interaction at the end of *North and South* can be seen as exemplary of the kind of reconceptualization of social relations that this book aims to forward, as can Rossetti's gestures toward a positive conception of intersubjective indeterminacy and Barrett Browning's promotion of a dialectical interplay between aes-thetic and intersubjective experience. In all of these instances, the model of selfhood counterposed to "fallenness" is one that is fun-damentally relational, open-ended, and participatory; this concep-tion of identity in turn lends tacit support to those instances where a writer aims to promote ethical norms of intersubjective mutuality or, in the case of Gaskell, more democratic processes of social transformation.

Here I want to extend the discussion of normativity, intersubjec-tivity, and agency to the poststructuralist terrain. Such an extension is profitable and instructive because of the deep parallels and con-tinuities between the kinds of moral and social questions that ex-ercised the Victorians and those that compel our attention today. Of course what I call "parallels" result in part from the inevitable ways in which contemporary concerns originally framed my read-ings of Victorian culture. Yet I believe there are historical continuities as well, insofar as the development of socially scientific approaches in the Victorian era eventually gave rise to dominant paradigms of thought in the twentieth century, predominantly those of sociology, linguistics, and structuralism, paradigms that continue to exert their force even on the "antisystematic" theories of poststructuralism. For despite the challenges that poststructuralism poses to the scientism of structuralism, it has nonetheless failed to redress adequately the fundamental problems of agency and normativity that plagued struc-turalism. Poststructuralism's primary emphases have been on in-determinacy and a radical alterity that functions at the symbolic or structural level. But this privileging of disruption at the systemic level derives from a residual objectivism within poststructuralism itself, one that profoundly disables the political and ethical projects of those cultural critics who employ poststructuralist paradigms in an untransformed way. It is this residual objectivism that allows us to discern similarities between contemporary and Victorian questions, despite manifold historical and cultural differences. For if a deep-seated objectivism characterizes the rhetoric of fallenness and inhibits the theorization of moral agency and intersubjectivity, the residual objectivism of poststructuralism has had similar effects on our own attempts at theoretical self-understanding.

We can take some measure of the continuities between Victorian and contemporary approaches to the question of agency by the interest that poststructuralist critics have brought precisely to protosociological or protomodernist aspects of Victorian discourse. Given Dickens's especially vivid sense of social determination, as well as his peculiarly modern conception of alienated self-reflexivity, it seems apt, for example, that D. A. Miller would privilege Dickens in his Foucauldian study of nineteenth-century realism.[2] Miller reads Dickens as everywhere revealing both the extent to which subjects are fully and thoroughly constituted by social forces, inscribed into the social order, and the many ways in which those same subjects seek to disavow that fact through elaborate rituals of secrecy. For Miller, the rituals of secrecy are merely a ruse of power, which manages social subjects by encouraging their belief that power does not itself construct their own sense of privacy. Miller's account of modern subjectivity reveals a "structural uniformity" of character in Dickens, in the nineteenth-century novel, and throughout modern disciplinary society.[3] Everyone participates in the illusion of interiority. As I have argued, however, there is a critical difference between "fallen" and protected characters in Dickens, insofar as the fallen character is denied, and denies herself, those illusions of freedom and privacy that constitute Miller's modern subject. Miller's failure to remark on this difference is ironic insofar as his own text everywhere recapitulates the Dickensian fallen subjectivity, which knows itself only as determined, which looks inward only to find an inscribed self. All the same, Miller's reading is in a deep sense true to Dickens, who himself is clearly haunted by the forms of

2. Two of the five novels chosen for individual study are by Dickens, who also figures prominently in Miller's introduction. D. A. Miller, *The Novel and the Police.*
3. Miller, *The Novel and the Police* 203.

subjectivity he assigns to the fallen. But, as I have stressed, we need not reproduce such extreme conceptions in our theoretical approaches.

For despite its importance as an emphatic intervention into naturalizing conceptions of vice, Dickens's bleak version of fallenness remains locked within a hypostatized subject/structure opposition. It is of course desirable to have larger social analyses inform our self-conceptions; but in Dickens, impersonal forces distortedly define identities and relations. The fallen read themselves as the mere effects of larger forces, and their self-understandings terminate in an estranging third-person perspective. The pure or protected characters similarly read the fallen as the victims of larger forces, hence the many scenes in which a male protagonist stands still before a fallen, falling, or drooping woman. This posture not only thwarts the possibility for mutuality, it entrenches an atomized notion of individuality. And I am suggesting here that such a notion is recapitulated in Miller, where it appears as the pathos of confessionalism, the highlighting of the critic's own solitary self and the illusions to which he, as a thoroughly modern subject, chooses to cling.

Not all poststructuralist critics are as pessimistic as Miller. Indeed, just as John Stuart Mill and other mid-Victorians sought to protect against the anxious feelings of fatalism that accompanied the endorsement of a new social science, many poststructuralist critics, having embraced a conception of constructed subjectivity, still seek to protect themselves against those feelings of fatalism that trouble their own political and ethical commitments, at the same time that they view with profound suspicion the kind of "moral freedom" that Mill sought to justify, or the kind of wholesale social transformation that Owen envisioned. However, like the Victorian rhetoric of fallenness, itself fascinated with structures and impersonal forces, poststructuralist approaches frequently have trouble conceiving the standpoint that is assumed by subjects in a nonreifying encounter. This limitation is ironic, precisely because much poststructuralist cultural criticism takes for its topic the processes of othering, both subtle and blatant, that underwrite economies of power and inform discursive practices. Likewise, the tasks of historical and cultural recovery in the contemporary human sciences often aim to reconstruct and thereby "give voice" to the suppressed or negated experiences of historically subordinated groups, groups defined through hierarchies of gender, race, class, and sexuality. To take a central example, the movement of cultural studies in Britain and North America largely derives from the felt need to reconstitute the lived practices of subcultures, social groups, and variously positioned subjectivities. Indeed, in his recent survey of cultural studies, Patrick Brantlinger offers the following as the main "lesson" of cultural studies: "In order to understand ourselves, the discourses of 'the Other'—of all the others—is that which we most urgently need to hear."[4]

Of course, throughout this study I myself have located a negative process of othering in the depictions of prostitutes and fallen women. Such a negative process, I have repeatedly asserted, is enabled and supported by a faulty and extreme conception of determined subjectivity. I suggest here that poststructuralist cultural criticism, which in many ways deeply influenced my desire to explore depictions of fallen otherness in Victorian culture, can itself end up reifying subjectivity in its more extreme constructionist formulations, thereby undermining its own normative project of overcoming repressive and disabling approaches to cultural difference. This problem has of course been recognized by many working in the field of cultural criticism, prompting reformulated approaches that emphasize "lived experience," autobiographical self-understanding, or the subject's own participation in its construction. Nonetheless, as I hope to show, these reformulations still fail to reconcile their appeals to reconfigured forms of social interaction with their accounts of subjectivity and selfhood. And this problem is of fundamental importance to the larger project of cultural criticism to which this book aims to contribute. For it seems to me we need to elaborate conceptions of subjectivity and social interaction that remain consistent with the normative principles that guide our practices of cultural interrogation and transformation; this consistency becomes especially important as we seek to answer the challenge that a multicultural society poses to our theoretical understandings. At the most basic level, we must forward the possibilities for mutual understanding even as we respect difference and acknowledge indeterminacy. In an attempt to contribute to such an admittedly daunting task, I elaborate and endorse a revised version of the Habermasian model of communicative action, one that can incorporate

4. Patrick Brantlinger, *Crusoe's Footprints* 3.

precisely those elements of sympathetic reciprocity and indeterminate otherness that I stress in my readings of Victorian texts.[5]

In doing so, however, I want to examine more closely what is widely regarded as the primary impasse or, in less skeptical formulations, the constitutive tension of poststructuralist thought: the incommensurability between its epistemological stance and its political claims, between its descriptions and its prescriptions, between the pessimism of its intellect and, if not the optimism, at least the intrusiveness of its moral and political will. I want to do so to avoid suggesting any simple conflation of Victorian and contemporary debates; this is an "Afterword" precisely because it seeks to extend the consideration of questions of agency to contemporary theory. "Poststructuralism" is of course a wide and varied terrain, but the shared tenets of its several manifestations—deconstructive, psychoanalytic, Marxist, Foucauldian—form something of a generalizable paradigm. Poststructuralism in its various guises forwards a critique of humanism and the unified subject of modern liberalism, and casts Enlightenment conceptions of truth, rationality, and autonomy as at once deluded and oppressive, derivatives of a falsely universal conception of human subjectivity that in turn relies upon and enables multiple forms of power and domination. The critiques of power and domination, however, entail implicit normative claims that remain external to the overarching antifoundationalist epistemology. Ever-encroaching and self-extending power networks in Foucault, the violence of metaphysics in deconstruction, reified or suppressed otherness in cultural and literary criticism—all of these make appeal at some level to a vision of unalienated relations and undamaged forms of social life. As Habermas writes in discussing the critique of reason as it has been waged through negative dialectics, deconstruction, and genealogy,

> Whether modernity is described as a constellation of life that is reified and used, or as one that is technologically manipulated, or as one that is totalitarian, rife with power, homogenized, impris-

5. Brantlinger himself concludes his survey of cultural studies with a call for a turn to the Habermasian model of communicative action; I offer, however, certain revisions of Habermas from a feminist perspective, and I provide a series of critiques of contemporary paradigms that differ from Brantlinger's. Brantlinger's is one of very few positive considerations of Habermas among literary studies. For an adaptation of the Habermasian conception of the public sphere for a feminist project, see Rita Felski, *Beyond Feminist Aesthetics*.

oned—the denunciations are constantly inspired by a special sensitivity for complex injuries and subtle violations. Inscribed in this
sensitivity is the picture of an undamaged intersubjectivity that the
young Hegel first projected as an ethical totality.[6]

The same normative appeal attends poststructuralist cultural criticism, which has itself grown out of the earlier critiques of modernity. In poststructuralist criticism, this normative appeal also
only fleetingly or awkwardly appears, since it is characteristically
subordinated to a perspective that construes the human subject as
the effect of larger forces and structures: as the point through
which language speaks, as the site of unconscious disruptions, or
as a position within a social grid traversed by the constitutive
forces of gender, race, and class. This third-person perspective—
what I earlier called the residual objectivism of poststructuralism—
relegates morality to the status of assertion or intimation and casts
into question its own viability as critique, since, as Peter Dews
points out, the philosophical position of poststructuralism "assumes the foundations of the classical forms of critique to be
necessarily and oppressively identitarian."[7]
Many who subscribe to the poststructuralist paradigm dismiss
the problems of grounding one's critique or being able properly
to account for one's own account, either by adopting a pragmatic
stance compatible with the antifoundationalist credo or by self-
consciously embracing the idea that their own critique is necessarily
complicit with those forms of power it purports to "unmask."[8] But
the problem of political will and normative assertion has generated
a more elaborate and sustained debate. Approaches to the issue
take several distinct forms, though many critics and theorists employ a combination of the forms. Some theorists posit a politically
efficacious resistance or disruption that is guaranteed as a systems
effect, thereby avoiding the rhetoric of voluntarism. Examples of
this first approach include deconstructionist intimations about the
inherent subversiveness of linguistic undecidability and psychoan-

6. Jürgen Habermas, *The Philosophical Discourse of Modernity* 337.
7. Peter Dews, *Logics of Disintegration* xvi.
8. For an example of the pragmatic stance, see Nancy Fraser and Linda J. Nicholson, "Social Criticism without Philosophy"; for examples of the admission of
complicity, see Miller, *The Novel and the Police*, and Nancy Armstrong, *Desire and
Domestic Fiction*.

alytic claims for the disrupting effects of the unconscious.[9] Others actively embrace the tension between epistemology and politics, affirming a "double gesture" that simultaneously avows a theoretical antihumanism and a political humanism. This approach is represented by theorists who have followed Gayatri Chakravorty Spivak's endorsement of "strategic essentialism."[10] Foucault's own shifts in perspective from the systemic to the local (as the site of resistances and "reverse discourses") also rely on a similarly motivated double move.[11] Still others, in part out of dissatisfaction with the double gesture, have sought to articulate political strategies that derive more directly from constructionist critique; Judith Butler is a prime example, as are the proponents of various oppositional politics.[12]

I argue here that none of these approaches adequately theorizes the normative appeals informing poststructuralist critique; and I hope to forward the discussion of poststructuralist politics and ethics by placing the debate in dialogue with Habermas's theory of communicative action. Habermas's project calls for a turn to "intersubjectivity" as a means of overcoming the impasse between a subject-centered paradigm and the theoretical and ethical failures of systems theories. For Habermas, the logocentrism of Western thought and the powerful instrumentality of reason are not absolute but rather constitute "a systematic foreshortening and distortion of a potential always already operative in the communicative practice of everyday life." The potential he refers to is the potential for mutual under-

9. Paul Morrison in "Paul de Man" shows how the claim of inherent subversiveness animates Derrida's defense of de Man. The politically inflected claim for the destabilizing effects of the unconscious is exemplified in the work of Jacqueline Rose, for example, *Sexuality in the Field of Vision*.

10. As I discuss later, Spivak has reconsidered her earlier position on strategic essentialism.

11. See Michel Foucault, *The History of Sexuality* 1:101. Foucault's formulations in this text, however, tend to move back and forth between a version of the first approach, whereby resistance is itself a function of systemic power, and a dual approach that shifts between the local and the systemic (see especially 92–102). Foucauldians such as Miller, who privilege the systems view, subscribe to a cynical version of the first approach: in this case resistance is a function of the system, yet it fundamentally perpetuates rather than destabilizes or transforms that system. See Miller, *The Novel and the Police*.

12. Judith Butler, *Gender Trouble*. I am here analyzing some prominent approaches within the field of cultural criticism, but my discussion cannot hope to cover the entire field of poststructuralist politics and ethics. For a useful survey that extends beyond the scope of this Afterword, see Martin Jay, "The Morals of Genealogy."

standing "inscribed into communication in ordinary language."[13] Habermas recognizes the dominance and reach of instrumental reason—his project is largely devoted to a systematic analysis of the historical conditions and social effects of that dominance—yet at the same time he wishes to retrieve an emancipatory model of *communicative* reason derived from a linguistic understanding of intersubjective relations.[14]

As I stated earlier, accounts that remain unable to mediate between the systemic and intersubjective perspectives, and that fundamentally privilege the former, ironically end up reifying subjectivity and otherness in a manner analogous to those forms of exclusion that are typically the object of critique. Habermas's announced shift from the paradigm of the philosophy of consciousness to the linguistically conceived paradigm of mutual understanding, by contrast, cogently addresses and resolves the problems generated by the impasse of poststructuralism as I outlined it above. This shift makes possible a nonmetaphysical grounding of critique by means of those very emancipatory communicative ideals that already inhere in acts of linguistic exchange. It renders explicit the ideal of undamaged intersubjectivity that the critique of systemic distortion necessarily implies and invokes. And it mediates between the prescriptive and descriptive in its employment of dialogic reciprocity as a regulative ideal that can guide political practices. It suggests, in other words, that if various forms of domination undermine, distort, or even foreclose the communicative ideal incipient in dialogical relations, then our task is not only to analyze those distortions but also to nurture the communicative ideals of recognition and respect. This is by no means to imply that such an ideal could ever be fully actualized or that "learning to listen" is an antidote adequate in and of itself to massive, structurally embedded inequalities. As Richard J. Bernstein writes,

13. Habermas, *Philosophical Discourse* 311.

14. See Jürgen Habermas, *The Theory of Communicative Action*. Habermas's work has inspired a wide range of scholars working in discourse ethics. Versions of the Habermasian call for a turn to "intersubjectivity" and dialogism have characterized important work by, among others, Seyla Benhabib, Richard J. Bernstein, and Nancy Fraser. Benhabib and Fraser have been crucial in the elaboration of feminist critiques of Habermas, and Benhabib in particular is important to the arguments I make here. See Seyla Benhabib, *Critique, Norm, and Utopia* and *Situating the Self*; Richard J. Bernstein, *Beyond Objectivism and Relativism*; and Nancy Fraser, *Unruly Practices*.

It would be a gross distortion to imagine that we might conceive of the entire political realm organized on the principle of dialogue or conversation, considering the fragile conditions that are required for genuine dialogue and conversation. Nevertheless, if we think out what is required for such a dialogue based on mutual under- standing, respect, a willingness to listen and risk one's opinions and prejudices, a mutual seeking of the correctness of what is said, we will have defined a powerful regulative ideal that can orient our practical and political lives.[15]

The theories of communicative reason and ethics profoundly shift the terms of the debate as they have been elaborated by the other approaches to the normative impasses of poststructuralism. The first approach is inadequate insofar as it locates subversion and transformation entirely beyond individual or collective agency. The double gesture, in calling for an oscillation between local acts of will and a systemic view of the social grid, objectifies social iden- tities and fails to show how or why we should want to privilege certain acts of will over others. The more consistent models of subversive or oppositional politics redress problems in the other two approaches yet still lack a positive normative dimension. I argue that the Habermasian theory not only overcomes the im- passes of the other approaches but also can itself be reformulated so as to accommodate less exclusively rationalistic conceptions of intersubjective reciprocity *and* so as to acknowledge more fully the indeterminacy of social relations. To make the case for a revised Habermasian model, I first examine in some detail the call for a "double gesture" that embraces both a theoretical antiessentialism and a "strategic essentialism." It is important to begin here because the double gesture self-consciously attempts to resolve the tension between theory and politics, and hence in certain ways might be seen as redressing the "cryptonormativism" that characterizes other approaches.[16]

15. Bernstein, *Beyond Objectivism and Relativism* 162–63.
16. I borrow the word "cryptonormative" from Habermas, who uses it to char- acterize Foucault's failure to maintain a merely neutral stance toward the positivity of power. Habermas, *Philosophical Discourse* 294.

Risks Necessary and Unnecessary

Back in 1978, in a long and influential article about sexual difference, politics, and the cinema, Stephen Heath wrote that the project of exposing the constructed character of sexual difference need not and perhaps should not be defined in opposition to the project of reconstructing the woman's gaze or of attempting to "distinguish positively feminine elements in particular film practices." In a phrase that was to be taken up by academic cultural critics and literary theorists in the mid- to late eighties, Heath surmised that "the risk of essence may have to be taken."[17] In a similar vein, Spivak began in interviews and essays in the mid-eighties to elaborate a concept of "strategic essentialism" that, from the vantage point of a deconstructive antihumanism, both justified and endorsed political uses of humanist categories such as the will, autonomy, rights, consciousness, and identity.[18] Numerous poststructuralist critics and theorists—aligned with feminism, cultural studies, and gay and lesbian studies—have in turn advocated some form of alliance between constructionism and essentialism, or between antihumanist theory and humanist claims and practices.[19] The double gesture that characterizes this paradoxical practice accepts and renders explicit the poststructuralist tension between theory and politics. It also seeks to redress a perceived problem of agency: rather than locating subversion and transformation entirely beyond individual or collective agency, it obtrusively insists on a kind of voluntarism, though one that remains informed by the antifoundationalist critique of the will.

An understanding of strategic essentialism cannot be gained simply from analyzing the origins of the term and its subsequent citations, for there are many manifestations of a similarly motivated double gesture that do not employ the term. In fact, within feminism, a version of strategic essentialism began to appear along with the

17. Stephen Heath, "Difference" 99.
18. See Gayatri Chakravorty Spivak, "Criticism, Feminism, and the Institution," "Strategy, Identity, Writing," and "Subaltern Studies."
19. For endorsements and elaborations of reconsidered understandings of essentialism, some of them explicitly endorsing a double gesture similar to Spivak's, see Diana Fuss, *Essentially Speaking*; Ann Snitow, "A Gender Diary"; Teresa de Lauretis, *Technologies of Gender* 26, and "Upping the Anti (sic) in Feminist Theory"; Paul Smith, *Discerning the Subject*; Biddy Martin, "Feminism, Criticism, and Foucault"; Rosa Braidotti, "The Politics of Ontological Difference"; Margaret Whitford, *Luce Irigaray*.

first sympathetic appropriations of poststructuralist thought. In *Sexual/Textual Politics*, for example, Toril Moi endorses Julia Kristeva's " 'deconstructed' form of feminism" but warns at the same time that "it still remains *politically* essential for feminists to defend women *as* women in order to counteract the patriarchal oppression that precisely despises women *as* women."[20] Moi does not make clear precisely what she means by "as women"; rhetorically, she enacts the very affirmation of unified identity for which the statement calls. One might also view the looseness of her formulation as a deliberate eclipsing of theoretical precision by political demand.

Moi's position exemplifies what has become a primary version of strategic essentialism, that is, the argument that a political pragmatism must accompany poststructuralist strategies of demystification and critique. Within this framework, however, essentialist categories are often cast as imperative in more than a narrowly pragmatic way. It isn't simply the case that we need categories such as rights and the subject of those rights in order to achieve distinct political goals; we also need myths of community and identity in order to counter dominant ideologies and underwrite collective forms of political practice. The more narrow approach assumes simply that we need to work within the existing system; the broader one makes a more fundamental claim about the role of myth and identity in human praxis. It makes a claim about a common human need (though usually not so baldly as that). As Ann Snitow writes, "Whatever the issue, feminists have gained a great deal by saying, 'We are "women," and this is what "women" want.' This belief in some ground of shared experience is the social basis from which any sustained political struggle must come."[21]

The argument for the political necessity of identity thinking thus claims that we must deliberately choose certain strategies whose abandonment in the name of poststructuralist rigor would be grossly misguided. Another version of strategic essentialism—or sometimes just another moment within a strategic essentialism argument—concentrates not so much on the future as on the past, arguing that, despite itself, essentialism has produced progressive political effects

20. Toril Moi, *Sexual/Textual Politics* 13. Moi reelaborates and further complicates this position in "Feminism, Postmodernism, and Style," arguing that we must "live out" the contradictions of not a double but a treble feminism, one that simultaneously affirms equality, difference, and deconstruction.

21. Snitow, "A Gender Diary" 12.

in the past. More a practice of reading than a plan of action, this approach revises and recuperates not only the past but also what are too often quickly dismissed as anachronistic or naive textual practices in the present. Spivak's approach to the Subaltern Studies project, a postcolonial historical reconstruction of Indian colonial "experience," exemplifies this particular facet of strategic essentialism. While Spivak sees an important constructionist emphasis in much of the work of these historians, she seeks also to explain and recuperate what her Western antihumanist training has caused her to view with considerable suspicion: an investment in the will, consciousness, and effective agency of the subaltern, a commitment to reconstructing the lost, negated, or covered-over experience of Indian colonial subjects. She accounts for these essentialist emphases by positing an unavoidable asymmetry between her work and the work of the historians, one constituted through the displacing axis of the "international division of labor": "The discourse of the unified consciousness of the subaltern *must* inhabit the strategy of these historians, even as the discourse of the micrologized or situated subject must mark that of antihumanists on the other side of the international division of labor."[22] Spivak not only explains but also privileges the work of these historians: by casting the subaltern as "the subject of his own history," the Subaltern Studies project importantly reveals "the *limits* of the critique of humanism as produced in the west."[23] What Spivak means here is that the critique of humanism remains blind to the ways in which the reconstruction of subjectivity, experience, and identity is of vital importance to groups who have been colonized.

Spivak's reading thus seems to grant the Subaltern Studies project a kind of autonomous critical function, insofar as she credits the historians with revealing the limits of antihumanism. Yet she simultaneously feels compelled to rescue the project from its own naiveté by reading it as a *"strategic* use of positivist essentialism in a scrupulously visible political interest."[24] Strangely, this formulation retains the notion of a strategy in a case where the effects seem not to have been calculated from a thoroughgoing poststructuralist vantage point. It's one thing to say that the historians' emphasis on

22. Spivak, "Subaltern Studies" 210.
23. Spivak, "Subaltern Studies" 209; my emphasis.
24. Spivak, "Subaltern Studies" 205.

humanist categories has a corrective effect on poststructuralist paradigms; that places their work in productive dialogue with Western deconstruction. But it's quite another thing to reinscribe their operative concepts as *strategies*, when they simply don't evince any such attitude toward them.[25] The strategy here lies in the critic's reading of the historians, not with the historians themselves. In a similar way, Diana Fuss recasts Luce Irigaray's essentialist language as an intentional strategy: "The point, for Irigaray, of defining women from an essentialist standpoint is not to imprison women within their bodies but to rescue them from enculturating definitions by men."[26] Essentialism here becomes a brilliantly conceived escape from oppressive constructions, or constructionism *tout court*. That such an escape is within her own terms necessarily deluded does not trouble Fuss, for she thinks it does political good to "believe" otherwise.[27]

Thus far I have laid out two different approaches to essentialism. The first, the politically pragmatic approach, endorses deliberate appropriations of essentialist and humanist categories: it is anticipatory and voluntaristic. The second, the recuperative, retroactive version, rereads and revises what have hitherto been dismissed as failed or faulty practices. It is backward looking rather than forward looking, a way of reading rather than a political prescription. The third and final approach to essentialism that I examine here paradoxically modifies the notion of intentional strategy altogether; it insists instead that essentialism is entirely *unavoidable* and hence something we must affirm and use. I first examine the way this

25. Her indication at one point that this strategy is "partially unwitting" highlights rather than resolves this issue. Spivak, "Subaltern Studies" 207.

26. Fuss, *Essentially Speaking* 61.

27. De Lauretis has made the most encompassing feminist reinscription of essentialism to date in "Upping the Anti (sic) in Feminist Theory." She argues, invoking Locke, that the essence appealed to in the writings of many so-called essentialists is a nominal and not a real essence; it is, in other words, a constructed essence. "It is a totality of qualities, properties, and attributes that such feminists define, envisage, or enact for themselves. . . . This is more a project, then, than a description of existent reality; it is an admittedly feminist project of 're-vision,' where the specifications *feminist* and *re*-vision already signal its historical location, even as the (re)vision projects itself outward geographically and temporally (universally) to recover the past and claim the future" (257). De Lauretis thus overcomes the tension between essentialism and constructionism by recasting the former as a version of the latter. Such an argument, however, involves a rather drastic reduction of cultural and radical feminisms, and ultimately has the effect of projecting a false unity on the diverse and contested field of feminism.

argument appears in Spivak's work and then move on to more recent feminist assertions that some form of double gesture is in fact inescapable.[28]

For Spivak, whose political criticism is strongly influenced by deconstruction, essentialism is not something that we could ever jettison or have done with, since it is a function of language—or logocentrism—itself. She makes a representative statement in a 1986 interview: "Since one cannot not be an essentialist, why not look at the ways in which one is essentialist, carve out a representative essentialist position, and then do politics according to the old rules whilst remembering the dangers in this? That's the thing deconstruction gives us; an awareness that what we are obliged to do, and must do scrupulously, in the long run is not OK."[29] Not OK, because essentialism enacts the violence of metaphysics generally and a host of exclusions historically, exclusions primarily of race and gender. Thus, although deconstructive critique must be supplemented by political practice, practice itself must be continually corrected by theory. Or, as Spivak puts it, not only does practice norm theory, but "theory always norms practice."[30]

While Spivak argues for the necessity of essentialism from within the paradigm of deconstruction, others such as Ann Snitow and Denise Riley have argued, in somewhat different terms, that the double gesture is simply constitutive of the history of feminism, or of feminism itself. In the opening paragraph of *"Am I That Name?": Feminism and the Category of "Women" in History*, Riley states, "Both a concentration on and a refusal of the identity of 'women' are essential to feminism. This its history makes plain."[31] In "A Gender Diary," Snitow offers a similar argument: "Feminism is inevitably a mixed form, requiring in its very nature such inconsistencies. . . . A common divide keeps forming in both feminist thought and action between the need to build the identity 'woman' and give it solid political meaning and the need to tear down the category 'woman' and dismantle its all-too-solid history."[32] Snitow's essay carefully works through the way this divide informs a number of classic de-

28. Again, as should be clear from the reinvocation of Spivak, more than one version of strategic essentialism can appear within a single argument.

29. Spivak, "Strategy, Identity, Writing" 45.

30. Spivak, "Strategy, Identity, Writing" 44.

31. Denise Riley, *"Am I That Name?"* 1.

32. Snitow, "A Gender Diary" 9.

bates within feminism—the essentialism/constructionism debate, the equality/difference debate, and the tension between cultural feminism and poststructuralism. Snitow argues that the divide cannot be overcome through thought alone and that it will only be overcome in a historical process. On this basis, she dismisses any attempt at what she calls "third course thinking" and asserts instead that " 'embracing the paradox' is just what feminism cannot choose but do."[33]

I suggest that Snitow fails to make a crucial distinction here. Recognizing the importance of a divide within the history of feminism, and understanding the powerful ways that divide informs the contemporary moment, does not mean that one is obliged to embrace that divide theoretically. Indeed, transmuting the historical debate into a theoretical postulate generates a series of problems, both practical and theoretical. At the least, a certain irony attends this position, insofar as it aims to get beyond debate and disagreement by insisting that we *all* affirm a contradiction. But as we shall see, the call to "embrace the paradox" is itself elaborated from, and fundamentally privileges, the poststructuralist position. In some ways this position reinscribes the problem of rescue and recuperation that marks the revisionist approach to essentialism. The recuperative stance harbors within itself, however, a more fundamental problem. By associating essentialism with practice and antiessentialism with an ultimate theoretical truth, the articulation of strategic essentialism generates a theory/practice split. In turning to Habermas, I will argue for a conception of theory that can render explicit, rather than undermine, the norms and self-understandings that are internal to practice. That is, theory need not be other than (and superior to) practice; ideally, it is practice itself as self-reflexive.

To further elaborate my critique of the double gesture, however, I must return to Spivak, who made the apparently even-handed claim that practice norms theory and theory norms practice, that each corrects the excesses or blindnesses of the other. In her reading of the Subaltern Studies project, as we have seen, Spivak argues for the importance of essentialist categories insofar as they point up a "limit" in the Western critique of humanism. But two things then crucially modify, if not altogether undermine, that point. First, as I

33. Snitow, "A Gender Diary" 19. Snitow is here citing—and criticizing—Linda Alcoff's attempt to transcend the paradox in "Cultural Feminism versus Post-Structuralism." For another argument precisely featuring and privileging feminism's elaboration of doubled strategies, see Smith, *Discerning the Subject*.

mention above, Spivak feels compelled to rescue the historians' practice by designating it as a strategy. Second, this retrieval is complemented by Spivak's own antihumanist reading of the subaltern's "identity" as "no more than a theoretical fiction to entitle the project of reading": "What had seemed the historical predicament of the colonial subaltern can be made to become the allegory of the predicament of *all* thought, *all* deliberative consciousness, though the elite profess otherwise."[34] This formulation should sound familiar to feminists, insofar as Lacanian feminism reads precisely in this fashion. The scapegoated feminine predicament reveals the truth of the whole: nobody has the phallus. Here, the negated subaltern reveals the truth of the whole: nobody has autonomous deliberative consciousness. In my view, however, to read historically disempowered or negated subject-positions as figures for an abstractly decentered subjectivity is to distort our understanding of *both* the decentered subject and the condition of specific oppressed groups. More important, Spivak generates a false dualism between a higher theoretical truth—the truth of decentered subjectivity—and what ultimately must then be seen as an enabling practical *lie*. That is, her conception of a strategic essentialism that both guarantees practice and then obligingly acts as a target for a knowing antihumanism ultimately works to disarticulate practice from theory, subordinating the former to the latter.

The idea that practice only works through what are ultimately dangerous fictions diminishes the extent to which the critique of naturalized identities can itself inform political practice. In terms less ominous than Spivak's, for example, Snitow nonetheless similarly suggests that those engaging in political activism are required to foster a forgetfulness of the kind of constructionist critique that led them to understand the workings of power in the first place:

> We begin: The category "woman" is a fiction; then poststructuralism suggests ways in which human beings live by fictions; then, in its turn, activism requires of feminists that we elaborate the fiction "woman" as if she were not a provisional invention at all but a person we know well, one in need of obvious rights and powers. Activism and theory weave together here, working on what remains the same basic cloth, the stuff of feminism.[35]

34. Spivak, "Subaltern Studies" 204.
35. Snitow, "A Gender Diary" 19.

The problem I have with this formulation lies in the way constructionism *belongs to* poststructuralism, while activism requires the
bracketing of constructionist critique (*pace* the weaving metaphor).[36]
In a refusal of these kinds of double gestures, some cultural critics
have insisted that we derive our politics more directly from constructionist critique. For example, Judith Butler argues for a feminist
politics "that will take the variable construction of identity as both
a methodological and normative prerequisite, if not a political
goal."[37] For Butler, the affirmation of unified identity is not a political
necessity; on the contrary, the disruption of naturalized conceptions
of identity should serve as the model for political practice as such.[38]
Butler thus aims to reconcile the normative and the theoretical and
does not insist on their irreducible opposition.

Yet Butler's theory remains limited insofar as it fails to account
sufficiently for the political ideals and values that inform progressive
practice, ones that extend beyond the recognition of constructedness. For Butler, the point is not simply to show that all subjectivity
is constructed but also to show that it is constructed within a dominant and oppressive heterosexual matrix. And in characterizing the
heterosexual matrix as dominant and oppressive, she means to emphasize, one can only assume, its failure to recognize and respect
other sexualities and subjective practices. But this is a normative
claim that only cryptically informs her account. Subverting identity
constitutes the methodology and the goal of feminist political practice; recognition and respect inform the discussion but are not given
theoretical primacy. Butler introduces the ideas of coalition and dialogue, but only to argue against the possibility of formulating any
notion of solidarity, which she in an unwarranted move equates
with unity: "Despite the clearly democratizing impulse that moti-
vates coalition building, the coalitional theorist can inadvertently
reinsert herself as sovereign of the process by trying to assert an
ideal form for coalitional structures *in advance*, one that will effec-

36. Snitow is actually careful elsewhere not to generate an opposition like this; it
is interesting that it emerges within her section on poststructuralism.
37. Butler, *Gender Trouble* 5.
38. Other critics have avoided strategic essentialist arguments by endorsing a
model of coalition based on a shared opposition to dominant power matrices. See
Lisa Duggan, "Making It Perfectly Queer"; Chandra Talpade Mohanty, "Cartographies of Struggle." These approaches importantly argue that we can articulate political
practices that integrate constructionist critique.

tively guarantee unity as the outcome."[39] But there's a difference between giving theoretical explicitness to tacitly supposed intersubjective ideals and decreeing what "unity" will be. While I am entirely in accord with Butler's idea that we should expect "divergence, breakage, splinter, and fragmentation" as part of the dialogical process of democratization, I think that she makes this point only to swerve away from giving theoretical prominence to the intersubjective ideals that inform this very point.[40]

Spivak's own reconsiderations on the topic of strategic essentialism revealingly devolve on the issue of dialogue and intersubjectivity. In an interview with Ellen Rooney for the journal *Differences*, Spivak expresses surprise as well as regret at the way strategic essentialism has been so widely heralded as a solution to theory's political impasses, suggesting that we must shift toward a new terrain, that of "building for difference."[41] Over the course of the questioning, Spivak manifests a repeated impatience with the very term *essentialism* and with the attempt to refine a theory about it. Arguing that we must talk of deconstructive practice in more "mundane" terms, she calls for "a sort of deconstructive homeopathy, a deconstructing of identity by identities."[42] Partly Spivak is answering the charge that she talks too much about herself:

> I believe that the way to counter the authority of either objective, disinterested positioning or the attitude of there being no author (and these two opposed positions legitimize each other) is by thinking of oneself as an example of certain kinds of historical, psychosexual narratives that one must in fact use, however micrologically, in order to do deontological work in the humanities. When one represents oneself in such a way, it becomes, curiously enough, a deidentification of oneself, a claiming of an identity from a text that comes from somewhere else. . . . To an extent, the way in which one conceives of oneself as representative or as an example of something is this awareness that what is one's own, supposedly, what is proper to one, has a history. That history is unmotivated but not capricious and is larger in outline than we are, and I think this is quite different from the idea of talking about oneself.[43]

39. Butler, *Gender Trouble* 14.
40. Butler, *Gender Trouble* 14.
41. Gayatri Chakravorty Spivak, "In a Word" 128.
42. Spivak, "In a Word" 130.
43. Spivak, "In a Word" 130–31.

A self-reflexive form of autobiographical historicizing thus enables productive deidentifications without the pretense of a rigid antiessentialism: "Being obliged to graph one's bio is very different from the attitude of claiming anti-essentialism."[44] In the interview Spivak thus reelaborates the concept of a necessary essentialism, one that, if accompanied by a "persistent critique," will prompt efficacious (homeopathic) deidentifications, thereby successfully curing people of the impulse to naturalize their histories and identities.[45] We are back, then, to a more basic claim about deconstruction's capacity for demythologizing critique, and hence back to a claim about the political efficacy of deconstruction. Yet despite the holistic connotations of the homeopathic metaphor, the form of the double gesture is still discernible as the internal oscillation, within the individual, between identification and deidentification. All the same, Spivak has abandoned the sharp opposition between strategic local practices and a demystifying theoretical deconstruction practiced "elsewhere"; and there is quite a difference between a persistent self-critique modeled on hermeneutic self-awareness (which her reformulation suggests) and an endorsement of decisionist essentializing.

Spivak's reconsiderations thus only partly recapitulate her earlier position. What I am more interested in, however, is the extent to which the category of otherness seems to have prompted her impulse to revise. That is, a redirective toward dialogical relations frequently accompanies Spivak's admission of the earlier argument's inadequacy. For example, in an attempt to derail what she takes to be a misguided emphasis on the theoretical question of a pristine antiessentialism, she introduces the new goal of "building for difference." And at the very end of the interview there is a sudden insistence on the importance of transactions with an audience:

> Many of the changes I've made in my position are because the audience has become a co-investigator and I've realized what it is to have an audience. You know what I'm saying? An audience is part of one. An audience shows us something. Well, that is the transaction, you know, it's a responsibility to the other, giving it

44. Spivak, "In a Word" 131.
45. Spivak, "In a Word" 126.

faces. It's not . . . I don't see this de-essentializing particularly, but really deconstructing the binary opposition between investigator and audience.[46]

When one co-investigates by inviting an audience to respond, then "positionality is shared with it."[47]

The realization of what it is to have an audience has disrupted and rendered inadequate Spivak's earlier position and in fact prompted her toward a conception of "shared positionality." I suggest, however, that "shared positionality" can function only as a threshold concept in Spivak's overall account, an account that still subordinates intersubjectivity to a systems perspective. Spivak makes an appeal to mutual understanding, but the form of *self-*understanding that underlies mutual understanding is conceived exclusively from a systemic perspective. In recognizing one's positionality, in "thinking of oneself as an example of certain kinds of historical, psycho-sexual narratives," one undergoes the salutary process of deidentification. In sharing positionality, presumably, one recognizes the other as similarly constructed, as equally an example of certain larger narratives without which self-representation remains impossible, and as equally capable of homeopathic deidentifications. One could presumably undergo a dialogue in which such forms of self-understanding were exchanged, mutually prompted, and critically examined. However, it still remains the case that such a conception of intersubjectivity is radically truncated insofar as it is routed only through the systemic perspective. The form of self-understanding embraced is one whereby the subject sees himself or herself not as constituted through intersubjective relations but rather as a member of an atomized, post hoc "community" of systems effects.

In response to the potentially reified conceptions of subjectivity that derive from a too-atomized version of positionality, some critics have focused instead on the individual as the site of heterogeneous, multiple identities. Thus, for example, as a white lesbian working-class student, or as a black middle-class heterosexual law professor, one becomes the site of intersecting and often conflicting positions that one is always "negotiating." Yet as Diana Fuss argues, risks of

46. Spivak, "In a Word" 153.
47. Spivak, "In a Word" 153.

essentialism and reification inhabit both singular and multiple conceptions of positionality, insofar as "the essentialism in 'antiessentialism' inheres in the notion of place or positionality."[48] Fuss herself endorses the Lacanian conception of identity as radically destabilizing, as at once necessary and impossible, "alienated and fictitious."[49] According to Fuss, a nonpsychoanalytic conception of constructed identity, whether singular or multiple, does not acknowledge the "subversive and destabilizing potential of the Unconscious" and engages in an unanxious taxonomy of "identifiable and unitary," even if ultimately conflicting, notions of identity.[50]

Unlike Fuss, I am less concerned here with the charge that social constructionist discourse can lend itself to fixed conceptions of identity than I am with the objectivism, or systems perspective, that often dominates the elaboration of subject positionality. Indeed, the notion of subject-positions ironically partakes of an inverted Cartesianism: the various anti-cogitos of poststructuralism simply define the human subject as res extensa rather than res cogitans and thereby reinstate a curiously scientistic model. Such a dualistic framework precludes the possibility of an intersubjective perspective that would define the human subject not as purely autonomous and self-present, nor as a mere place on intersecting grids, but rather as constituted through its ongoing relations to others as they are mediated by language, social systems, and history. The Lacanian paradigm of split subjectivity, while it may avoid the essentialism of place, does not further such an understanding but rather insists on an internally destabilized or "precarious" subject. Moreover, that internal destabilization is the product of a dualistic subject-structure model. Coherent self-identity is disrupted by a systemic force: the unconscious as the symbolic order or what Dews calls the "transindividual dimension of language."[51] For Lacan, language remains in crucial ways an interruptive and not an enabling medium.

It is certainly true that many poststructuralist accounts have attempted to forward nonmechanistic theories of subject constitution, particularly by emphasizing that subjects perform, enact, or participate in their own constructions. A kind of participation does, for example, emerge in Foucault's accounts of constructed subjectivity,

48. Fuss, Essentially Speaking 29.
49. Fuss, Essentially Speaking 102.
50. Fuss, Essentially Speaking 105, 103. This emphasis exists in some tension with her arguments in favor of strategic essentialism.
51. Dews, Logics of Disintegration 83.

but it subordinates intersubjective relations to the workings of a systemic form of power. In his very last works on the classical period in Greece, Foucault significantly shifted his attention precisely to ethical relations; however, the highly influential *Discipline and Punish* and *The History of Sexuality, Volume I* focus overwhelmingly on the singular subject's participation in his or her own construction, the various means by which modern individuals "willingly" internalize the workings of disciplinary power. Spivak's own conception of "being obliged to graph one's bio" follows in the wake of this project to understand the drama of subject constitution, as does Judith Butler's emphasis on the potential for adopting a parodic relation toward the construction one is "in." To conceive of the subject as a participant in its own constructions, however, is not the same as conceiving of the subject as a participant in social communities.[52] The self-disciplining, self-inscribing, or self-parodic subject is one whose most fundamental relation is to the system and not to other subjects. Indeed, Foucauldian as well as Lacanian models fundamentally tend to read intersubjective relations as displaced confrontations between the subject and the system. The Lacanian rewriting of the oedipal scenario as a confrontation with the Law partakes of this displacement, as does the Foucauldian account of the Panopticon and the self-disciplining subject. In the Panopticon, which Foucault presents as the model of modern disciplinary society, the gaze of the concrete other becomes a mere lieutenant for a structure of anonymous and global surveillance.

Insofar as these forms of dramatizing subjectivity reduce the participatory to the systemic, they only partially describe the social world. We can certainly trace the historical and social determinants of this self-alienating mode of apprehension, which undeniably forms a part of modern self-understandings and powerfully informs the various modernist and postmodernist aesthetics. I suggest, however, that we have no obligation to reproduce this self-alienating mode as an absolute fact about the social world or modern history. The systemic anti-cogito that characterizes the poststructuralist sensibility ("The system thinks me, therefore I am not") produces an utterly atomized social field, one that precludes entering into the

---

52. Foucault's concept of reverse discourses would be a cogent counterexample, since these are waged by, and on behalf of, discursive *groups*. Foucault, *History of Sexuality* 1:101.

standpoint that is assumed by subjects in nonreifying encounters. But such dominant theoretical approaches can be challenged and reconceived.

Intersubjectivity: Reconceiving the Subject

The theory of communicative action enables us to resolve the most problematic aspects of those arguments that resort to cryptonormativism or a paradoxical double gesture. It gives due prominence to the intersubjective ideals that inform critiques of othering and calls to respect differences. The accounts I discussed in the previous section fail to mediate between the systems perspective and the perspective of intersubjective and transformative praxis. In the case of the double gesture, political and theoretical practice are fundamentally irreconcilable. In the case of those more consistent accounts that attempt to derive practice from poststructuralist theory, accounts of dialogical practice and intersubjective relations are refracted through a systems perspective.

Habermas's approach can advance the debate over the politics of poststructuralism only if it is significantly revised in a less rationalistic and formalistic direction. But the conception of communicative reason is of vital importance for any theory that seeks to advance and justify democratic ideals. Habermas's account of the relations of reciprocity and recognition that are presupposed in any action oriented toward reaching understanding disallows the radical rupture between ethics and epistemology, and between practice and theory, in much poststructuralist and postmodern thought. By bringing to light those aspects of our intersubjective relations that are constituted communicatively, Habermas articulates a discourse ethics. This discourse ethics insists that the higher level of argumentation required in any self-reflexive democratic process is an extension of the more primary mode of action that is oriented toward reaching understanding. Thus, Habermas's theory enjoins us to see in our politics or ethics those regulative ideals of recognition and respect that are already presupposed in ordinary communication, presupposed even as they are simultaneously thwarted and distorted by social hierarchies and systemic domination. For Habermas, an ethics of discourse requires that norms be validated through a procedure of public argumentation among all those who are affected; only those norms that produce a consensus can be said to be valid.

In Habermas's account, there is thus a dialectical and not an incommensurable relation between the systemic and the intersubjective perspectives, and between the theory and the practice. The intersubjective ideal internally prompts systemic critique, and the concept of communicative reason underlies critique's claim to emancipatory and transformative potential. Thus, even though Habermas wishes to redeem a normative conception of reason and of understanding, his project must be recognized as equally devoted to uncovering the many forces and structures that thwart the ideal speech situation.[53] Habermas sees democratic possibilities as endangered not simply by faulty theoretical models that deny communicative reason but also more directly by social and historical conditions that disable reciprocal relations. In order to counter the development of industrial capitalism and its attendant structures of bureaucracy and "rationalization," we must emphasize and nurture those procedures and modes of interaction that are most conducive to the communicative ideal.

In Habermas's theory, then, our status as subjects who are constituted through intersubjective relations is preserved, yet also placed in productive dialogue with an understanding of larger systems and histories. The Habermasian foregrounding of an intersubjective ideal emphatically does not mean that we abandon systemic analyses of the social world in favor of a celebratory, local insistence on community, human interrelatedness, or friendly conversation.[54] We can ensure proper democratic processes only if we understand and engage those forces, both historical and structural, that determine the social world and powerfully condition what our capacities and arenas for action will be. The systemic perspective not only

53. Many fault Habermas and his followers for too naive a conception of consensus, for engaging in a form of wishful thinking. Such a complaint often fails to register the fact that Habermas is redressing an overemphasis on dissensus in postmodernist theory as well as in the Frankfurt School's failure to conceptualize noninstrumental forms of reason. Hence, his account necessarily places a very strong stress on mutual understanding.

54. My reading of Elizabeth Gaskell might be summoned to clarify this distinction, insofar as she on the one hand exhibits a myopic, mystified intersubjective ideal (through her endorsements of domestic communing and maternity) and on the other manages, at the ending of *North and South*, to forward a transformative model of participatory action that is more widely public, socially conscious, and self-reflective.

allows us to understand the structurally embedded inequities that distort human interaction but also can itself meaningfully inform an intersubjective relation, insofar as it allows us more fully to understand another's history and social situatedness.[55] It is practice itself, however, that prompts the move to the systemic theoretical perspective; and theory has done its work properly only if its account enables a reconfiguring of lived intersubjective relations.

As I mentioned earlier, the need to integrate a participatory or first-person perspective into cultural criticism has made itself felt in several ways in recent years. In a crucial sense, the attempt to mediate the tension between structural and "lived" accounts has defined the field of cultural studies. As Richard Johnson has written, cultural studies "is about the historical forms of consciousness or subjectivity, or the subjective forms we live by, or, in a rather perilous compression, perhaps a reduction, the subjective side of social relations."[56] For Johnson as well as for Stuart Hall, cultural studies is always concerned both to use and to modify structuralist accounts. Likewise, much of the most important work being done in gender studies, postcolonialism, and gay and lesbian theory centers precisely on the reconstruction of experience in light of constructionist and poststructuralist critique. These cultural analyses involve subtle dialectical understandings of the relation between structural positions and subjective experience.[57] Such approaches, insofar as they aim to mediate between systemic and lived perspectives, share an affinity with the dialectical model I'm endorsing here; and they certainly redress the dominance of the systemic perspective that I earlier criticized. However, what the theory of communicative reason would contribute to these approaches is a more explicit and integral normative self-understanding.

If the theory of communicative reason remains central to any consistent elaboration of a democratic or plural politics, it still, as I have suggested, stands in need of substantial revisions if it is to answer adequately to the complex indeterminacies of the social world and

55. Allowing the systemic perspective to "meaningfully inform" the intersubjective relation is not the same as asking that it *define* that relation, as in the case of Spivak's "shared positionality," a concept I criticized earlier.

56. Richard Johnson, "What Is Cultural Studies Anyway?" 43.

57. See Teresa de Lauretis, *Alice Doesn't* and *Technologies of Gender*; Biddy Martin and Chandra Talpade Mohanty, "Feminist Politics"; Linda Alcoff, "Cultural Feminism versus Post-Structuralism"; Biddy Martin, "Lesbian Identity and Autobiographical Difference[s]"; Mohanty, "Cartographies of Struggle."

to the inseparability of feeling from action oriented toward reaching understanding. As Seyla Benhabib's feminist critique of Habermas has shown, an elaboration of affective interaction can significantly deepen the concept of mutual understanding. As part of a larger analysis of modern theories of justice and moral development, Benhabib argues that Habermas's account is elaborated only from the perspective of the "generalized" and not from that of the "concrete" other. Consequently, Habermas fails to recognize the affective specificity of reciprocal recognition, which in turn provides the basis for the principles of need as opposed to justice. As Benhabib writes, "Human situations are perspectival, and to appreciate such perspectives involves empathy, imagination, and solidarity."[58]

Benhabib insists on the equal but separate importance of the perspectives of generalized and concrete otherness. The perspective of the generalized other serves as the basis for a principle of equality; and the perspective of the concrete other introduces the more concretely realized ethical principles of care, friendship, empathy, solidarity, and intimacy. Benhabib's account thus redresses the overemphasis on reason in the Habermasian ideal of mutual understanding. Concerned as he is to rescue reason from its detractors, Habermas does not acknowledge the extent to which the norms of mutual understanding and reciprocal recognition are internally dependent on empathy and compassion.

Habermas has met these criticisms only partway, and with an underlying recalcitrance. He acknowledges the importance of empathy to the procedure of roletaking, but thereby its importance is admitted only in the application, and not in the universal justification, of procedural ethics.[59] Habermas argues that once we move historically from a traditional to a rationalized lifeworld, we can abstract questions of justice from questions of the good life. For Habermas, it is only the former that constitute the proper domain of moral theory; questions of the good life, by contrast, remain imbued with particularity and relativity—they cannot be justified, only adjudicated. Such an overly formalistic and Kantian approach to ethical theory (only seemingly tempered by Hegelian historicizing) ultimately creates an artificial rupture between questions of

58. Benhabib, *Critique, Norm, and Utopia* 349; also see Seyla Benhabib, *Situating the Self* chap. 5.
59. Jürgen Habermas, *Moral Consciousness and Communicative Action* 182.

justice, which for Habermas can be universalized, and questions of the good life, which "are accessible to rational discussion only *within* the horizon of a concrete historical form of life or an individual life style."[60] In a subsidiary move, Habermas relegates nonrational dimensions of intersubjectivity to the realm of the concrete and protects the norm of mutual understanding from any affective resonances or disruptions. Such limiting abstractions must be abandoned in favor of an approach that fully integrates particularity and affect into the norm of mutual understanding.

In response to those moral theorists who argue that an ethics of responsibility or care must accompany an ethics of justice, Habermas has claimed that the only universally justifiable complement to the perspective of justice is *solidarity*, and not benevolence, care, or responsibility. Although the justification of solidarity may appear to integrate an affective dimension into the theory, it turns out to refer merely to the necessary maintenance of our life as shared: the principle of solidarity "is rooted in the realization that each person must take responsibility for the other because as consociates all must have an interest in the integrity of their shared life context in the same way."[61] The principle of solidarity thus does not refer to the irreducible affective dimensions of our interactions with others but rather conceives of responsibility toward others as an acknowledgment that we must maintain the webs of relation that constitute our social world. But there is no reason why the norm of mutual understanding cannot be amplified so as to embrace the affective forms that accompany and enable recognition and respect. Indeed, to fail to do so is to truncate the conception of intersubjectivity that underlies systemic critique. Here Habermas himself generates distortions that issue in part, one can only surmise, out of blindness to his own biases of gender and culture.

In his attempt to further substantiate his theory of moral justification through appeal to theories in developmental sciences, Habermas has also undermined the more radical implications of his shift from a subject-centered to a communicative paradigm. Of vital importance in the theory of communicative action is the conception of the subject as intersubjectively decentered and inherently rela-

60. Habermas, *Moral Consciousness* 178.
61. Jürgen Habermas, "Justice and Solidarity" 47.

tional.[62] Yet in my view Habermas's infatuation with developmental sciences both reflects and reinforces a too-stable conception of individual identity. I think we need to accentuate and further elaborate the ways in which the intersubjective relation itself works against the rigidities of identity thinking, and this despite the seeming stability invoked by the norm of "reaching understanding." As Benhabib has argued, the true negation of identity logic resides precisely in our relation to the other:

> The true negation of identity logic would imply a relation to an "other" who could at every point remind the self that it was not a mere projection or extension of the self, but an independent being, another self. The limits of the compulsion to identity are revealed when the object of identification is itself capable of acting in such a way as to differentiate between identity and difference, between self and other. If identity logic is the attempt to blur limits and boundaries, then those limits can be reestablished via the act of an other self who is capable of rejecting the narcissistic self-extension of the other. The true negation of identity logic would be an epistemological relation in which the object could not be subsumed under the cognitive categories of the self without that it—the object—could also regard these categories as adequate to capture its own difference and integrity. Identity logic can only be stopped when difference and differentiation are internal to the very self-identification of the epistemological object and subject, and this is only the case when our object is another subject or self.[63]

The norms embedded in the speech act need not, and indeed should not, translate into an unproblematic exchange of self-identical meanings by two placeholding consciousnesses. Indeed, as Dews has argued in his analysis of Habermas's conceptions of intersubjectivity, the ideal of reaching understanding is required precisely because of the "constitutive tension of linguistic intersubjectivity," a tension that exists "even in the absence of structural inequalities of power": "Communication is not simply a matter of the transferral of identical meanings from one consciousness to another, but involves the si-

---

62. See Drucilla Cornell, "Toward a Modern/Postmodern Reconstruction of Ethics" 299, for an eloquent description of subjectivity as intersubjectively decentered.

63. Benhabib, *Critique, Norm, and Utopia* 221.

multaneous maintenance of the distinct identities of—in other words: the non-identity between—the partners in communication. This non-identity cannot fail to enter into the interpretation of meaning."[64]

Habermas's primary emphasis on the principle of justice (as that which enforces relations of equality) and his reconstruction of moral stages of development have tended to diminish the profound importance of intersubjective tension and social plurality, even as procedural ethics remains in the service of adjudicating between concrete individual and collective constituencies. He also risks installing a too-unified conception of subjectivity and social identity. I argue instead that the regulative ideal of mutual understanding must be enlarged and recast so as to embrace both the concreteness of otherness and the indeterminacy of social identities and relations. For it is precisely the indeterminate nature of social relations that keeps ever before us the possibility of political transformation. Such transformations do not occur automatically, as implied in the mechanistic models of systemically guaranteed resistances and subversions, but rather through processes of mutual understanding and dialogue.

With the aim of opening up but also justifying Habermas's theory, I want to place Habermas in relation to Ernesto Laclau and Chantal Mouffe, two of his most trenchant critics.[65] In *Hegemony and Social Strategy: Towards a Radical Democratic Politics*, Laclau and Mouffe aim to redress what they identify in classical Marxism as the reduction of the concrete to the abstract on the level of social as well as historical understanding. Classical Marxism reduces divergent subject-positions to a single (class) position; likewise, any historical moment, including the present, is apprehended only as a point within a trajectory determined a priori. Reading from within the more open-ended and versatile concept of *hegemony*, Laclau and Mouffe describe the subject and the social through a concept of textual polysemy: "The category of the subject is penetrated by the same ambiguous, incomplete, and polysemical character which overdetermination as-

---

64. Dews, *Logics of Disintegration* 221.
65. In *New Reflections on the Revolution of Our Time*, Ernesto Laclau begins by defining his project in opposition to Habermas's, yet never really directly engages his theories. However, he does append to the volume an essay by Slavoj Žižek that casts the ideal speech situation as a fetish. See also Chantal Mouffe, "Radical Democracy" 31–32.

signs to every discursive entity."[66] We must recognize and trace overdeterminations rather than perceive subjects as unitary or fixed; this is the first step toward enabling "the possibility of the deepening of a pluralist and democratic conception."[67]

The problem Laclau and Mouffe set for themselves is to avoid an absolute dispersion or atomism while still assiduously renouncing any regressive appeal to a transcendental subject. Crucial to their reconception is the principle of "antagonism," a category of social interaction defined not positively but rather *against* a notion of "opposition" that regressively conceives identities that face off as a priori fixities. Antagonism—unstable, ever shifting—reflects the partial and precarious nature of all identification. Laclau and Mouffe bring before us the force of such precariousness precisely through the evocation of an encounter: "The presence of the 'Other' prevents me from being totally myself":

> Insofar as there is an antagonism, I cannot be a full presence for myself. But nor is the force that antagonizes such a presence: its objective being is a symbol of my non-being, and, in this way, it is overflowed by a plurality of meanings which prevent its being fixed as full positivity. Real opposition is an *objective* relation—that is, determinable, definable—among things; contradiction is an equally definable relation among concepts; antagonism constitutes the limits of every objectivity, which is revealed as a partial and precarious *objectification*.[68]

For Laclau and Mouffe, antagonism is a function of the radical contingency of the social; but rather than serving to render politics impossible, it serves as the precondition for transformation, and precisely at the level of social alliances. The radical nonfixity of identity gives us the freedom collectively to construct new hegemonies that will emerge through mutually transforming encounters between variously constituted groups. Such social processes are vital to progressive social transformation: "For there to be a 'democratic equivalence' we need the construction of a new 'common sense' which changes the identity of the different groups in such a way that demands are articulated equivalentially with those of the oth-

66. Ernesto Laclau and Chantal Mouffe, *Hegemony and Socialist Strategy* 121.
67. Laclau and Mouffe, *Hegemony and Socialist Strategy* 166.
68. Laclau and Mouffe, *Hegemony and Socialist Strategy* 125.

ers."[69] In this conception no form of fixed identity can be said to constitute the groups whose identity is produced and transformed through their various encounters and struggles with one another: "Equivalence is always hegemonic insofar as it does not simply establish an 'alliance' between given interests, but modifies the identity of the forces engaging in that alliance."[70]

Laclau and Mouffe's "radical relationalism of social identities" derives from a poststructuralist linguistic model and hence might seem, in this respect, to elaborate the ambiguities and instabilities of identity from a systems perspective. Yet we must keep in mind the primacy of intersubjective "antagonism," which is not elaborated from such a perspective. Indeterminacy becomes simply the condition of our irreducibly social identities that enables us endlessly to renegotiate and recreate our relations to others, as both individuals and members of nonreified collectives. That is, indeterminacy serves as the precondition but not the guarantee of political transformation. Only in and through the relations between subjects and groups are identities constituted and transformed; so in an important sense, and quite self-consciously, Laclau and Mouffe avoid the objectivism that inhabits poststructuralist systems theory while still forwarding a general theoretical account of the social.

An important question remains, however: does the concept of antagonism as constitutive of the social entirely foreclose or undermine any conception of communicative reason? In their more recent work, these thinkers have stressed the importance of the situated social agent through a reconstructed conception of Gadamer's phronesis (detached from its traditionalist resonances and reconceived more along the lines of the Wittgensteinian language game).[71] Although Laclau and Mouffe themselves see Habermas as engaged in the deluded project of attempting to guarantee the political efficacy of Enlightenment ideals, I suggest that there are tacit similarities between Habermas's conception of communicative action as the site of emancipatory potential and Laclau's developing account of hegemonic struggle. In an article that extends many of the claims in *Hegemony and Socialist Strategy*, Laclau elaborates in further detail how antifoundationalism can serve as the ground for a profound political optimism. He does so precisely by specifying a communi-

69. Laclau and Mouffe, *Hegemony and Socialist Strategy* 183.
70. Laclau and Mouffe, *Hegemony and Socialist Strategy* 183–84.
71. See Mouffe, "Radical Democracy"; Laclau, "Politics and the Limits of Modernity" 63–82.

cative model of social praxis, arguing that society should be "understood as a vast argumentative texture through which people construct their own reality." He further claims that "inasmuch as argument and discourse constitute the social, their open-ended character becomes the source of a greater activism and a more radical libertarianism."[72]

But if Laclau is to justify a transformative praxis through a conception of society as fundamentally discursive, he must presuppose communicative norms, even in the face of the radical disruptions of antagonism. In order to appropriate the radically open and transformable character of social identities for a new hegemony—in order to articulate a common sense—we must presuppose some form of communicative understanding, unless we are to imagine that such articulations take place behind the backs of social subjects. It seems to me that the turn to phronesis is itself an attempt to render more explicit those communicative and reconstructive processes involved in mutually transforming intersubjective alliances. Yet it also seems that an unacknowledged intersubjective ideal underlies the whole concept of a new common sense. We may acknowledge that power is constitutive of all interactions, and that identity is indeterminate, and still aim to foster regulative ideals of equality and reciprocal respect. Otherwise, what meaning does "democracy" or "the left" have? In other words, if the Habermasian account must be revised to give prominence to social indeterminacy and concrete social positions, then the ideas of "equivalences" and "common sense" must be deepened through an acknowledgment of the intersubjective ideals that underlie them. Insofar as it serves merely as the foundation of a procedural model, communicative reason does not need to be yoked to essentializing conceptions of identity, whether individual or social. A regulative ideal of mutual understanding does not render identity determinate, it merely renders politics possible.

Laclau and Mouffe generate an entirely promising vision of communicative politics in their thoroughgoing reconceptualization of rights. According to them, a radical democratic politics would be based on a demand to rights constituted through variable contexts and not determined a priori:

> The idea of 'natural' rights prior to society—and indeed, the whole of the false dichotomy individual/society—should be abandoned,

72. Laclau, "Politics and the Limits of Modernity" 79.

and replaced by another manner of posing the problem of rights. It is never possible for individual rights to be defined in isolation, but only in the context of social relations which define determinate subject positions. As a consequence, it will always be a question of rights which involve other subjects who participate in the same social relation.[73]

Given the multiplicity of subject-positions, as well as the fundamental unevenness of the social, any demand for rights must thus take into account the rights claims of other groups: a reconstructed principle of equality must thus be balanced by a reconstructed principle of liberty, which recognizes differences and hence leads to the notion of plurality. Similarly, Benhabib wishes to balance the category of the general other (which would correspond to the struggle for equality) with the category of the concrete other (which enables and ensures a *plural* democracy). More important to the argument I have been making in this Afterword, Laclau and Mouffe's different manner of posing the problem of rights, their emphasis on social contexts and indeterminacy, still relies, if only implicitly, on a fundamental appeal to the forms of mutual recognition on which rights rest. Hence I find peculiar their refusal to recognize the importance of the theory of communicative action.

There is a discernible similarity between the impasses of the Victorian rhetoric of fallenness and the impasses of those poststructuralisms that allow a systems perspective to dominate their account of the social world. This book has argued that mutually transforming reciprocal recognition, a condition of any democratic and emancipatory practice, is an experience fundamentally foreclosed in conventional representations of Victorian fallenness as well as in those poststructuralisms that allow a systems perspective to dominate their account of the social world. Such contemporary recapitulations fail to express the fundamentally intersubjective, participatory, and open-ended nature of the social world. In this Afterword, I have tried to elaborate those theoretical positions that might help us to further such an understanding of the social world, just as my readings of Victorian texts stressed critical or revisionist moments. We might in fact contemplate those challenges anew in light of the

73. Laclau and Mouffe, *Hegemony and Socialist Strategy* 184.

discussion I have offered here, to see to what extent they manifest the kind of acknowledgment of intersubjective practices that I have argued is vital to democratic possibilities. Gaskell's vision at the end of *North and South* comes closest to the Habermasian communicative ideal, and her works generally do not separate sympathy or feeling from the ideal of mutual understanding. D. G. Rossetti's "Jenny," insofar as it critiques the objectifying stance of the speaker, indirectly suggests positive aspects of intersubjective indeterminacy; and Barrett Browning does so more explicitly through her insistence on a productive interplay between aesthetic and intersubjective experience. While I would not want to reduce these historical texts to their usefulness for contemporary social theory, I do believe that their challenges to the Victorian rhetoric of fallenness have resonances for contemporary theory.

But this Afterword has been most concerned to demonstrate that the systems-dominated poststructuralist paradigms do not adequately theorize their normative commitments. The project of communicative ethics, as I have tried to show, allows us to do more than describe and reinscribe the impasses of constructionism. In place of reductive or distorting social and linguistic determinisms, it offers a more coherent and comprehensive theory of the mutually constitutive agencies and antagonisms that make up our intersubjective practices.

Works Cited

Abrams, Philip. *The Origins of British Sociology: 1834–1914*. Chicago: University of Chicago Press, 1968.

Acton, William. *Prostitution Considered in Its Moral, Social, and Sanitary Aspects, in London and Other Large Cities, with Proposals for the Mitigation and Prevention of Its Attendant Evils*. London: John Churchill, 1857.

Alcoff, Linda. "Cultural Feminism versus Post-Structuralism: The Identity Crisis in Feminist Theory." *Signs* 13 (1988): 405–36.

Anderson, Amanda. "Prostitution's Artful Guise." *Diacritics* 21 (1991): 102–22.

Arac, Jonathan. *Commissioned Spirits: The Shaping of Social Motion in Dickens, Carlyle, Melville, and Hawthorne*. New York: Columbia University Press, 1989.

Armstrong, Nancy. *Desire and Domestic Fiction: A Political History of the Novel*. New York: Oxford University Press, 1987.

Auerbach, Nina. *Romantic Imprisonment: Women and Other Glorified Outcasts*. New York: Columbia University Press, 1985.

———. *Woman and the Demon: The Life of a Victorian Myth*. Cambridge: Harvard University Press, 1982.

Barlow, John. *Man's Power over Himself to Prevent or Control Insanity*. London: William Pickering, 1843.

Basch, Françoise. *Relative Creatures: Victorian Women in Society and the Novel*. New York: Schocken, 1974.

Benhabib, Seyla. *Critique, Norm, and Utopia: A Study of the Foundations of Critical Theory*. New York: Columbia University Press, 1986.

———. *Situating the Self: Gender, Community and Postmodernism in Contemporary Ethics*. New York: Routledge, 1992.

Bernheimer, Charles. *Figures of Ill Repute: Representing Prostitution in Nineteenth-Century France*. Cambridge: Harvard University Press, 1989.

Bernstein, Richard J. *Beyond Objectivism and Relativism: Science, Hermeneutics, and Praxis.* Philadelphia: University of Pennsylvania Press, 1983.

Bick, Suzann. " 'Take Her Up Tenderly': Elizabeth Gaskell's Treatment of the Fallen Woman." *Essays in Arts and Sciences* 18 (1989): 17–27.

Bodenheimer, Rosemarie. *The Politics of Story in Victorian Social Fiction.* Ithaca: Cornell University Press, 1988.

——. "Private Grief and Public Acts in *Mary Barton.*" *Dickens Studies Annual* 9 (1981): 195–216.

Boone, Joseph Allen. *Tradition Counter Tradition: Love and the Form of Fiction.* Chicago: University of Chicago Press, 1987.

Braidotti, Rosa. "The Politics of Ontological Difference." In *Between Feminism and Psychoanalysis,* ed. Teresa Brennan, 89–105. London: Routledge, 1989.

Brantlinger, Patrick. *Crusoe's Footprints: Cultural Studies in Britain and America.* New York: Routledge, 1990.

Bray, Charles. *The Philosophy of Necessity; or, the Law of Consequences; as Applicable to Mental, Moral, and Social Science.* 2 vols. London: Longman, Orme, Brown, Green, and Longmans, 1841.

Brooks, Peter. *Reading for the Plot: Design and Intention in Narrative.* New York: Knopf, 1984.

Browning, Elizabeth Barrett. *Aurora Leigh and Other Poems.* Ed. Cora Kaplan. London: The Woman's Press, 1978.

——. *The Letters of Elizabeth Barrett Browning.* Ed. Frederic G. Kenyon. 2 vols. London: Macmillan, 1897.

——. *The Letters of Elizabeth Barrett Browning to Mary Russell Mitford 1836–1854.* Ed. Meredith B. Raymond and Mary Rose Sullivan. 3 vols. Winfield, Kans.: Armstrong Browning Library of Baylor University, Browning Institute, Wedgestone Press, and Wellesley College, 1983.

Browning, Robert, and Elizabeth Barrett Barrett. *The Letters of Robert Browning and Elizabeth Barrett Barrett, 1845–1846.* Ed. Elvan Kintner. 2 vols. Cambridge: Belknap Press of Harvard University Press, 1969.

Bulmer, Martin, Kevin Bales, and Kathryn Kish Sklar. "The Social Survey in Historical Perspective." In Bulmer, Bales, and Sklar, eds., *The Social Survey* 1–48.

——, eds. *The Social Survey in Historical Perspective, 1880–1940.* Cambridge: Cambridge University Press, 1991.

Butler, Judith. *Gender Trouble: Feminism and the Subversion of Identity.* New York: Routledge, 1990.

Carlisle, Janice. *John Stuart Mill and the Writing of Character.* Athens: University of Georgia Press, 1991.

Chase, Cynthia. *Decomposing Figures: Rhetorical Readings in the Romantic Tradition.* Baltimore: Johns Hopkins University Press, 1986.

Clark, Robert. "Riddling the Family Firm: The Sexual Economy in *Dombey and Son.*" *ELH* 51 (1984): 69–78.

Cockshut, A. O. J. *The Imagination of Charles Dickens.* New York: New York University Press, 1962.

Collins, Philip. *Dickens and Crime*. London: Macmillan, 1962.

Cooper, Helen. *Elizabeth Barrett Browning: Woman and Artist*. Chapel Hill: University of North Carolina Press, 1988.

Corbett, Mary Jean. *Representing Femininity: Middle-Class Subjectivity in Victorian and Edwardian Women's Autobiography*. New York: Oxford University Press, 1992.

Cornell, Drucilla. "Toward a Modern/Postmodern Reconstruction of Ethics." *University of Pennsylvania Law Review* 133 (1985): 291–380.

Craik, W. A. *Elizabeth Gaskell and the English Provincial Novel*. London: Methuen, 1975.

Crick, Brian. "Mrs. Gaskell's *Ruth*: A Reconsideration." *Mosaic* 9 (1976): 85–104.

Cullen, Michael J. *The Statistical Movement in Early Victorian Britain: The Foundations of Empirical Social Research*. New York: Harvester Press, 1975.

Culler, Jonathan. *The Pursuit of Signs: Semiotics, Literature, Deconstruction*. Ithaca: Cornell University Press, 1981.

David, Deirdre. *Intellectual Women and Victorian Patriarchy: Harriet Martineau, Elizabeth Barrett Browning, and George Eliot*. Ithaca: Cornell University Press, 1987.

Davidoff, Leonore, and Catherine Hall. *Family Fortunes: Men and Women of the English Middle Class, 1780–1850*. Chicago: University of Chicago Press, 1987.

Davis, Tracy C. *Actresses as Working Women: Their Social Identity in Victorian Culture*. London: Routledge, 1991.

de Lauretis, Teresa. *Alice Doesn't: Feminism, Semiotics, Cinema*. Bloomington: Indiana University Press, 1984.

——. *Technologies of Gender: Essays on Theory, Film, and Fiction*. Bloomington: Indiana University Press, 1987.

——. "Upping the Anti (sic) in Feminist Theory." In Hirsch and Keller, eds., *Conflicts in Feminism* 255–70.

Dews, Peter. *Logics of Disintegration: Post-Structuralist Thought and the Claims of Critical Theory*. London: Verso, 1987.

Dickens, Charles. *David Copperfield*. Harmondsworth: Penguin,1966.

——. *Dombey and Son*. Harmondsworth: Penguin, 1970.

——. "Home for Homeless Women." *Household Words* 7 (1853).

——. *Letters from Charles Dickens to Angela Burdett-Coutts 1841–1865*. Ed. Edgar Johnson. London: Jonathan Cape, 1953.

——. "A Nightly Scene in London." *Household Words* 36 (1856).

——. *Oliver Twist*. Harmondsworth: Penguin, 1966.

Dixon, Hepworth. *The London Prisons*. London: Jackson and Walford, 1850.

Duggan, Lisa. "Making It Perfectly Queer: Theory, Politics, and Paradox in the 90s." *Socialist Review* 22 (1992): 11–33.

Easson, Angus. *Elizabeth Gaskell*. London: Routledge and Kegan Paul, 1979.

Ellis, Mrs. [Sarah Stickney]. *The Women of England, Their Social Duties, and Domestic Habits*. New York: D. Appleton, 1839.

Emsley, Clive. *Crime and Society in England 1750–1900*. London: Longman, 1987.

Felski, Rita. *Beyond Feminist Aesthetics: Feminist Literature and Social Change*. Cambridge: Harvard University Press, 1989.

Forster, John. *The Life of Charles Dickens*. 3 vols. London: J. M. Dent and Sons, 1966.

Foucault, Michel. *The History of Sexuality: An Introduction*. Vol. 1. Trans. Robert Hurley. New York: Random House, 1978.

Fraser, Nancy. *Unruly Practices: Power, Discourse, and Gender in Contemporary Social Theory*. Minneapolis: University of Minnesota Press, 1989.

Fraser, Nancy, and Linda J. Nicholson. "Social Criticism without Philosophy: An Encounter between Feminism and Postmodernism." In *Feminism/Postmodernism*, ed. Linda J. Nicholson, 19–38. New York: Routledge, 1990.

Fryckstedt, Monica Correa. *Elizabeth Gaskell's "Mary Barton" and "Ruth": A Challenge to Christian England*. Stockholm: Almqvist and Wiksell International, 1982.

Fuss, Diana. *Essentially Speaking: Feminism, Nature, and Difference*. New York: Routledge, 1989.

Gallagher, Catherine. "George Eliot and *Daniel Deronda*: The Prostitute and the Jewish Question." In Yeazell, ed., *Sex, Politics, and Science* 39–62.

——. *The Industrial Reformation of English Fiction: Social Discourse and Narrative Form, 1832–1867*. Chicago: University of Chicago Press, 1985.

Ganz, Margaret. *Elizabeth Gaskell: The Artist in Conflict*. New York: Twayne, 1969.

Gaskell, Elizabeth. *The Letters of Mrs. Gaskell*. Ed. J. A. V. Chapple and Arthur Pollard. Cambridge: Harvard University Press, 1967.

——. *Mary Barton*. Harmondsworth: Penguin, 1970.

——. *North and South*. Harmondsworth: Penguin, 1970.

——. *Ruth*. New York: Oxford University Press, 1985.

Gerin, Winfred. *Elizabeth Gaskell: A Biography*. Oxford: Clarendon Press, 1976.

Graver, Suzanne. *George Eliot and Community: A Study in Social Theory and Fictional Form*. Berkeley: University of California Press, 1984.

Greg, William Rathbone. *The Creed of Christendom: Its Foundations Contrasted with Its Superstructure*. 1851. Toronto: Rose Belford, 1878.

[——]. "Prostitution." *Westminster Review* 53 (1850): 448–506.

Habermas, Jürgen. "Justice and Solidarity: On the Discussion Concerning 'Stage 6.'" Trans. Shierry Weber Nicholsen. *The Philosophical Forum* 21 (1989–90): 32–52.

——. *Moral Consciousness and Communicative Action*. Trans. Christian Lenhardt and Shierry Weber Nicholsen. Cambridge: MIT Press, 1990.

——. *The Philosophical Discourse of Modernity*. Trans. Frederick Lawrence. Cambridge: MIT Press, 1987.

——. *The Theory of Communicative Action*. Trans. Thomas McCarthy. 2 vols. Boston: Beacon Press, 1984–87.

Halevy, Elie. *The Growth of Philosophic Radicalism*. Trans. Mary Morris. London: Faber and Faber, 1972.

Hapke, Laura. "He Stoops to Conquer: Redeeming the Fallen Woman in the Fiction of Dickens, Gaskell, and Their Contemporaries." *Victorian Newsletter* 69 (1986): 16–22.

Harasym, Sarah, ed. *The Post-Colonial Critic*. New York: Routledge, 1990.

Hardy, Barbara. *The Moral Art of Dickens*. New York: Oxford University Press, 1970.

Harman, Barbara Leah. "In Promiscuous Company: Female Public Appearance in Elizabeth Gaskell's *North and South*." *Victorian Studies* 31 (1988): 351–76.

Harris, Daniel. "D. G. Rossetti's 'Jenny': Sex, Money, and the Interior Monologue." *Victorian Poetry* 22 (1984): 197–215.

Heath, Stephen. "Difference." *Screen* 19 (1978): 50–112.

Helsinger, Elizabeth K., Robin Lauterbach Sheets, and William Veeder. *The Woman Question: Society and Literature in Britain and America, 1837–1883*. Vol. 3. Chicago: University of Chicago Press, 1983.

Hemyng, Bracebridge. "Prostitution in London." In *London Labour and the London Poor* (1861–62), by Henry Mayhew, 4:210–72. New York: Dover, 1968.

Hirsch, Marianne, and Evelyn Fox Keller, eds. *Conflicts in Feminism*. New York: Routledge, 1990.

Horn, Pierre L., and Mary Beth Pringle, eds. *The Image of the Prostitute in Modern Literature*. New York: Ungar, 1984.

Irigaray, Luce. *Speculum of the Other Woman*. Trans. Gillian C. Gill. Ithaca: Cornell University Press, 1985.

Jay, Martin. "The Morals of Genealogy: Or, Is There a Post-Structuralist Ethics?" *Cambridge Review* 110 (1989): 70–74.

Johnson, Barbara. *A World of Difference*. Baltimore: Johns Hopkins University Press, 1987.

Johnson, Richard. "What Is Cultural Studies Anyway?" *Social Text* 6 (1987): 38–80.

Jordan, John O. "The Social Sub-Text of *David Copperfield*." *Dickens Studies Annual* 14 (1985): 81–92.

Kalikoff, Beth. "The Falling Woman in Three Victorian Novels." *Studies in the Novel* 19 (1987): 357–67.

——. "Victorian Sexual Confessions." *Victorian Institute Journal* 18 (1990): 99–112.

Kanner, Selma Barbara. "Victorian Institutional Patronage: Angela Burdett-Coutts, Charles Dickens, and Urania Cottage, Reformatory for Women, 1846–1858." Diss., UCLA, 1972.

Kaplan, Cora. Introduction, *Aurora Leigh and Other Poems*, by Elizabeth Barrett Browning, 5–36. London: The Women's Press, 1978.

Kettle, Arnold. "The Early Victorian Social-Problem Novel." In *From Dickens to Hardy,* ed. Boris Ford (vol. 6 of *The Penguin Guide to English Literature*), 164–81. Harmondsworth: Penguin, 1958.

Kucich, John. "Transgression and Sexual Difference in Elizabeth Gaskell's Novels." *Texas Studies in Language and Literature* 32 (1990): 187–213.

Laclau, Ernesto. *New Reflections on the Revolution of Our Time.* London: Verso, 1990.

———. "Politics and the Limits of Modernity." In Ross, ed., *Universal Abandon?* 63–82.

Laclau, Ernesto, and Chantal Mouffe. *Hegemony and Socialist Strategy: Towards a Radical Democratic Politics.* London: Verso, 1985.

Langbauer, Laurie. *Women and Romance: The Consolations of Gender in the English Novel.* Ithaca: Cornell University Press, 1990.

Langbaum, Robert. *The Poetry of Experience: The Dramatic Monologue in Modern Literary Tradition.* New York: W. W. Norton, 1963.

Lansbury, Coral. *Elizabeth Gaskell: The Novel of Social Crisis.* New York: Barnes and Noble, 1975.

Leavis, F. R., and Q. D. Leavis. *Dickens the Novelist.* London: Chatto and Windus, 1970.

Leighton, Angela. " 'Because Men Made the Laws': The Fallen Woman and the Woman Poet." *Victorian Poetry* 27 (1989): 109–27.

Lewes, G. H. "*Ruth* and *Villette.*" *Westminster Review* 59 (1853): 474–91.

Logan, William. *An Exposure, from Personal Observation, of Female Prostitution in London, Leeds, and Rochdale, and Especially in the City of Glasgow; with Remarks on the Cause, Extent, Results, and Remedy of the Evil.* Glasgow: G. Gallie and R. Fleckfield, 1843.

Lucas, John. *The Literature of Change: Studies in the Nineteenth-Century Provincial Novel.* New York: Barnes and Noble, 1977.

———. "Mrs. Gaskell and Brotherhood." In *Tradition and Tolerance in Nineteenth-Century Fiction,* ed. David Howard, John Lucas, and John Goode, 141–205. London: Routledge and Kegan Paul, 1966.

McKeon, Michael. *The Origins of the English Novel 1600–1740.* Baltimore: Johns Hopkins University Press, 1987.

Mahood, Linda. *The Magdalenes: Prostitution in the Nineteenth Century.* London: Routledge, 1990.

Mandelbaum, Maurice. *History, Man, and Reason: A Study in Nineteenth-Century Thought.* Baltimore: Johns Hopkins University Press, 1971.

Marcus, Steven. *The Other Victorians: A Study of Sexuality and Pornography in Mid-Nineteenth Century England.* New York: Basic Books, 1964.

Marsh, Joss Lutz. "Good Mrs. Brown's Connections: Sexuality and Story-Telling in *Dealings with the Firm of Dombey and Son.*" *ELH* 58 (1991): 405–26.

Martin, Biddy. "Feminism, Criticism, and Foucault." In *Feminism and Foucault: Reflections on Resistance,* ed. Irene Diamond and Lee Quinby, 3–18. Boston: Northeastern University Press, 1985.

———. "Lesbian Identity and Autobiographical Difference[s]." In *Life/Lines:*

Theorizing Women's Autobiography, ed. Bella Brodzki and Celeste Schenck, 77–103. Ithaca: Cornell University Press, 1988.

Martin, Biddy, and Chandra Talpade Mohanty. "Feminist Politics: What's Home Got to Do with It?" In *Feminist Studies/Critical Studies*, ed. Teresa de Lauretis, 191–212. Bloomington: Indiana University Press, 1986.

Martineau, James. *Types of Ethical Theory*. 2 vols. Oxford: Clarendon Press, 1901.

Mermin, Dorothy. *The Audience in the Poem: Five Victorian Poets*. New Brunswick: Rutgers University Press, 1983.

——. *Elizabeth Barrett Browning: The Origins of a New Poetry*. Chicago: University of Chicago Press, 1989.

Michie, Helena. *The Flesh Made Word: Female Figures and Women's Bodies*. New York: Oxford University Press, 1987.

Mill, John Stuart. *Autobiography*. In *Collected Works of John Stuart Mill*, vol. 1: *Autobiography and Literary Essays*, ed. J. M. Robson and Jack Stillinger. 1981.

——. "Bentham." In *Collected Works of John Stuart Mill*, vol. 10: *Essays on Ethics, Religion, and Society*, ed. J. M. Robson, 77–115. 1969.

——. "Coleridge." In *Collected Works of John Stuart Mill*, vol. 10: *Essays on Ethics, Religion, and Society*, ed. J. M. Robson, 119–63. 1969.

——. *Collected Works of John Stuart Mill*. Ed. J. M. Robson. 33 vols. Toronto and London: University of Toronto Press and Routledge and Kegan Paul, 1963–91.

——. *On Liberty*. In *Collected Works of John Stuart Mill*, vol. 18: *Essays on Politics and Society*, ed. J. M. Robson, 213–310. 1977.

——. *The Subjection of Women*. In *Collected Works of John Stuart Mill*, vol. 21: *Essays on Equality, Law, and Education*, ed. J. M. Robson, 259–348. 1984.

——. *A System of Logic Ratiocinative and Inductive*. Ed. J. M. Robson. Vols. 7 and 8 of *Collected Works of John Stuart Mill*. 1974.

——. *Utilitarianism*. In *Collected Works of John Stuart Mill*, vol. 10: *Essays on Ethics, Religion, and Society*, ed. J. M. Robson, 203–59. 1969.

Miller, D. A. *The Novel and the Police*. Berkeley: University of California Press, 1988.

Miller, James. *Prostitution Considered in Relation to Its Cause and Cure*. Edinburgh: Sutherland and Knox, 1859.

Mitchell, Sally. *The Fallen Angel: Chastity, Class, and Women's Reading, 1835–1880*. Bowling Green, Ohio: Bowling Green University Popular Press, 1981.

Mohanty, Chandra Talpade. "Cartographies of Struggle: Third World Women and the Politics of Feminism." In *Third World Women and the Politics of Feminism*, ed. Chandra Talpade Mohanty, Ann Russo, and Lourdes Torres, 1–47. Bloomington: Indiana University Press, 1991.

Moi, Toril. "Feminism, Postmodernism, and Style: Recent Feminist Criticism in the United States." *Cultural Critique* 9 (1988): 3–22.

——. *Sexual/Textual Politics: Feminist Literary Theory*. New York: Methuen, 1985.

Morrison, Paul. "Paul de Man: Resistance and Collaboration." *Representations* 32 (1990): 50–74.

Mort, Frank. *Dangerous Sexualities: Medico-Moral Politics in England since 1830*. London: Routledge and Kegan Paul, 1987.

Mouffe, Chantal. "Radical Democracy: Modern or Postmodern?" In Ross, ed., *Universal Abandon?* 31–45.

Nead, Lynda. *Myths of Sexuality: Representations of Women in Victorian Britain*. Oxford: Basil Blackwell, 1988.

Nord, Deborah Epstein. "The Urban Peripatetic: Spectator, Streetwalker, Woman Writer." *Nineteenth-Century Literature* 46 (1991): 351–75.

Nunokawa, Jeff. "For Your Eyes Only: Property, Capital, Sexuality, and the Body of the Oriental in *Dombey and Son*." In *Macropolitics of Nineteenth-Century Literature: Nationalism, Exoticism, Imperialism*, ed. Jonathan Arac and Harriet Ritvo, 138–58. Philadelphia: University of Pennsylvania Press, 1991.

Owen, Robert. *Essays on the Formation of Human Character*. London: B. D. Cousins, 1840.

Parent-Duchâtelet, Alexandre. *La prostitution à Paris au XIXe siècle*. Ed. Alain Corbin. Paris: Seuil, 1981. First published in 1836 as *De la prostitution dans la ville de Paris*.

Pinch, Adela. "Female Chatter: Meter, Masochism, and the *Lyrical Ballads*." *ELH* 55 (1988): 835–52.

Pollard, Arthur. *Mrs. Gaskell: Novelist and Biographer*. Cambridge: Harvard University Press, 1966.

Poovey, Mary. "Speaking of the Body: Mid-Victorian Constructions of Female Desire." In *Body/Politics: Women and the Discourses of Science*, ed. Mary Jacobus, Evelyn Fox Keller, and Sally Shuttleworth, 29–46. New York: Routledge, 1990.

——. *Uneven Developments: The Ideological Work of Gender in Mid-Victorian England*. Chicago: University of Chicago Press, 1989.

Reed, John R. *Victorian Will*. Athens: Ohio University Press, 1989.

Riley, Denise. *"Am I That Name?": Feminism and the Category of "Women" in History*. Minneapolis: University of Minnesota Press, 1988.

Rose, Jacqueline. *Sexuality in the Field of Vision*. London: Verso, 1986.

Rosenblum, Delores. "Face to Face: Elizabeth Barrett Browning's *Aurora Leigh* and Nineteenth-Century Poetry." *Victorian Studies* 26 (1983): 321–39.

Ross, Andrew, ed. *Universal Abandon? The Politics of Postmodernism*. Minneapolis: University of Minnesota Press, 1988.

Rossetti, Dante Gabriel. *The Collected Works of Dante Gabriel Rossetti*. Ed. William M Rossetti. 2 vols. London: Ellis and Scrutton, 1886.

Rowell, Geoffrey. *Hell and the Victorians*. Oxford: Clarendon Press, 1974.

Rubenius, Aina. *The Woman Question in Mrs. Gaskell's Life and Works*. Cambridge: Harvard University Press, 1950.

Ryan, Alan. *John Stuart Mill*. New York: Pantheon, 1970.

Schor, Naomi. *Breaking the Chain: Women, Theory, and French Realist Fiction*. New York: Columbia University Press, 1985.

Seltzer, Mark. *Bodies and Machines*. New York: Routledge, 1992.

——. "The Naturalist Machine." In Yeazell, ed., *Sex, Politics, and Science* 116–47.

Sheets, Robin. "Pornography and Art: The Case of 'Jenny.' " *Critical Inquiry* 14 (1988): 315–34.

Showalter, Elaine. *The Female Malady: Women, Madness, and English Culture, 1830–1980*. New York: Penguin, 1985.

——. *A Literature of Their Own: British Women Writers from Brontë to Lessing*. Princeton: Princeton University Press, 1977.

Sigsworth, E. M., and T. J. Wyke. "A Study of Victorian Prostitution and Venereal Disease." In *Suffer and Be Still: Women in the Victorian Age*, ed. Martha Vicinus, 77–100. Bloomington: Indiana University Press, 1972.

Smith, F. Barry. "Sexuality in Britain, 1800–1900: Some Suggested Revisions." In *A Widening Sphere: Changing Roles of Victorian Women*, ed. Martha Vicinus, 182–98. Bloomington: Indiana University Press, 1977.

Smith, Paul. *Discerning the Subject*. Minneapolis: University of Minnesota Press, 1988.

Snitow, Ann. "A Gender Diary." In Hirsch and Keller, eds., *Conflicts in Feminism* 9–43.

Spencer, Herbert. *Social Statics: Or, the Conditions Essential to Human Happiness Specified, and the First of Them Developed*. London: John Chapman, 1851.

Spivak, Gayatri Chakravorty. "Criticism, Feminism, and the Institution." Interview with Elizabeth Grosz (1984). In Harasym, ed., *The Post-Colonial Critic* 1–16.

——. "In a Word." Interview with Ellen Rooney (1988). *Differences* 1 (1989): 124–56.

——. "Strategy, Identity, Writing." Interview (1986). In Harasym, ed., *The Post-Colonial Critic* 35–49.

——. "Subaltern Studies: Deconstructing Historiography." *In Other Worlds: Essays in Cultural Politics*, 197–221. New York: Routledge, 1988.

Stallybrass, Peter, and Allon White. *The Politics and Poetics of Transgression*. Ithaca: Cornell University Press, 1986.

Steinmetz, Virginia V. "Images of 'Mother-Want' in Elizabeth Barrett Browning's *Aurora Leigh*." *Victorian Poetry* 21 (1983): 351–67.

Stoneman, Patsy. *Elizabeth Gaskell*. Bloomington: Indiana University Press, 1987.

Swann, Karen. " 'Christabel': The Wandering Mother and the Enigma of Form." *Studies in Romanticism* 23 (1984): 533–53.

Tait, William. *Magdalenism: An Inquiry into the Extent, Causes, and Consequences of Prostitution in Edinburgh*. Edinburgh: P. Rickard, 1840.

Talbot, James Beard. *The Miseries of Prostitution*. London: James Madden, 1844.

Tillotson, Kathleen. *Novels of the Eighteen-Forties*. Oxford: Clarendon Press, 1954.

Tobias, J. J. *Crime and Police in England 1700–1900*. Dublin: Gill and Macmillan, 1979.

Valverde, Mariana. "The Love of Finery: Fashion and the Fallen Woman in Nineteenth-Century Social Discourse." *Victorian Studies* 32 (1989): 169–88.

Walkowitz, Judith R. *City of Dreadful Delight: Narratives of Sexual Danger in Late-Victorian London*. Chicago: University of Chicago Press, 1992.

——. *Prostitution and Victorian Society: Women, Class, and the State*. Cambridge: Cambridge University Press, 1980.

Wardlaw, Ralph. *Lectures on Female Prostitution: Its Nature, Extent, Effects, Guilt, Causes, and Remedy*. Glasgow: James Maclehouse, 1842.

Watt, George. *The Fallen Woman in the 19th-Century English Novel*. Totowa, N.J.: Barnes and Noble, 1984.

Webb, R. K. "The Gaskells as Unitarians." In *Dickens and Other Victorians*, ed. Joanne Shattock, 144–71. New York: St. Martin's Press, 1988.

Whitford, Margaret. *Luce Irigaray: Philosophy in the Feminine*. London: Routledge, 1991.

Williams, Raymond. *Culture and Society, 1780–1950*. 1958. New York: Columbia University Press, 1983.

——. Introduction. *Dombey and Son*, by Charles Dickens, 11–34. Harmondsworth: Penguin, 1970.

Wordsworth, William. *The Prelude 1798, 1805, 1850*. Ed. Jonathan Wordsworth, M. H. Abrams, and Stephen Gill. New York: W. W. Norton, 1978.

Yeazell, Ruth Bernard. *Fictions of Modesty: Women and Courtship in the English Novel*. Chicago: University of Chicago Press, 1991.

——, ed. *Sex, Politics, and Science in the Nineteenth-Century Novel*. Selected Papers from the English Institute, 1983–84, n.s. 10. Baltimore: Johns Hopkins University Press, 1986.

——. "Why Political Novels Have Heroines: *Sybil, Mary Barton*, and *Felix Holt*." *Novel* 18 (1985): 126–44.

Yeo, Eileen Janes. "The Social Survey in Social Perspective." In Bulmer, Bales, and Sklar, eds., *The Social Survey* 49–65.

Zwinger, Lynda. "The Fear of the Father: Dombey and Daughter." *Nineteenth-Century Fiction* 39 (1985): 420–40.

Index

Reading Women Writing

A SERIES EDITED BY

Shari Benstock and Celeste Schenck

Library of Congress Cataloging-in-Publication Data

Anderson, Amanda.
    Tainted souls and painted faces : the rhetoric of fallenness in Victorian culture /
Amanda Anderson.
        p.   cm. — (Reading women writing)
Includes bibliographical references and index.
    ISBN 0-8014-2781-9 (cloth).   —ISBN 0-8014-8148-1 (paper)
    1. English literature—19th century—History and criticism. 2. Women and
literature—Great Britain—History—19th century. 3. Prostitution—Great Britain—
History—19th century. 4. Moral conditions in literature. 5. Prostitutes in literature.
6. Sex role in literature. I. Title. II. Series.
    PR468.W6A53 1993
    820.9'353—dc20   93-17254